What the Great Ate

What the Great Ate

A Curious History of Food and Fame

Matthew Jacob and *Mark Jacob*

WITH ILLUSTRATIONS BY RICK TUMA

THREE RIVERS PRESS

NEW YORK

Library of Congress Cataloging-in-Publication Data
Jacob, Matthew.
  What the great ate: a curious history of food
and fame / Matthew Jacob and Mark Jacob; with
illustrations by Rick Tuma.
    p. cm.
  Includes bibliographical references.
  1. Celebrities—Biography—Anecdotes.
2. Celebrities—History—Anecdotes. 3. Food
habits—History—Anecdotes. 4. Fame—History—
Anecdotes. I. Jacob, Mark. II. Title.
  CT105.J28 2010
  920.073—dc22   2009052321

ISBN 978-0-307-46195-7

PRINTED IN THE UNITED STATES OF AMERICA

Design by Elizabeth Rendfleisch
Illustrations by Rick Tuma

10 9 8 7 6 5 4 3 2 1

First Edition

CONTENTS

HISTORY'S FIRST CELEBRITIES—its first "greats"—were Adam and Eve. And what was the most famous thing about them? What they ate, of course: the forbidden fruit. An apple, right? Well, maybe not.

The book of Genesis chronicles how Eve plucked fruit from a tree that was "good for food" but doesn't stipulate that the forbidden item was an apple. Genesis is vague on another point as well. It doesn't specify where Eden was, though some have assumed it was the Holy Land. If so, apples are out. Archaeological research indicates that apples didn't grow in the Middle East during ancient times.

Some scholars speculate that the forbidden fruit was an apricot, a peach, a pomegranate, or a fig. According to one theory, the tale of the apple arrived much later when Christian missionaries shared Bible stories with Teutonic tribes that had a strong attachment to the apple as the symbol of their earth mother.

When it comes to the history of food, extracting hard facts from mushy myths is difficult and often impossible. Some stories that are incredibly interesting are simply incredible.

The Roman emperor Elagabalus supposedly ordered six hundred ostriches killed so that his cooks could prepare ostrich-brain pies. Legend also says he fed dead slaves to eels to fatten them up. But the tales of Elagabalus are too fanciful for us to trust.

The bedrock of *What the Great Ate* is well-chronicled fact. Where legends are repeated, they are identified as such. Where apocryphal tales are cited, they're doubted or debunked.

We define a person as great if he or she has significantly influenced human development. But let's be crystal clear: "Great" does not mean "good." Joseph Stalin and Adolf Hitler were undoubtedly great; they altered history. Certainly, the world would have been better if their parents had forgotten to feed them. Even so, something can be learned from their dining habits. We'll tell stories about Stalin's tyranny at the dinner table and Hitler's paranoia about his birthday cake.

Our primary mission is to explain what the great actually ate—such as the sauerkraut savored by actor Gary Cooper, the breakfast cereal enjoyed by Saddam Hussein, and the "pig's delight" that was the Supreme Buddha's final dish. But we'll also examine how famous people used food as an artistic inspiration, a corporate symbol, even as a weapon. The human diet is governed by an almost sacred code, which is why most of us are either horrified or giddy when people start freelancing with food. The 1931 film *The Public Enemy* included many scenes of violence, including murder, but audiences were most shocked when the mobster played by James Cagney grabbed half a grapefruit and pushed it into his girlfriend's face.

This book is a fusion of two subjects that fascinate us—the lives of the people who shaped our world and the amazing lore that surrounds food. It is supposed to entertain, but it's not mere trivia. Eating is a primary instinct. How did it influence the higher accomplishments, such as writing, composing, and theorizing? What food-related obsessions guided humankind's development? And what is the fuel for genius?

Elvis Presley, justifying his gargantuan appetite, used to say, "The input has to be as great as the output."

Actress Sophia Loren once declared: "Everything you see I owe to spaghetti."

Yet food was a source of shame—not pride—for novelist Edith Wharton as she lingered on her deathbed, voicing regret over food she had eaten decades earlier.

In fact, meals have changed history. Food has been blamed for the deaths of kings and popes. A pretzel nearly ended the presidency of George W. Bush.

And food has reflected important truths. In the run-up to the American-led invasion of Iraq in 2003, U.S. lawmakers, upset at the lack of support from France, ordered congressional cafeterias to rename french fries "freedom fries." The action symbolized a nation pushing headlong toward war and brooking no dissent.

But we won't become lost in Higher Meaning. We promise to have fun.

Take the story of Georges Feydeau and the lobster. The French writer once ordered lobster at a restaurant, but the crustacean on his plate was missing a claw. The waiter explained that lobsters often fought each other in the restaurant's tank. "Then take this one away and bring me the victor," Feydeau ordered.

Perhaps Feydeau wasn't all that great, but he did produce that one great remark.

Consider this book as a tapas bar—not one big, fat entrée but, instead, a variety of tasty and surprising delights.

George Orwell wrote rather disparagingly that "a human being is primarily a bag for putting food into." But that's not a bad thing to be, if the bag is great enough and the food is good enough.

Bon appétit.

CHAPTER 1

Chicken à la King

The world's most powerful rulers ate with authority

*E*va Perón's 1946 visit to France was supposed to showcase Argentina's emergence as a major economic and cultural power. But the visit proved to be a lemon.

Argentina's first lady was used to the rustic steak-and-fries cuisine of her native country, and Paris's rich, refined cuisine did not agree with her stomach. Food seemed to vex her in other ways during the trip. She was undoubtedly peeved by the French newspaper that sarcastically opined, "Madame Perón will be made palatable to the French workers and peasants by being dressed as a piece of Argentine frozen beef."

The last straw was her dinner at the chic Restaurant des Ambassadeurs. A pair of clowns dressed as a camel approached her table and presented her with a bouquet of flowers—the bouquet was delivered through the camel's rear end. Appalled by the gesture, she stalked out of the restaurant.

Asparagus is typically cooked for a short time, only until it is tender. And apparently this is the way it has been cooked for centuries. That would explain why the Roman emperor **Augustus** reportedly coined the expression *velocius quam asparagi coquantor*—"faster than you can cook asparagus."

As a teenage king in the seventeenth century, **Louis XIV** of France devoured large portions that led to frequent bouts of diarrhea. He consumed several soups during the typical day, wrote the duc de Saint-Simon, "and everything that was served to him was full of spices, double at least of what one ordinarily puts in, and very strong."

One day in 1689, the adult Louis embraced a moment of self-sacrifice. After wars had drained the royal treasury, he ordered his gold dinner service melted down and sold. Thereafter, Louis ate his meals on silver plates and dishes.

When **Mao Ze-dong** urged his fellow Chinese to embrace the "class struggle," his exhortations were often food-laden.

Reflecting on his rural youth, Mao recalled, "For twenty-odd years, I grew up eating honeydew, being ignorant about everything." The masses, he once declared, see the "comfort of the capitalists, and they want to dip their own fingers in the gravy." And, lest the world forget, "a revolution is not a dinner party."

Before he rose to power in Italy, **Benito Mussolini** and his political allies frequently settled their disputes with adversaries by dueling with swords, even though it was illegal. Not wanting to alarm his wife's mother, who then lived with his family, Mussolini would use code language to inform his wife that he would be dueling later that day. "Today we're making spaghetti," he would tell her.

Nero, the famously narcissistic Roman despot, presided over the death of a species—an herb called *silphium* that once grew wild in what now is Libya. *Silphium* was so prized by ancient gastronomes that it was overharvested. For decades, it appeared to be extinct, until a single surviving plant was found. Nero's loyalists picked it and delivered it to the emperor, who promptly ate the last *silphium* ever found on Earth.

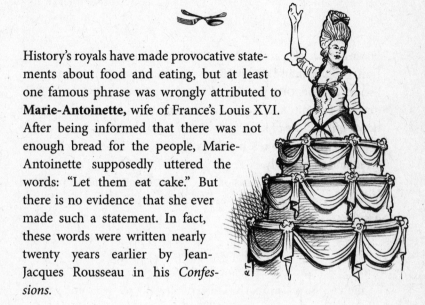

History's royals have made provocative statements about food and eating, but at least one famous phrase was wrongly attributed to **Marie-Antoinette,** wife of France's Louis XVI. After being informed that there was not enough bread for the people, Marie-Antoinette supposedly uttered the words: "Let them eat cake." But there is no evidence that she ever made such a statement. In fact, these words were written nearly twenty years earlier by Jean-Jacques Rousseau in his *Confessions.*

Many years before he became Israel's prime minister, **Ariel Sharon** was a guest at a dinner hosted by New York Mayor Ed Koch. The mayor recalled that "he ate off my plate! I've never seen anything like it."

The experience prompted Koch to deliver some tough love to Sharon in the mayor's trademark terse style. "I love you, and I worry you're going to die," he told Sharon. "You're fat and you eat too much."

The medieval king **Charlemagne** is believed to have possessed an asbestos tablecloth. At the end of the meal, he reportedly impressed banquet guests by throwing the tablecloth into a fire so that the crumbs would be consumed—leaving the tablecloth white and clean.

Long before Islamic fundamentalists forced him from power in Iran, **Mohammad Reza Pahlavi**—the shah—had to contend with the revolution that periodically occurred in his stomach. Reza loved the traditional Iranian dish of mutton's head and foot, but he ate only a little of it because his stomach couldn't tolerate it. The shah's belly dealt much better with chicken dishes, which he ate often and thoroughly.

"If you saw the remains of the chicken he ate," said his personal servant, "you'd think the bones had been washed with [the detergent] Fab."

In the year 888, **Guido,** the Duke of Spoleto, was viewed as a contender to assume the throne of the Frankish kingdom. But his frugal dining habits helped derail his bid. The archbishop of Metz, one of Guido's critics, snapped, "No one who is content with a modest meal can reign over us."

When the Roman emperor **Vitellius** was presented with the Shield of Minerva, he was preparing to eat, not to enter battle. The shield was his favorite dish—a hodgepodge of pike livers, peacock brains, flamingo tongues, and other exotic ingredients.

Vitellius made sure he was well fed by securing dinner invitations from several households on the same evening—and honoring all of them. He was such a glutton that he couldn't restrain himself from eating the meat that was placed on altars as religious offerings.

In the first years after the Cuban revolution of the late 1950s, the premier **Fidel Castro** bragged that the fifty-four flavors served by Havana's Coppelia ice-cream parlor well surpassed the choices offered by the capitalist ice-cream chain of Howard Johnson. Many years later, as Cuba's economy struggled, customers of Coppelia were lucky to find two flavors available.

As economic conditions deteriorated in Argentina after World War II, the country's president, **Juan Perón,** informed his citizens that he had been examining their garbage bins. The amount of meat and bread that the Argentine people discarded each day, he contended, was enough to feed a city as large as Buenos Aires.

In 1792, supporters of the French Revolution arrested **King Louis XVI** in the town of Varennes. But a leader of the revolt spread the false rumor that Louis had been captured in the village of Sainte-Menehould after insisting on stopping there to eat pigs' feet. Sainte-Menehould was known as a regional center of gastronomy, especially for pigs' feet, also called trotters.

The king's prodigious appetite made the tale believable. On his wedding day, for example, the teenage Louis devoured an enormous amount of food. He had been urged not to overindulge— lest it hinder his ability to consummate the marriage—but the future king had replied, "Why not? I sleep so much better that way."

Soviet dictator **Joseph Stalin** craved bananas but insisted on quality. According to one biographer, he "got very cantankerous" when served a substandard banana.

The Roman emperor **Nero** once spoke of mushrooms as "food of the gods." He had at least one good reason to pay tribute to mushrooms. They were the vehicle used to poison his stepfather, **Claudius,** and create the vacancy that Nero filled. Agrippina, Claudius's fourth wife, is suspected of dousing Claudius's mushrooms with poison.

Nicolae Ceaușescu ruled Romania with an iron fist from 1967 to 1989, and he never ate anything unless a food tester had first sampled it to make certain it wasn't poisoned.

A portable chemical lab accompanied Ceaușescu on his foreign trips to verify that ingredients for his meals were not poisonous or radioactive, and an aide supervised the preparation of the communist premier's meals. These foods were placed in a special cart that was locked and then wheeled out of the kitchen—under the watchful eye of a bodyguard—and into the dining room. Unlocking the food cart was no simple matter; the elaborate code for the lock was changed every day. Once the cart was unlocked, Ceaușescu's food was served by a designated waiter who traveled with the dictator.

The regime of Soviet dicator **Joseph Stalin** took a different precaution for poison prevention. At mealtimes, he would be presented with several identical plates of food. He would choose only one of them.

Over the years, **Mao Ze-dong** became frustrated with the elaborate meal testing that was used to ensure that his food was safe. "It upsets everyone for no reason," he complained.

If **Montezuma** were alive today, the Aztec emperor would probably prefer to dine in libraries, not restaurants. No one was permitted to speak loudly or make any other noise during his meals. Although the emperor ate in the presence of many people, a gilt wooden screen was placed in front of Montezuma to provide privacy. Only a few elderly nobles who stood near him at attention were allowed to watch the emperor eat.

During the 1970s, North Korea's dictatorial heir, **Kim Jong-il,** established a health institute named for his ruling father, **Kim Il-sung.** Researchers were instructed to find ways to help the elder Kim live a long and pleasant life. One of the institute's major recommendations was particularly bizarre: North Korea's aging leader was advised to eat dog penises that were at least seven centimeters long.

As he concluded a visit to Great Britain, **King Carlos I** of Portugal was asked by his host, **King Edward VII,** what had impressed him the most during his trip.

"The roast beef," he replied.

Slightly disappointed by his guest's reply, King Edward probed, "Is that all?"

"Well," added the Portuguese monarch, "the boiled beef is quite good too."

Adolf Hitler's meals generally consisted of side dishes. Meat was virtually unheard of at the German leader's dinner table. But his Austrian cook—an enthusiastic carnivore—tried to sneak a bit of meat broth or fat into Hitler's meals.

The Führer discovered the attempted deception and limited his cook's fare to only two items: clear soup and mashed potato.

Just before he crossed the English Channel to visit France in 1534, England's **King Henry VIII** wanted to ensure that an ample supply of his favorite foods awaited him. A dispatch was sent across the channel to those guarding the king's provisions.

"It is the king's special commandment," the dispatch declared, that all of the artichokes "be kept for him."

In 1969, when **Benazir Bhutto** moved to the United States to attend college at Harvard-Radcliffe, certain foods emerged as her favorites. Pakistan's future prime minister drank gallons of apple cider during her brief years in New England. And she recalled devouring "unconscionable numbers" of peppermint-stick ice-cream cones, sprinkled with chocolate-flavored jimmies.

Most emperors enjoy lives of rich foods and elegant entertaining. Yet when Japan's **Emperor Ogimachi** began his reign in 1567, the Imperial Court was teetering on the edge of poverty. Tax collections declined, and the operator of a large silver mine stopped paying tribute to the emperor.

At one Imperial Court dinner, the meal was nothing more than wheat vermicelli soup. The nobles in the emperor's court were thrilled to receive gifts as simple as a few biscuits or a bundle of dried persimmons.

On May 14, 1610, the royal carriage transporting **King Henri IV** of France became stalled in traffic at Les Halles, site of Paris's largest food market. French author Émile Zola called Les Halles "Paris's stomach"—a place where one observed "the bourgeoisie munching, digesting, peacefully ruminating its joys and flaccid morals." Les Halles' moral meter took a steep dive on that May day when a religious zealot named François Ravaillac approached Henri's carriage and stabbed the French king twice, killing him.

As potatoes were brought from the Americas to Europe and became popular, new varieties were developed. In nineteenth-century England, several were named for members of the British royal family.

One was called the **Victoria**. Another was named the Purple-Eyed **King Edward**.

As a young man, **Mustafa Kemal Atatürk**—Turkey's future leader—told a poetry-writing friend that life "is but a dry chestnut." He ate a lot of dry chestnuts, sometimes while drinking an anise-flavored spirit called raki. It was a beverage, he said, that "makes one want to be a poet."

Once Atatürk became president of Turkey, drinking and dining were no longer a topic for starry-eyed stanzas. In a 1925 speech, he declared that one of the nation's critical needs was to train waiters to provide good table service. He also noted that restaurant menus offered too many dishes, which he argued was bad for health and bad for the economy.

Ugandan dictator **Idi Amin** once told an adviser before dinner, "I want your heart. I want to eat your children." Were his remarks a gruesome metaphor or a disturbingly literal confession? Opinions vary.

His exiled health minister, Henry Kyemba, stated that "on several occasions he told me quite proudly that he had eaten the organs or flesh of his human victims." But Otonde Odera, Amin's Kenyan cook, scoffed at rumors that his former boss was a part-time cannibal. According to Odera, the dictator consumed "normal food," and a spicy rice dish called *pilau* was one of his favorites.

Even cooking normal food for Amin was not without its drama. Odera was imprisoned for four nights out of suspicion that he was trying to poison the dictator.

The Roman emperor **Tiberius** ate melons at nearly every meal. He also adored cucumbers and sought to have them grown throughout the year, never traveling without them.

In 1568, after her forces were defeated by her half brother's army near the city of Glasgow, **Mary Queen of Scots** felt she had only one option left—flee to England and seek the support of her cousin, Elizabeth I.

With her enemies in hot pursuit, Mary shaved off her hair to disguise her appearance. During her three-day journey south, she survived on sour milk and oatmeal. But drinking rancid milk was nothing compared to the fate that awaited Mary in England.

During his years as president of the Philippines, **Ferdinand Marcos** consumed a diet built around sardines and vegetables. One of his favorite vegetables was called malunggay. According to a Filipino newspaper, Marcos was "a malunggay addict" who consumed soup full of the vegetable's green, oval-shaped leaves. This is believed to be the vegetable that Marcos referred to in his diary as "guaranteed to stop the aging process."

In July 1959, a carbonated cold war broke out at a trade fair in Moscow. Soviet premier **Nikita Khrushchev** and U.S. Vice President **Richard Nixon** vigorously debated capitalism and communism over cups of Pepsi-Cola at the soft-drink company's pavilion. Nixon had invited Khrushchev to the pavilion to sample two versions of Pepsi—one made with American water and one with Russian water. Khrushchev declared that the Moscow version of Pepsi obviously tasted better and instructed others around him to try this version of the cola.

It isn't clear whether Nixon suggested the soda tasting to Khrushchev as a favor to a Pepsi executive who, the night before, had told the vice president he was desperate "to get a Pepsi in Khrushchev's hand."

Catherine de Medicis, the Italian-born wife of France's King Henri II, had a legendary appetite. At one point, Catherine nearly died from a gluttonous binge that included a classic Florentine dish called *cibrèo*. Think of it as an Italian version of soul food: *Cibrèo* is made with the gizzard, liver, testicles, and cockscomb of a young rooster, which is mixed with beans and egg yolks, and then served on toast.

A few years before his election as Iran's president, **Mahmoud Ahmadinejad** was serving as mayor of Tehran. Although he had many decisions to make, where to eat lunch wasn't one of them. Each day he brought a sack lunch from home. In 2005, then President Ahmadinejad became annoyed at a reporter who asked him if he still brought lunch from home each day.

"That continues," he replied. "Is there a problem with that? What's wrong if you want to eat the food that your wife has cooked?"

Canadian Prime Minister **Pierre Trudeau** was well schooled in food and wine, but he was clueless when it came to cooking. "If a meal was not provided, he would eat spaghetti out of a can," remembered one friend.

Charles de Talleyrand-Périgord was a skilled French diplomat who briefly served as the nation's prime minister in 1815. He once used his wicked wit to express his dissatisfaction with a meal. While dining with a French governmental minister, Talleyrand tasted the fish and found it was cold.

"That is a magnificent carp," said the minister. "How do you like it? It came from my estate in Virsur Ainse."

"Did it?" asked Talleyrand. "But why did you not have it cooked *here*?"

Winston Churchill is often credited for a similarly sharp-tongued quote: "Well, dinner would have been splendid if the wine had been as cold as the soup, the beef as rare as the service, the brandy as old as the fish, and the maid as willing as the Duchess." Yet it is highly doubtful that this quip originated from the British prime minister. Among other reasons for skepticism, one editor opined that the notoriously impatient Churchill "would not have stayed for the second course of such a meal."

Rumanika, polygamist king of the Karagwe region of East Africa in the mid-1800s, kept his wives well fed—whether they liked it or not. They drank a steady diet of milk sucked by straw from a gourd and became so fat that they could not stand up and instead rested on the floors of their royal huts. If any wives resisted, they were force-fed by a man who stood over them with a whip.

Benito Mussolini's table manners were deplorable. He once hosted Greek Prime Minister **Elefthérios Venizélos** for a formal dinner but didn't speak a single word to Venizélos. Instead, Mussolini directed all of his conversation to the waiters.

If it had been up to Mussolini's wife, Rachele, those annoying ceremonial dinners would have ended much sooner. In 1936, she tried but failed to persuade her husband to leave office as Italian premier. Rachele even suggested the very words he should use to explain his resignation to **King Vittorio Emmanuel III.**

She urged Mussolini to tell the king, "I have restored peace and prosperity at home and made Italy great and powerful abroad. Now the Italians aren't all 'ice-cream sellers' anymore."

The people who prepared meals for the British crown during the fourteenth century were not following precise directions. The Forme of Cury, a collection of recipes for dishes served to **King Richard II** and his barons, offered crude instructions. One of its recipes advised cooks, "Take rabbits and smite them to pieces; seethe them in grease."

Ten years before he was elected president of Poland, **Lech Wałęsa** was leading a strike at a shipyard in Gdansk. During the strike, he faced a midday dilemma: which to do first—go home to eat lunch or answer questions from eager journalists?

On some days, his decision was easy. Whenever his wife, Danka, telephoned him to say she had fried his favorite fish for lunch, Wałęsa would tell reporters, "Gentlemen, you're just going to have to wait."

What is the best way to prepare a huge turbot that has been caught in the Adriatic Sea? The first-century Roman emperor **Domitian** found this question so critical but perplexing that he arranged an informal council of advisers to seek suggestions. In Domitian's day, coastal areas were patrolled by the emperor's agents, who would strong-arm fishermen to hand over their best fish to Domitian.

Years before **Pol Pot** and his Khmer Rouge communists took control of Cambodia in 1975, the ruling Sangkum Party published a booklet predicting what communist rule would mean for the nation. "There would be no delicious food to eat," predicted Sangkum. "If you ate more than allowed, the government would learn about it from your children in secret and you would be taken out and shot."

Although these warnings may have struck many Cambodians as far-fetched rhetoric, the future would show they weren't far off the mark. One of the achievements that Pol Pot's regime proclaimed was that it had successfully achieved communal eating throughout most of the country.

Oliver Cromwell, the seventeenth-century Lord Protector of England, was not always the stern, humorless man that history has portrayed. He liked to play practical jokes. One evening, Cromwell was dining with his advisers when suddenly—as he had prearranged—a drumbeat was heard. Cromwell's footguards entered the dining room, grabbed food haphazardly off the table, and quickly departed, leaving behind a stunned table of advisers.

In the eighteenth century, **King Stanislaw Leszczyński** of Poland suffered a big demotion. Backed by Russian troops, a group of Polish nobles forced him into exile. His consolation prize was to preside over the duchy of Lorraine in what is now France. There he was introduced to a cake called *kugelhopf* that he enjoyed. But Leszczyński had a complaint: the cake's texture was slightly dry.

Although he was forced to settle for the title of duke, he would not accept a merely satisfactory *kugelhopf*. He reportedly began soaking the cake in rum, and the resulting taste pleased him greatly. He named his amended version of the cake after his favorite literary hero—Ali Baba. Today many restaurants serve an almost identical dessert called *baba au rhum*.

In the early 1950s, a team of British chemists developed a method for pumping huge amounts of air into sweetened milk solids. The result was a product called Mr. Whippy Super-Soft Ice Cream. One member of this research team was the United Kingdom's future prime minister, **Margaret Thatcher.**

France's **King Henri III** drank only water because his stomach couldn't tolerate wine. During the early years of his reign, courtiers were allowed to mill about him as he ate meals. But the king returned from a lengthy visit to Poland with new dining habits. His meals were no longer public events; a balustrade was erected to ensure that visitors kept their distance while he ate.

Many years before he became president of the Czech Republic, **Václav Havel** endured the same fate as many other political dissidents: imprisonment. Writing from his cell in 1980, Havel asked his wife, Olga, to send him personal items, including a toothbrush, toothpaste, skin lotion, and a razor for shaving. Because the communist authorities set strict limits on a parcel's weight, he suspected that Olga might not be able to fit all of the requested items into the parcel.

"But [send] nothing at the expense of cigarettes, tea and chocolate," Havel stressed. Tea and chocolate, he wrote, were two examples of "the whims that give me inner comfort."

During the 1920s, Perugina, the Italian confectionery company, placed an ad in newspapers that offered **Benito Mussolini**'s personal testimonial: "I tell you, and I authorize you to repeat it, that your chocolate is truly exquisite."

Queen Victoria remembered her childhood as rather dull, including the food she was served. As a girl, she promised herself that she would eat whatever she wanted as an adult and that mutton would not be on her menu.

Chinese leader **Mao Ze-dong** insisted on the highest-quality foods and was fussy about how they were prepared. Chairman Mao's rice preferences required farmers to husk the harvested rice slowly and by hand in order to preserve a membrane between the husk and kernel that Mao believed enhanced the rice's taste. A special farm was established to grow rice for Mao's table, and the water used for its rice paddies was considered to be the country's best. His poultry and milk were also produced at specially designated farms that had won him over for their quality.

Mao's favorite foods were frequently shipped to him from distant regions of China. Once, a special fish from the southern province of Hubei was transported alive six hundred miles—in a plastic bag with oxygenated water—to Mao's private residence, where it was prepared for the Chinese leader's next meal.

Although French President **Valéry Giscard d'Estaing** loved hunting, he didn't care much for eating the prey he had killed. Scrambled eggs and smoked salmon were two of his preferred foods.

August 9, 1978—during Giscard's presidency—was a momentous date in French history. For the first time in more than a century, the national government stopped setting the price of bread.

A nineteenth-century biographer wrote of **Mary Queen of Scots** that "her appetite was better than her digestion." A Catholic cardinal in France who was Mary's guardian wrote that "if she had her way and ate as much as she liked, her stomach would often suffer for it."

Her fragile health lends credence to the story that *marmalade* originated from the French phrase: *Marie est malade*—"Mary is sick." According to this account, orange preserves were the only thing Mary could eat when she was ailing. Yet the credibility of this charming tale is shattered by the fact that the word *marmalade* appeared in the English language eighteen years before Mary's birth.

A lot of books and articles claim that Ethiopian emperor **Menelik II** ate pages ripped out of a Bible in hopes of restoring his health during the 1910s. Although this story is highly doubtful, the retelling of it may have helped inspire a publisher in 2002 to release an edible book for children that was appropriately titled *Eat This Book*—its pages were made from potato starch.

The habits of staff and servants annoyed Russia's **Catherine the Great** during her 1780 visit to Narva, a city in modern-day Estonia. While she was there, Catherine wrote that female attendants at a dinner table stood so close behind her chair and "breathed such hot air on me that I didn't feel the cold." At one point, she wrote, "I was terrified that [an attendant] was going to rub my plates with rhubarb the way they rub them with garlic."

Catherine was generally a light eater. One of her favorite dishes was boiled beef with pickled cucumbers. A typical dinner at Catherine's imperial residence included soup, boiled chicken, roast leg of mutton or beef, hash duck, and stewed mushrooms.

She fussed over the eating habits of her children, including

Prince Alexander. Her children were forbidden to drink any beverage without first eating a piece of bread.

According to his former personal chef, North Korean ruler **Kim Jong-il** always asked for extra portions of *toro,* his favorite type of sushi. Although Kim knew only a few words of English then, for some reason he would utter the English words "one more" to inform his chef that he was ready for more *toro.*

"How can you be expected to govern a country that has 246 varieties of cheese?" French President **Charles de Gaulle** was quoted as asking in 1962.

But it's disputable whether he really posed this question. Some say he uttered a similar comment eleven years earlier in which the number of cheeses was 265.

Either figure underestimates by hundreds the number of French cheeses. Of all of the varieties of *fromage* in his native country, de Gaulle's favorite was an aged, orange-hued cheese called Mimolette.

Queen Victoria's sister, Feodora, had two suggestions for the British monarch: Eat more slowly and add less salt to meat. One of Victoria's ministers, Lord Melbourne, advised the queen to eat only when she was hungry. She scoffed at the recommendation by replying that she was *always* hungry.

The queen's appetite was put to an extreme test when she married Prince Albert in 1840. One of their wedding gifts was a thousand-pound wheel of cheddar cheese.

Vicente Fox Quesada's presidential experience moved from carbonation to nation. He became president of Coca-Cola Mexico in 1975, and Mexican voters elected him their president in 2000.

Soon after he left office as Mexican president, Fox offered advice to aspiring politicians, urging them to "learn to eat very fast, the minute they put your plate down, because they will immediately introduce you to speak, and then you will stand at the podium looking out longingly at the delicious cake the audience is enjoying. Then they will hand you another cup of coffee and whisk you out the door, hungry and light-headed, and a bit cranky."

A host of slaves and domestic staff labored hard to ensure that Egyptian kings ate well—even after these rulers died. Within the ornate tomb that was built for **King Den,** who died around 3000 BCE, attendants placed several amphorae filled with foods. After all, the king would need nourishment in the next world. Each amphora was sealed with fat, a method of preserving food that survives today in the French bistro dish called duck confit.

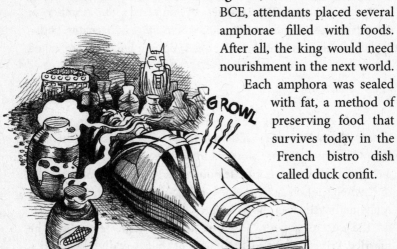

France's **King Louis XV** was not only an eager diner but was also willing to do some of the cooking himself. Louis XV would prepare omelets, lark pâté, and other dishes.

On Sundays, boiled eggs always graced Louis' plate. On that day, French people paraded to the king's palace to watch him dine. Perhaps they admired Louis' ability to clip off one end of an egg with a single stroke of his fork—a performance followed by a royal attendant's anticlimactic announcement: "The king is about to eat his egg!"

King George IV of Britain adored peaches, especially when they were stewed in brandy. He became accustomed to eating two peaches every evening when they were in season. One year, poor weather damaged the peach trees supplying the royal household. The king was given the bad news: He would need to reduce his consumption to one peach nightly. But George chose an alternative that a biographer called "an excellent compromise between frugality and epicurism"—he would eat two peaches every other night.

In 1925, soon after he was elected as a delegate to the Communist Party Congress, future Soviet premier **Nikita Khrushchev** met Joseph Stalin—the party's supreme leader. Khrushchev was so eager to get a front seat near Stalin at these meetings that he generally skipped breakfast to arrive early.

Montezuma introduced Europeans to chocolate in the sixteenth century, but the chocolate they tasted was a far cry from the version that is widely eaten today. The Aztec ruler consumed his chocolate as a cold, unsweetened beverage that was typically flavored with vanilla and hot chilies. Chocolate was reportedly the only beverage that Montezuma drank.

In 1604, a Spaniard played the role of food critic when he wrote that the beverage called *chocolatl* "is loathsome to such as are not acquainted with it, having a skumme or frothe that is very unpleasant to taste."

On New Year's Eve 1995, several days before he died, the terminally ill former French President **François Mitterrand** gathered with friends at his home and enjoyed his legendary "last supper" while stretched out on a chaise longue.

The meal began with several servings of oysters, but the evening's height of gastronomy was reached when Mitterrand reportedly devoured an illegal delicacy: ortolan. The small, endangered songbird is typically drowned in Armagnac brandy, its feathers plucked, and then it is roasted and eaten whole—bones and all.

Mitterrand reportedly ate his ortolan the traditional way, concealing his face behind a napkin as he ate the bird. It is debated whether this tradition reflects the notoriety of eating a forbidden food or the desire to capture fully the aromas of the bird. A Mitterrand biographer wrote that after ten minutes of concealing himself, Mitterrand emerged from the napkin "capsized with happiness, his eyes sparkling" and ready to face his impending death.

Qianlong, one of the longest-reigning emperors of China's Qing dynasty, ate very well but very fast. According to a French priest who frequented the emperor's court during the 1770s, Qianlong ate meals of "quantity" and "magnificence" but never took more than fifteen minutes to devour them.

The road to South Africa's presidency was a rocky one for **Nelson Mandela.** He spent more than twenty-seven years in prison while the country's white rulers struggled to maintain the system of racial apartheid.

While imprisoned, Mandela redirected much of his passion to a fruit and vegetable garden. To provide compost for the garden, Mandela collected the bones that remained after prison meals and persuaded fellow inmates to hammer these bones into a powder that was added to the soil.

By 1975, he and other prisoners had grown two thousand chilies, nearly a thousand tomatoes, two watermelons, and other assorted plants. Mandela's obsessive oversight of the garden was almost unnerving to fellow prisoners. One of them wrote that "he is fanatical about it."

In December 1928, **Indira Gandhi**—the woman who was destined to become India's prime minister—made a bad impression by showing up at a Calcutta event wearing drab clothes. But her public image was redeemed several days later when a rumor spread widely among Indians—who love their bananas—that she had devoured six of them for breakfast.

Soviet dictator **Joseph Stalin** brought both his appetite and practical-joke playing to dinner parties. Once he placed a tomato on the seat of a Politburo member and laughed riotously when the member sat on it and created an unpleasant noise heard throughout the room. At another dinner, Stalin secretly ordered an attendant to add extra pepper to one guest's food.

Although the Soviet premier found these incidents humorous, they were also a control mechanism. According to one Stalin biographer, these practical jokes reflected the dictator's desire "to keep people on edge."

Nikolai Bulganin, a high-ranking communist official, once said, "You come to Stalin's table as a friend, but you never know if you'll get home by yourself or if you'll be given a ride—to prison!"

For a period of time after leaving office as Canada's prime minister, **Brian Mulroney** had his mail forwarded to him in care of New York City's Le Cirque restaurant.

A British intelligence report from 1945 had some revealing observations about Germany's leader: "**Hitler** eats rapidly, mechanically. For him food is merely an indispensable means of subsistence."

Hitler was not talkative at the dinner table: "Quite often Hitler will sit there throughout the entire meal, turned to his own thoughts, seemingly without listening to the talk going on around him."

When Mexican revolutionaries overthrew and executed Emperor Maximilian in 1867, his wife, **Empress Carlota**, was fortunate enough to have been in Europe. But news of the revolt left Carlota emotionally unhinged as she traveled to Rome.

Fearful that someone was trying to poison her, she limited her diet to oranges and nuts. The petrified empress even examined the shells of nuts for signs that someone had tampered with them. She ordered her carriage driver to stop at the city's Trevi fountain so she could collect water unlikely to be poisoned. To ease Carlota's worries of tainted food, chickens were kept in her hotel suite in Rome and then slaughtered and cooked on a charcoal stove that had been hastily installed within the suite.

One morning, the empress interrupted the pope's breakfast, dipped her fingers into his hot chocolate, and licked them. "This at least is not poisoned," she declared to shocked Vatican officials.

By the spring of 2009, flight attendants were probably dreading the day when Australian Prime Minister **Kevin Rudd** boarded one of their flights. In January of that year, an airline staffer was driven to tears by Rudd's persistent demand for a meat-free meal. In 2008, the prime minister reportedly got testy with another flight attendant because the in-flight meal featured sandwiches instead of hot food.

One day in 1978, the people of New York City presented Romanian dictator **Nicolae Ceaușescu** with food, but not in the form he was accustomed to receiving it.

Soon after protesters had thrown food at the communist leader's motorcade, the city's mayor, Ed Koch, paid a visit to Ceaușescu's hotel suite. "This is an outrage," Romania's president fumed, declaring that his life had been threatened.

"A couple of tomatoes and a few eggs?" replied the mayor.

"They could have been hand grenades," Ceaușescu angrily retorted.

Mayor Koch offered a conciliatory request. "Let's be friends, Mr. President, and maybe one day we can eat together in a Romanian restaurant here," said Koch.

Ceaușescu asked his staff to draft a press statement about the mayor's visit. "Just say, 'Problems of common interest were discussed,'" he instructed.

To keep his spirits from languishing during his lengthy time in prison, **Nelson Mandela**—the man destined to become South Africa's president—dreamed of the meals his wife, Winnie, used to cook for him. Referring to one of his wife's most scrumptious dishes, Mandela wrote to her, "If I don't get that dish when I return [home] some day I will dissolve the marriage on the spot."

The secret 1971 visit by U.S. Secretary of State **Henry Kissinger** to China opened the door to normalized relations between the two nations. But it also left some of his Chinese hosts with strange impressions of American tastes.

Attendants who worked at the official guesthouse in Beijing found that bowls full of candy placed in Kissinger's guest quarters were empty the next day. Even the wrappers were gone, prompting the attendants to inform Chinese leader **Mao Ze-dong** that the Americans had eaten the sweets, wrapper and all. They didn't realize that Kissinger and his aides had packed up the candies as souvenirs of their trip.

Diet was a subject that was never far from **Adolf Hitler**'s thoughts. Although he was not a strict vegetarian, he often sang the virtues of a vegetable-centered diet to those around him. Hitler's secretary said that during the final months of World War II, the Führer's talk was confined generally to two subjects: his diet and his dog.

Hitler's personal library included roughly a thousand books on the subjects of diet and nutrition. Several of these books had his handwritten notes scribbled along the margins.

Getting invited to a banquet hosted by the English court during the sixteenth century must have been a thrill. But for the monarchy, it was sometimes a case of "been there, done that." Royal feasts could last for several hours. Once, **King Henry VIII** relieved his boredom at a banquet by throwing sugarplums at the guests.

When he was eating—not tossing—his food, Henry heartily indulged in a variety of foods: baked lampreys and game pies stuffed with oranges and even dolphin, which was then considered a delicacy.

Around 1950, **Joseph Stalin** took a sudden fancy to canned pineapple. The Soviet dictator's fondness for the fruit was so intense that he instructed a subordinate to send a telegram to the communist regime in China. Aware that pineapples grew well in southern China, Stalin ordered his staff to ask the Chinese to "provide us a place where we can build a factory to can pineapples."

A Soviet colleague warned him that **Mao Ze-dong** was likely to view such a proposal as a slap at China's sovereignty. But Stalin insisted that a telegram be sent.

Within a couple of days, Mao responded. "If you are interested in canned pineapple, give us credits, we will build a factory, and we will supply you with the product of the factory as a way of paying back the credits."

After reading Mao's telegram, Stalin began cursing.

Throughout history, world leaders have been forced out of office for a variety of reasons, but one of the most bizarre ousters occurred on September 9, 2008. On that day, a court in Thailand ruled that Prime Minister **Samak Sundaravej** must vacate his office because he had violated the nation's constitution. His transgression? Samak had accepted payments of $2,350 for appearing on four episodes of a televised Thai cooking show called *Tasting and Complaining*.

Before **King Louis XIV** assumed control of France's affairs in 1651, his mother, **Anne of Austria,** served as regent. Even though many European nobles were eating with forks by the mid-seventeenth century, Anne would have nothing to do with this utensil. She ate meat with her fingers throughout her life.

Like any good son, Louis followed his mother's example. Yet going fork-free was not just a personal preference for him. When the Duke of Burgundy and his brothers arrived at the king's court for a meal, they brought their own forks with them, but Louis refused to let them use these utensils in his presence.

Italian premier **Benito Mussolini** felt that meals should not take more than three minutes and that no one should devote more than ten minutes per day to eating. This hurry-up style of dining probably contributed to Mussolini's stomach ailments. Those gastrointestinal maladies prompted him to rely mostly on a liquid diet. He drank three liters of milk on a typical day.

King George III of Great Britain had an appetite for mutton—and for some reason, he generally ate his mutton while standing.

At his coronation banquet, the king and queen ate with abandon, prompting the poet Thomas Gray to lament that the royals were eating "like farmers."

In December 2003, U.S. soldiers discovered Iraq's vanquished dictator, **Saddam Hussein,** hiding near the city of Tikrit. In the ensuing months, while guarding the captured Saddam, troops learned about his tastes by delivering him breakfast each morning.

Saddam loved Kellogg's Raisin Bran Crunch cereal. One morning, when soldiers brought the deposed dictator a different cereal, Saddam was quick to protest: "No Froot Loops!"

The visit by France's **King Henri III** to Venice in 1574 was celebrated with a strange meal in which 1,286 items—everything from bread to forks to centerpieces—were made out of spun sugar.

Israeli Prime Minister **Golda Meir** had two menus—one for cooking and one for diplomacy. She once invited U.S. Senator Frank Church, a member of the Foreign Relations Committee, to breakfast at her residence. After he arrived, she abruptly left the room. A confused Church soon found her in the kitchen, cooking their breakfast. "You came to help?" she asked. The prime minister instructed him to go into the living room, where she would bring him breakfast.

Then Meir placed an order: "There are a few things you can help me with—Phantoms, land-to-air missiles, and help Russian Jews to emigrate."

Caracalla, the third-century Roman emperor, was praised by a contemporary for grinding his own grain for the barley cake he later consumed.

Adolf Hitler had a sweet tooth, especially when it came to the rich pastries of his native Austria. Yet on his birthday in 1923, Germany's future chancellor was in no mood to eat. In an apartment filled with well-wishers, Hitler confidant Ernst Hanfstaengl recalled the cakes "with swastikas and eagles in whipped cream all over them." When asked by Hanfstaengl why he wasn't eating a piece of cake, Hitler replied that he feared being poisoned. The apartment's landlord, he said, was a Jew.

CHAPTER 2

Eating Their Words

Writers plotted a novel approach to dining

*E*RNEST HEMINGWAY ATE some unusual foods in his life—
dolphin liver, for example. But the strangest food he consumed was
an improvised meal during his teen years.

While hunting with his father, thirteen-year-old Ernest and
his friend killed a porcupine that had injured a dog with its quills.
Ernest's father was furious that the boys had killed the porcupine.
As punishment, he ordered the boys to cook and eat the animal.
Years later, the friend recalled the wretched experience: "We
cooked the haunches for hours, but they were still about as tender
and tasty as a piece of shoe leather."

On another occasion, dinner turned into a pop quiz. The elder
Hemingway cooked local game that he and Ernest had hunted
and killed, then blindfolded his son and asked him to identify the
different animals from their taste.

After hearing from a doctor that low blood sugar fed his lifelong
craving for booze, **Sinclair Lewis** started devouring hefty portions
of sweets in order to curb his alcohol consumption. In one day,
the author of *Babbitt* consumed an entire two-pound box of Louis
Sherry chocolates. But not all of his sweets freed him from alco-

hol. He concocted a chocolate cookie recipe that required a shot of bourbon.

Irish playwright **Samuel Beckett** ate out frequently, probably because neither he nor his wife had a knack for cooking. When Beckett dined at the Parisian restaurant Aux Iles Marquises, he insisted on sitting far away from the restaurant's lobster and trout tank, which he found upsetting.

Growing up in Harlem during the Great Depression, novelist **James Baldwin** ate a lot of corned beef. In an essay, Baldwin recalled: "My mother fried corned beef, she boiled it, she baked it, she put rice in it, she disguised it in corn bread, she boiled it in soup, she wrapped it in cloth, she beat it with a hammer, she banged it against the wall, she threw it into the ceiling."

In 1878, **Mark Twain** and his family embarked on a sixteen-month trip to Europe. Twain found European coffee to be a "feeble, characterless" beverage. The bread was "cold and tough," and the butter lacked salt and was made of "goodness knows what." And steak? "They have it in Europe, but they don't know how to cook it."

When playwright **Neil Simon** struggled with a scene, he used small bags of treats to motivate himself. Simon would tell himself things like: "Okay, finish this scene and you can eat some Fritos."

e. e. cummings was usually a late riser who ate a huge breakfast. He enjoyed eggplant, shish kebab, and other Middle Eastern foods. A menu from Khoury's, a Syrian restaurant that was one of his favorites, is among the documents in the collection of cummings papers held by the New York Public Library.

In 1822, **James Fenimore Cooper** founded the Bread and Cheese Club. Despite its name, the club's focus was not loaves and Limburger. It was essentially a social club, although its members did plenty of eating. The club gathered on Thursday evenings at a New York City tavern, and each meeting concluded with a supper.

In December 1850, Cooper battled stomach ailments and grumbled that his wife was far too pleased to act as his dietary czar. "You cannot imagine the old lady's delight at getting me under, in the way of food," he groused. "I get no meat, or next to none . . . This morning, being Xmas, I had a blow-out of oysters, and at dinner it will go hard if I do not get a cut into the turkey." It's unknown whether Mr. or Mrs. Cooper won this yuletide war of wills.

Eggs can be poached, boiled, scrambled, or fried. But during a trip through Scotland, **John Keats** didn't want to see another egg—no matter how it was cooked. "No supper but eggs and oat cake," Keats complained about the food he and a friend endured, adding that "we have lost the sight of white bread entirely—now we have eaten nothing but eggs all day—about 10 apiece and they have become sickening."

Keats's greatest culinary passion was Bordeaux red wines, or what the British call claret. Keats rhapsodized over claret that "fills the mouth with a gushing freshness." A friend of Keats claimed that the poet once covered his tongue with cayenne pepper just to stimulate his taste buds and enhance his enjoyment of claret.

When short story writer **Flannery O'Connor** took a seat at the dinner table, one of her mother's rules required young Flannery to eat her vegetables before moving on to other foods on her plate.

In a 1960 interview, O'Connor recalled a letter she'd received from a woman who complained "that my book left a bad taste in her mouth. I wrote back to her and said, 'You weren't supposed to eat it.'"

During the 1950s, **Gabriel García Márquez** was a struggling Colombian writer living in Paris who lacked the money to enjoy the city's premier restaurants. When he returned in 1968 as a literary success, García Márquez said his stomach wanted to make up for the lavish meals his poverty had denied him years earlier. He told an interviewer, "I wanted to eat all things I had not eaten, drink all the wine I could not afford to buy. And I hated it. I hate Paris."

García Márquez struggled to maintain a healthy body weight. "I am on an eternal diet," he said in 1988. "Half my life I couldn't eat what I wanted because I couldn't afford to, the other half because I have to diet."

Canadian-born writer **Saul Bellow** liked to both cook and eat. But he panicked in 1985 when a houseguest presented him with two pounds of corned beef from the Chicago deli owned by Bellow's cousin. Bellow loved corned beef, but he'd just learned that his cousin's deli had been closed temporarily—a decision made after some of the deli's customers had fallen ill with salmonella poisoning. Bellow's devotion to corned beef forced a compromise: He ate a slice, but only after thoroughly heating it.

Dr. Seuss's classic children's book *Green Eggs and Ham* wouldn't have been as charming if author **Ted Geisel** had stayed with an early draft and called the dish "green ham and eggs." By swapping the ham and the eggs, he invented a nifty phrase that rhymed with the name of his character Sam-I-Am.

A few years after the death of writer **Gertrude Stein** in 1946, her longtime companion published *The Alice B. Toklas Cookbook*, which featured a recipe for hashish fudge. Toklas's recipe came from a friend, and she claimed to be unfamiliar with it before publication.

The recipe is misnamed: The cannabis required is not hashish but rather garden-variety marijuana leaves. And although the recipe may have inspired some people to bake marijuana brownies when pot use soared in later decades, Toklas's version was not the sort of thing that could be whipped up easily by stoners in a dorm room. It included sugar, butter, black peppercorns, nutmeg, cinnamon, coriander, dates, figs, almonds, peanuts, and "a bunch of canibus sativa . . . pulverized."

For most of his adult life, **Walt Whitman** ate heavy, high-fat meals. In 1885, Whitman's friend John Burroughs cut right to the chase. "I am almost certain," he told Whitman, "you eat too heartily and make too much blood and fat." Burroughs advised Whitman to eat only "a little meat once a day" and to stop eating meat and oysters for breakfast.

Franz Kafka had chronic digestive problems, which prompted him to adopt a lacto-vegetarian diet. Kafka drank large quantities of milk, which he considered a crucial ingredient for good health. He also embraced the teachings of Horace Fletcher, the American dietary evangelist who advised people to chew their food one hundred times per minute.

Initially, Kafka's relentless chewing was not well received by everyone. "For months on end," he wrote to his girlfriend, "my father had to hide behind his newspaper during dinner, until he got used to it." Kafka's dietary habits rendered him virtually skin and bones. In 1912, he called himself "the thinnest person I have ever known."

During the later years of his life, Kafka was increasingly drawn to Zionism. He fantasized about settling in Palestine and becoming a waiter in a Tel Aviv restaurant.

If an apple a day keeps the doctor away, then what does a banana keep at bay? Shyness, or so **Aldous Huxley** believed. One day in 1952, the author of *Brave New World* took a vigorous walk with his friend, musical composer-author Robert Craft. The two men capped the day at a Beverly Hills ice-cream parlor, where Huxley ordered a banana split. The author told Craft that introverts "should eat bananas every day."

The French boarding school that **Honoré de Balzac** entered in 1807 nurtured the boys' culinary savoir-faire. Each boy was given a small plot on which he could grow his own vegetables. A small shop within the school made and sold pigeon pâté. Balzac described the "gastronomic commerce" that emerged during mealtimes—the cacophony generated by dozens of boys bartering with one another, trading food off their plates.

Rarely since the Garden of Eden has the consumption of a fruit created as much angst as it did on June 17, 1921. "Eating cherries today in front of the mirror I saw my idiotic face," **Bertolt Brecht** wrote in his diary. "Those self-contained black bullets disappearing down my mouth made it look looser, more lascivious and contradictory than ever."

A bread-and-water diet is usually associated with prisoners in a bygone era, but the law-abiding **Percy Shelley** happily embraced that regimen as his primary form of sustenance. The English poet found it difficult to walk past a bakery without stopping to buy a loaf. He usually ate bread by itself, but sometimes he nibbled on raisins while munching his bread. A friend of Shelley reported that the poet's pockets "were generally well-stored with bread. A circle upon the carpet, clearly defined by an ample verge of crumbs, often marked the place where [Shelley] had long sat at his studies."

The summer meals that **Mark Twain** enjoyed as a boy on his aunt and uncle's Missouri farm were so sumptuous, he wrote, that "it makes me cry to think of them." The "main splendor" for Twain was the way his aunt cooked fried chicken, hot biscuits, and cornbread. "These things have never been properly cooked in the North," added the man born Samuel Clemens.

Raymond Chandler made his name by writing short stories and novels that firmly established the crime genre. Yet he once considered writing a book titled *Cookbook for Idiots.* The topics he envisioned the book covering included "How to Make Coffee That Doesn't Taste Like Colored Water" and "Really Good Mashed Potatoes Are as Rare as Virgins, but Any Fool Can Make Them if He Tries."

As a graduate student, **Pearl Buck** was part of the committee that welcomed Eleanor Roosevelt to Cornell University for a speech and luncheon. Buck described the lunch—created by Cornell's Home Economics Department—as "mostly raw cabbage" and "an uneatable meal." Being the wife of a politician, Mrs. Roosevelt simply thanked the department for lunch.

Buck lived for so many years in China that her dietary habits reflected those of the Chinese; she ate little meat and avoided dairy products. When the Pulitzer Prize–winning writer returned to the United States in 1934, Buck detected a "rank wild odor" among her native citizens, and she attributed it to the American diet. "I remembered how my Chinese friends had used to complain of the way white folk smelled and so they did," she wrote.

Buck must have cared deeply about food. Her autobiography, *My Several Worlds,* contains an exhaustive list of the Chinese dishes she relished, including "the plum flower fragrant salted fish of Chao-chow," but it doesn't mention either of her two husbands.

Lend an ear to **Garrison Keillor:** "People have tried and they have tried, but sex is not better than sweet corn."

When he was annoyed at the dinner table, Polish-born novelist **Joseph Conrad** would flick pellets of bread—a habit he also carried to restaurants. When his wife once served him calf's head for a meal, he petulantly turned his back to the table and remained in that position until she removed the offending dish.

Langston Hughes rarely deferred his dreams of dining. When he arrived at the home of friend Irma Cayton, he would typically ask, "Irma, what are we going to eat, huh?" A student reporter at Morehouse College talked with Hughes over a meal and wrote afterward that the black poet-playwright "not only has a soul that grows deep 'like the rivers,' but he has also a digestive tract deeper than a river, for he can really put away food."

Hughes sent a cordial reply to a Dutch writer who had criticized Hughes's *Poetry of the Negro* collection. He invited the critic to visit America and eat soul food with him—"we could go downstairs and eat some good old pig feet and sauerkraut with cornbread."

Unfortunately, *where* Hughes could eat his vittles was severely restricted by the segregationist policies that prevailed across many states. In Delaware, Hughes lamented, an African American could buy a hamburger "but in a sack to eat outside."

Su Dongpo was not only one of China's greatest poets, but he served as a provincial governor during the eleventh century. And he was a superb cook.

After many of his constituents honored him with gifts of pork, Su cut the meat into pieces and braised them in a wine-flavored sauce. The recipe produced a red-tinged pork that he shared with the public. It was such a hit that the dish survives today as Dongpo pork.

Eighteenth-century poet and essayist **Samuel Johnson** didn't think much of cucumbers, as friend James Boswell recalled. Johnson believed that "a cucumber should be well sliced, and dressed with pepper and vinegar, and then thrown out as good for nothing."

Chilean poet **Pablo Neruda**'s 1951 trip through Asia was a culinary adventure. He drank Mongolian rice whiskey that was made from fermented camel's milk. "Shivers still run up and down my spine when I recall its taste," said Neruda.

He was aghast when officials in China told him it would be "almost impossible" for him to be served Chinese food. "Comrade, please prepare my papers for my return to Paris," he instructed a colleague. "If I can't have Chinese food in China, I'll have it in the Latin Quarter, where it is not a problem." His hosts quickly led Neruda to an excellent Chinese restaurant.

George Bernard Shaw was a stern vegetarian who argued that meat eating was a form of cannibalism. Another reason Shaw went meatless was that he deplored the "steam and grease, the waiter looking as if he had been caught in a shower of gravy and not properly dried . . . the reek of the slaughterhouse that convicted us all of being beasts of prey." Shaw hoped that vegetarianism would alleviate his migraine headaches; it did not.

Shaw was content to make his dinner from the likes of brown bread, apples, cheese, and green beans. And he fancied chocolates and other sweets.

Edith Wharton grew up in a world where rich and decadent foods were always plentiful. So it's hardly surprising that she wrote in her novel *The Age of Innocence* that the brownstones of Manhattan produced a "uniform hue (that) coated New York like a cold chocolate sauce."

While lying on her deathbed, Wharton was haunted by a memory. "Oh, the shame of it!" she cried. "I feel it still." She could not shake the memory of an incident more than sixty years earlier when she disappointed her mother by polishing off a plate of apricots she had been forbidden to eat.

Johann Wolfgang von Goethe observed that northern Italians were more attractive than those who lived farther south. The German poet and author of *Faust* attributed this to the different way in which the two groups ate polenta.

Vladimir Nabokov had a passion for writing and butterflies. But his interest in butterflies went beyond collecting them. The author of *Lolita* confided to a *Sports Illustrated* reporter that he had eaten butterflies in Vermont. "I didn't see any difference between a monarch butterfly and a viceroy," he related. "The taste of both was vile. . . . They tasted like almonds and perhaps a green cheese combination."

Robert Frost grew up in a household with no standard mealtimes. Bread, fruit, and other foods were frequently left in a bowl in the family's living room—available whenever Robert and his siblings returned home from their outdoor activities.

For Frost's wife, Elinor, food preparation was a rustic activity. A neighbor recalled that when dinnertime approached, Elinor "would take a bucket of potatoes into the field and sit on the grass to peel them—without water to my astonishment—and that, as far as I could see, was often the only preparation for a meal."

One of Frost's favorite dining destinations was the Waybury Inn near Middlebury, Vermont, where he began every dinner with a daiquiri. But he never drank more than one.

A tumbler of cream, a few tablespoons of rum, beef broth, an egg beaten into a glass of sherry, soup, and a pint of champagne. These are strange concoctions for anyone to ingest on the same day. Yet **Charles Dickens** apparently consumed all of these items every day for the last ten weeks of his 1868 visit to America.

When it came to food, Dickens was all talk and no action. "He was accustomed to talk and write a good deal about eating and drinking," said one acquaintance, "but I have rarely seen a man eat and drink less."

In *Remembrance of Things Past,* French novelist **Marcel Proust** writes nostalgically of an Aunt Léonie who gave the book's narrator a madeleine, a French butter cookie, after "dipping it first in her own cup of real [tea] or of lime-flower tea."

Proust's chronically ill health did not curb his adventurous approach to eating. In 1919, he replied to a formal dinner invitation by writing, "I am not on any sort of diet, I eat anything, I drink anything, I don't think I care for red wine, but I like all the white wines in the world, and I like beer and cider." His only dietary requirement, Proust added, was that he wanted to bring his own bottle of mineral water.

Although he adored the city of Paris, novelist **J. R. R. Tolkien** was not smitten with its food. "I detest French cooking," he declared, adding that he preferred "good plain food." Tolkien also liked simple beverages like tea. As a prep-school student, Tolkien and a few other boys formed a secret tea-drinking club, sneaking tea and refreshments into school buildings. According to one biographer, Tolkien "spent the greater part of his waking hours" in the 1920s having tea with one person or another.

After Tolkien's parents died, the teenage J.R.R. and his younger brother were sent to live in a boardinghouse. The brothers and a fellow boarder—Tolkien's future wife, Edith—would hoist extra food up to their rooms by using a basket attached to a rope. The maid cooperated with their scheme.

The three **F. Scott Fitzgerald** essays that *Esquire* published in 1936 were written by the author while he resided in a cheap North Carolina hotel, surviving on apples and meat dished out of tins.

The way Fitzgerald behaved around food was as raucous as the Jazz Age he depicted in *The Great Gatsby*. At dinner parties, Fitzgerald might start crawling underneath the table. Or he might try to eat soup with his fork. One evening in New York City, Fitzgerald and a friend entered Child's restaurant, and Fitzgerald soon began mixing poached eggs, hash, and ketchup in his friend's derby cap.

After he and his wife, Zelda, became estranged, Fitzgerald lived with his lover, Sheilah Graham, who encouraged his capricious eating habits. They prepared bizarre dishes of food, and Fitzgerald sometimes ate courses in reverse order, starting, for example, with a dessert soufflé.

On the morning of October 19, 1976, **Saul Bellow** and his wife were preparing to share an English muffin when the telephone rang. His agent informed him that he'd won the Nobel Prize for Literature.

John Steinbeck's 1939 novel *The Grapes of Wrath* chronicled the lives of underdogs—ordinary people struggling to survive during the Great Depression. Yet Steinbeck was a pull-yourself-up-by-your-bootstraps kind of guy, especially when it came to hunger. Reflecting on life during the Depression, the California native once wrote, "Given the sea a man must be very stupid to starve. That great reservoir of food is always available. I took a large part of my protein food from the ocean." Not only that, Steinbeck added, in northern California "you can raise vegetables of some kind all year long."

Steinbeck practiced what he preached. "John pretty much lived off the land, scraping around for food," one acquaintance recalled. For a few years, the novelist was even self-sufficient when it came to red wine, producing a homemade product that a friend described as "foul but strong."

Nobel Prize–winning German author **Günter Grass** deplored the cramped living quarters of his childhood during the 1940s. And a tasty dessert couldn't ease his distress.

"Not even the vanilla pudding with almond slivers that Father, who loved to cook for the family, made from ingredients he skimmed off his meager deliveries and hoarded for special occasions was of any help," he wrote.

After he heard that the library in the French town of Cavaillon couldn't afford to purchase his books, the novelist-playwright **Alexandre Dumas** struck a deal with the town. In exchange for the 194 volumes that Dumas had written up to that point, town officials sent him an annuity each year of a dozen Cavaillon melons, highly coveted for their taste.

When **Maya Angelou** was seven, she and her brother moved from rural Arkansas to St. Louis to live with their mother and her relatives. "Their food astonished us. They ate liverwurst and salami, which we had never seen. Their sliced bread was white and came in greasy, slick waxed paper," she recalled.

Years later, after setting a formal dinner table for her and her boyfriend one evening, Angelou exchanged harsh words with him. She grabbed the corners of the tablecloth and lifted it up, allowing the food, china, and glassware to slide into the center. Angelou dragged the ensemble into the living room and dropped it in front of her boyfriend. "Here's dinner if you want it," she declared. "I'm leaving."

As a young boy, English novelist **D. H. Lawrence** sometimes made potato cakes and toffees in his family's kitchen. He was also an avid cook as an adult. His wife, Frieda, remarked, "I cook when he'll let me, but he does it much better himself."

In 1862, **Victor Hugo**'s wife planned a special dinner party for France's literary stars. Its purpose was to persuade writers to publicly support Hugo's controversial novel *Les Misérables*. Several invitees declined to attend, including **George Sand,** who explained that she always ate too much when she dined away from home.

Two years later, Hugo's publisher organized a meal to promote another of his books. But authorities banned the banquet, fearing it would incite public discord. A journalist wrote that the book was such a collection of "conceits, rigmaroles and gibberish" that the publisher needed "to puff it with food."

Oscar Wilde had rich, bohemian tastes. "Poke him and he would bleed absinthe and clotted truffles," said actress Elizabeth Robins.

Wilde loved to stay and dine at London's Savoy Hotel, but the publicity the hotel received during Wilde's homosexuality trial lost it at least one customer. After a Savoy waiter testified at the trial that he'd delivered a sixteen-shilling supper of chicken and salad for two persons to Wilde's hotel room, the judge was aghast. "I know nothing about the Savoy," the judge confessed, "but I must say that in my view 'Chicken and salad' [for that price] is very high! I am afraid I shall never have supper there myself."

Nineteenth-century Russian novelist **Fyodor Dostoyevsky** was a chronic complainer, and food was high on his list of grievances.

After he and his comrades were imprisoned by the Czarist regime, Dostoyevsky criticized the food. The authorities responded by giving him fifty lashes.

Even the food outside of prison raised his ire—no matter where he ate it. In Germany, he whined about having tea at Die Grosse Wirtschaft because either the tea was too weak or no jam was brought to the table. And one couldn't trust the German waiters, he complained, who "have no qualms about adding things to your bill that you never ordered, just hoping you won't bother to check it!" During a dinner in Italy, Dostoyevsky attacked a waiter so bitterly that the server was moved to ask, "Don't you realize that I'm a human being, too?"

Dostoyevsky would even gripe about what others consumed. He teased his wife, Anna, for drinking "a cup of the worst coffee in the world, which you nevertheless gulp down with tremendous appetite."

Anna complained that Dostoyevsky's son Paul—from a previous marriage—constantly engaged in "petty tricks" to make her look like a poor housekeeper: "Sometimes he would drink up all the cream before [Fyodor] came into the dining room so that we would have to rush to the shop to buy more, which of course would be rancid, and so [Fyodor] would have to wait for his coffee. Or [Paul] would eat a grouse just before dinnertime so that two were served instead of three, and there wouldn't be enough."

George Orwell seemed to revel in the dreary food of England during World War II. He'd devour overcooked cod with bitter turnip tops and then annoy those within earshot by announcing, "I'd never have thought they'd have gone so well together!" Orwell ate boiled eels that his wife, Eileen, had left for the cat—and he found them delicious. He and Eileen would donate part of their wartime food rations to others.

Even though Orwell often typed drafts until three o'clock in the morning, his second wife, Susan, still insisted that he come to the breakfast table promptly at eight o'clock.

Washington Irving spent nearly twenty years of his life on the road. His diaries reveal just how difficult it was for a traveler to find a wholesome meal in the era before Fodor's travel guides.

While traversing upstate New York, the *Legend of Sleepy Hollow* author ate "an uncomfortable breakfast" in a boardinghouse. In eastern France, Irving and his companion found that the locals "did not understand the mystery of bread & butter with coffee as the French eat nothing with it but dry bread."

In the Italian city of Bologna, wrote Irving, a traveler faced the "necessity of bargaining for every meal before he eats it or else paying the most extravagant price."

In a restaurant outside of Paris, Irving complained that "grease seemed to be the grand ingredient in the sauces." The farther they ventured from Paris, the worse the food tasted. Irving guessed that a chicken they were served at one inn had been "on the table for a longer space of time than ever it [had] in the farm yard."

During his destitute years in New York City, the muckraking journalist **Jacob Riis** would stand outside a basement window of Delmonico's restaurant at the same time every evening. The payoff, Riis wrote, was "a generous supply of meat-bones and rolls from a white-capped cook who spoke French." Years later, Riis's prosperity allowed him to eat at Delmonico's and "other swell restaurants through the windows of which I had so often gazed with hungry eyes."

Food and writing were the twin pillars of **John Steinbeck**'s life. "As long as I can eat and write more books, that's all that I require," he declared. Steinbeck said he wrote much of his 1947 novel *The Wayward Bus* at his kitchen table "amid jampots and pieces of cold toast and stale coffee."

Before he became famous, however, Steinbeck sometimes scrambled to find his next meal. When he moved to New York City in 1925, he survived for several weeks on canned sardines and moldy crackers. When Steinbeck moved back to California, he and his wife often ate at one of the cheap, sawdust-floored restaurants that lined the San Francisco waterfront. During these years, dinner for Steinbeck sometimes consisted of hamburger and stolen avocados. But by the 1940s, Steinbeck was a celebrated novelist whose dining venues were distinctly upscale.

When Steinbeck played the role of chef, the result was often a big mess. He once told his wife that his sons were thrilled that he planned to make his "world-shaking macaroni for dinner . . . because it means that there will be tomato sauce all over the kitchen and all over me. My dinners are not only food. They are decorations also."

When he worked as a Western Union telegram messenger in the 1950s, American playwright **Edward Albee** often ate dinner at a cafeteria in the Manhattan Towers Hotel. "You could get a huge, huge bowl of borscht," he said, "and all the black bread you could eat for thirty-five cents."

Dinner parties that Albee attended were filled with almost as much drama as his plays. During one sponsored by Albee's foundation, a young playwright lifted his hands so other diners could see that he had just slit his wrists. "Oh, that's the wrong way to do it," Albee said calmly. "Let's go upstairs and fix that." At a dinner party given by theater critic Mel Gussow, Albee got into a verbal catfight with another guest, producer Joseph Papp. Albee proposed an insulting toast to Papp and then called Papp's *A Chorus Line* a "piece of shit." Papp returned the insults, and all civility left the dining room. The next day, Albee wrote an apology to Gussow that began, "What a splendid party except for that Edward Albee person!"

During an 1845 visit to Boston, **Edgar Allan Poe** took it on the chin from the city's newspaper critics. Poe penned a public reply declaring that Bostonians had "no soul," the poetry they produced was "not so good" and their hotels were "bad," but their pumpkin pies were "delicious."

Virginia Woolf had a lot to say about food. The morning meal she ate in the English town of Wilton disappointed her because a "breakfast which has been laid over night is never an exhilarating meal." A stout relative who joined her for a meal ate "an enormous luncheon, almost demolishing a pineapple." Dinner at an Indian curry restaurant in London was "rather nasty." In Greece, she was dazzled by "the experience for the first time of sitting on the ground & eating grapes from the tree in the open air."

While **Johann Wolfgang von Goethe** was in Naples, friends tried to stop him from drinking a glass of water with insects floating in it. Goethe dismissed their concerns and drank the water. If people were willing to eat crabs and eels, he reasoned, a few insects were no big deal.

The menu for **Truman Capote**'s legendary 1966 Black and White Ball wasn't nearly as chic as the masks and outfits were. The midnight buffet featured chicken hash, spaghetti Bolognese, scrambled eggs, sausages, pastries, and coffee. But this was no ordinary chicken hash; it was the Plaza Hotel's own recipe, which Capote fancied. It was prepared with hollandaise sauce, sherry, and heavy cream—no potatoes—and it dished out more than six hundred calories a serving.

French playwright **Molière** once told a friend, "My wife's soups are like brandy; you know all the ingredients she puts in them." In 1667, Molière became so ill that he resorted to a milk-only diet for two months.

Six years later, minutes before Molière passed away, he had a final snack and was helped into bed. His last morsel of food was distinctly Italian, not French. His cook, Renée Vannier, brought him Parmesan cheese.

Emily Dickinson charmed friends and family with her poetry and baked goods. When the Dickinsons' cook-housekeeper quit, Emily started baking the family's bread. She continued to do so even after a replacement was hired, mostly because her father preferred her bread.

Dickinson told a close friend that "people must have puddings," and according to the friend, she spoke "*very* dreamily, as if they were comets."

Food was never far from **Anton Chekhov**'s mind, especially when he traveled outside of his native Russia. During a lengthy trip through Ukraine and Siberia, Chekhov rated the duck soup as "pure filth," and considered the tea to be "real mattress juice." However, he was willing to grade these regions on a curve: "If you ask for milk or water, no one shoves his fingers into the glass."

As he listened to a tour guide in Rome drone on, Chekhov found himself daydreaming about eating cabbage soup. In Monaco, there were restaurants in which each dish was "a veritable artistic composition before which one goes to one's knees in veneration," he wrote. Chekhov complained to a friend who had canceled plans for their trip to North Africa: "And already I was dreaming every night that I was eating figs!"

When **Samuel Beckett** lived briefly in Berlin, his regular haunt was a restaurant called the Giraffe. While there one day, Beckett was asked, "Why is there no expression of hope in your work?" After lingering silence, Beckett picked up a crumb of bread from the tablecloth, stared at it, then replied—borrowing the words of Dante—"I would have written over the gates of Heaven what is said to be written over Hell—abandon all hope ye who enter here." Then Beckett dropped the crumb and added, "That's what I think of hope."

By the time a bride and groom cut the wedding cake, the real drama of the day is over. But this was not the case when novelist **John Steinbeck** married his second wife, Gwyn Conger, in 1943. For starters, the bakery delivered the wedding cake late. Then, just as the newlyweds began to cut the cake, two policemen interrupted and said they had a warrant for Steinbeck's arrest. The crowd gasped when one of the cops said, "A young woman outside claims that you are the father of her child."

Moments later, all was well and the cake was cut. Two of Steinbeck's friends had played a practical joke on the couple.

Marcel Proust should have been called the Count of Caffeine. He once ended a dinner at Paris's Hotel Ritz by drinking sixteen demitasses of espresso.

It's not every day that a person—even a famous one—gets an invitation to dine at the White House. But **William Faulkner** had a simple explanation for why he declined the dinner invitation from First Lady Jacqueline Kennedy. "That's a long way to go just to eat," he said.

Even the weapons of wartime weren't enough to make **Ernest Hemingway** abandon a hearty meal. While in Europe during 1944, he was dining with army officers when a mortar shell ripped through a nearby wall without exploding. The officers quickly scurried into a potato cellar, but Hemingway remained at the table, cutting his meat and drinking his wine.

Leo Tolstoy bought a large estate in the Russian plains of Samara, roughly six hundred miles southeast of Moscow, partly because he loved the region's koumiss—fermented mare's milk. Koumiss was considered to be a healthful tonic. Taking a koumiss "cure" meant living solely on the milk for a few months. Tolstoy took the cure at least a couple of times in his life.

Once when Tolstoy was suffering from severe stomach pains,

his wife's sympathy was tempered by the question she asked him: What did he expect after he ate three cucumbers, one right after the other?

As a young adult, **Victor Hugo** could eat half an ox at one sitting, then fast for three days. Later, while he was living in exile in the Channel Islands, a pattern took hold for his mornings. He would rise at dawn, swallow two raw eggs, drink a cup of cold coffee, and then begin writing. Hugo ate a lot of root vegetables but moderate amounts of meat. He drank water colored with a little wine.

When Hugo returned to France in 1870 after a lengthy exile, his first dinner back in the motherland was simple: bread, cheese, and wine. His mistress, Juliette, kept some of the bread as a memento.

For Juliette, food provided the language of eroticism. She once wrote this note to Hugo: "I drank everything you left in your glass, and I shall nibble your little piece of chicken wing. I shall eat with your knife and sup from your spoon."

Hot dogs helped ignite the romance between Beat Generation writer **Jack Kerouac** and his first wife, Edith Parker. Kerouac first met Parker in 1940 at Lou's Deli in New York City, where they ordered hot dogs with sauerkraut. Parker wrote that her "nervousness over being so taken by Jack" was part of the reason she devoured five hot dogs. Kerouac later told Parker that he fell in love after seeing her eat all those hot dogs.

The couple was divorced in 1946. By the end of their marriage, Parker wrote that she and Jack "barely managed to subsist on mayonnaise sandwiches."

In 1949, as Kerouac began writing *On the Road,* his modus

operandi was consistent: He slept until noon, ate breakfast, and then proceeded to write. Kerouac loved Chinese food, especially pork dishes, and his favorite dessert was apple pie à la mode.

Because **Anton Chekhov** enjoyed oysters, it might have amused him if he could have known that the coffin carrying his remains was transported by rail in a freight car emblazoned OYSTERS in large letters. This may have created the confusion that led dozens of Chekhov's mourners who arrived at the rail station to gather behind a different coffin that was unloaded from the train.

Indian poet-novelist **Rabindranath Tagore** had plenty of scorn for those who ate a heavy lunch. The Nobel laureate once wrote, "It is an imbecile thing to eat a bellyful of food at midday, which stupefies one's imagination and other higher faculties."

In an 1892 letter, Tagore confessed that he had committed a "major blunder"—exhausting his personal supply of tea and cocoa.

"Part of the secret of success in life," wrote **Mark Twain,** "is to eat what you like and let the food fight it out inside."

While living in Paris after World War I, **Ernest Hemingway** almost never paid for a restaurant meal, regularly sponging off companions. He and his first wife, Hadley, subsisted mostly on leeks.

Hemingway found respite from his hunger by gazing at Cézanne paintings at a Paris museum. The Cézannes, wrote

Hemingway, looked "more beautiful if you were belly-empty, hollow-hungry." He considered it "good discipline" to look at these paintings.

Pablo Neruda's second wife was a nutrition buff who urged the Chilean poet to limit his portion of *dulce de alcayota*—a sweet jam made from spaghetti squash—to only a spoonful. But Neruda would hear none of it. "I will eat all the alcayota until I turn into an alcayota!"

Those who visited **Honoré de Balzac** during mealtime had to be ready to duck. Balzac shoved food into his mouth and sprayed it about as he chewed. He ate food off his knife in the manner of a peasant. Balzac's typical breakfast was two boiled eggs and bread. For dinner, he drank a glass or two of Vouvray, his favorite wine.

In 1831, Balzac was already three months behind his deadline for submitting a novel to the publisher. Balzac sent the anxious publisher half the manuscript—along with word that a pâté would soon follow.

Balzac briefly adopted a milk-only diet during the 1830s to combat stomach problems. He also reduced his food portions in order "not to transmit the fatigue of digestion to the brain."

A meal with **Oscar Wilde** was never ordinary. When a hotel waiter informed him that some nice fish were available that day, Wilde begged to differ. "If you knew the breeding habits of fish," he said, "you would scarcely call them *nice*."

In 1897, Wilde met a group of French artists and poets in Dieppe for a dinner that was so rowdy that municipal authorities sent Wilde a formal letter warning that further misconduct could force his expulsion from the country.

Edgar Allan Poe left Philadelphia in 1844 and arrived in New York City, hoping to find more stable work to support his family. His first letter home was uncharacteristically upbeat, mostly about the food at his boardinghouse. Poe raved about the "elegant ham, and 2 [dishes] of veal piled up like a mountain and large slices— 3 dishes of the cakes, and every thing in the greatest profusion. No fear of starving here."

H. G. Wells accepted a dinner invitation from **George Orwell** in 1941, warning Orwell that he couldn't eat any rich foods. But Wells ate a lavish meal, capped by a dessert of plum cake. Several days later, he sent Orwell an angry note: "You knew I was ill and on a diet, [but] you deliberately plied me with food and drink."

Much to her chagrin, **Charlotte Brontë**'s literary gifts got her invited to a lot of dinner parties, which she considered a "hideous bore." The reason was her own nerves. "I always feel under awkward constraint at table," the author of *Jane Eyre* once confided to a friend. Dining with or without company became difficult by the mid-1840s, when Brontë developed a toothache that persisted for years.

When **Charles Dickens** hosted a dinner party, the menu was written on paper and displayed on a sideboard. Dickens often amused guests by reading the menu aloud and offering a sarcastic commentary. He might read "croquettes of chicken" and remark, "Weak, very weak—decided lack of imagination here."

The physicians who treated **Anton Chekhov** for tuberculosis offered some strange dietary prescriptions. One doctor advised him to eat as many as eight eggs each day. Another physician recommended a diet that was centered on what Chekhov called "stupid" cocoa and oatmeal.

Coffee, according to **Truman Capote,** was the subject of the "greatest quarrel" he ever had with his domestic partner, Jack Dunphy. An admirer of upscale Medaglia d'Oro coffee, Dunphy became incensed when Capote returned from the grocery store without it. Furious at Dunphy's reaction, Capote roamed through their summer home and threw objects at will. For the rest of the summer, Dunphy made do with ordinary coffee.

Samuel Beckett told a woman he had not enjoyed their sexual encounter. Making love without being in love, he explained to her, was like having "coffee without brandy."

Soon after his father took his own life in 1928, **Ernest Hemingway** asked his mother to send him the suicide weapon. His mother shipped it—accompanied by a chocolate cake.

CHAPTER 3

Soul Food

Prophets and philosophers didn't live on bread alone

THE **SUPREME BUDDHA,** Siddhartha Gautama, ate his way to enlightenment.

According to legend, a woman named Sujata took the milk from one thousand cows and fed it to five hundred cows, and then milked those cows and fed half that number, and so on. She used the milk from the final eight cows to prepare a sweetened dish of milk-rice, which was served to Gautama in a golden bowl. Gautama divided the meal into forty-nine rice balls and consumed them. He then tossed the golden bowl in a river, declaring, "If today I am to attain full enlightenment, may this golden bowl swim upstream." And indeed it did.

The meal of forty-nine rice balls sustained Gautama for the next forty-nine days, a time when he ate nothing, sat under a bodhi tree, and became Buddha.

Aristotle believed that food was "cooked" in the human intestines.

While the most powerful Middle Eastern men of the prophet **Muhammad**'s time ate in splendid dining halls, he preferred to dine outdoors on a woven palm mat. He took only one meal a day, and not too elaborately. The Messenger of God was a carnivore, enjoying camel, gazelle, and other meats available to desert dwellers.

Among his other foods: pumpkin, dates, milk, mutton broth, melons, grapes, and barley bread dipped in olive oil. Cucumbers were a particular favorite.

One of the miracles of **Jesus Christ,** described in the Bible, is his multiplying of five loaves of bread and two fish so that they fed five thousand people. The type of fish is not identified by the Bible, but scholars believe it probably was tilapia, which has been eaten in the Middle East for millennia but has become popular in the United States only in recent decades.

Tilapia is sometimes called **St. Peter**'s fish, based on another biblical account. Jesus told the apostle Peter to go fishing and pull up the first fish that took his hook. Inside the fish's mouth was a shekel coin, which Jesus and Peter used to pay their taxes.

The Chinese philosopher **Confucius** wrote about peaches around 500 BCE, more than a century before the fruit was documented in any other part of the world.

According to legend, Confucius was dining with Duke Ai of Lu and his courtesans when the duke's servants presented the philosopher with millet and a peach. Confucius ate the millet and then enjoyed the peach. The courtesans laughed and laughed at his breach of custom—eating the millet before the peach instead of afterward. How ridiculous.

"If only I were master of my stomach once more!" declared German philosopher **Friedrich Nietzsche,** referring to his frequent indigestion.

To address the problem, Nietzsche experimented with a wide variety of diets. He tried vegetarianism. He tried living on milk and eggs alone. He tried eating hardly anything at all. At various times, he refused to consume mustard, vinegar, pepper, cabbage, cauliflower, black bread, onions, and cheese.

But the philosopher who famously stated that "God is dead" had faith in something called Liebig's meat extract. The product, a thick liquid that could be mixed with water to produce a beef broth, was believed to be an appetite stimulant. Because it took about thirty-four pounds of South American beef to produce one pound of the extract, many consumers thought it was particularly nourishing. But in fact it had few nutrients, if any.

For all his grace in the pulpit, the **Reverend Martin Luther King Jr.** was a mess at the dinner table.

Friends said the civil rights leader was a wildly enthusiastic lover of soul food whose favorite dining utensils were his hands. King "never did learn the finer arts of eating," said one friend. Another described a meal at a New York restaurant in which King's companions laughed at him because, instead of "putting on the dog in terms of table manners, he brought his same old country habits of eating."

The Nobel Peace Prize winner often devoured chitterlings, fried chicken, and black-eyed peas.

"He loved anything that was 'soul,'" said Emma Anderson, a member of Calvary Baptist Church in Chester, Pennsylvania.

It's no surprise that Anderson admired King's discerning appetite: One of his favorite foods was her sweet potato pie.

St. Augustine, the North African philosopher whose fourth-century writings profoundly influenced Western Christian beliefs, recalled how he was attracted to sin at the age of sixteen. He and fellow young hoodlums raided a tree full of pears even though the fruit was "tempting neither in appearance nor taste."

"We came away with great loads of pears," he wrote, "not to feast on ourselves but to throw to the pigs. Even if we did eat a few, it was only because we relished doing what was forbidden."

Mohandas Gandhi was a strict vegetarian, vowing "not to live upon fellow animals." He explained that "the basis of my vegetarianism is not physical but moral. If any said that I should die if I did not take beef tea or mutton, even under medical advice, I would prefer death."

He regretted that he could not forsake the consumption of all animal products.

"I would give up milk if I could, but I cannot," he said. "I have made that experiment times without number. I could not, after a serious illness, regain my strength unless I went back to milk. That has been the tragedy of my life."

One day in 1784, elderly French philosopher **Denis Diderot** wanted to conclude his meal by eating an apricot. Diderot was well known for overeating, and his wife advised him not to consume the fruit. He replied: "But how the devil can that hurt me?" Diderot ate the apricot and died minutes later.

It's odd that statues of the **Supreme Buddha,** Siddhartha Gautama, often show him as a fleshy creature, considering how frequently he was on some sort of fast. In one instance, a meal consisted of one sesame seed, one grain of rice, one jujube, one pulse pod, one kidney bean, and one mungo bean.

The Buddha was said to have described his own scrawniness by saying that "because I ate so little, my gaunt ribs became like the crazy rafters of a tumble-down shed; because I ate so little, the pupils of my eyes appeared lying low and deep; because I ate so little, my scalp became shriveled and shrunk as a bitter white gourd."

For **Jean-Paul Sartre,** food was both sustenance and symbol.

"It is not a matter of indifference whether we like oysters or clams, snails, or shrimp, if only we know how to unravel the existential significance of these foods," the French philosopher wrote.

And indeed, Sartre's diet said a lot about him. He found crabs and lobsters revolting because they reminded him of insects. He liked cakes and other pastries because "the appearance, the putting together, and even the taste have been thought out by man and made on purpose." He preferred canned fruits and vegetables to fresh produce, thinking that the processing made the food more of a man-made product, and therefore better. Fresh produce, he believed, was "too natural."

The prophet **Muhammad** sometimes fasted for two or three days, and always ended his fasts by eating a date. The tradition continues today as Muslims typically break their daytime fast during Ramadan by eating dates. The Prophet's wives were told that they must feed every beggar who approached them, even if they could provide only half a date.

The overheated room where philosopher **René Descartes** cooked up his greatest insights was known as his "oven."

The Gospel According to Matthew says that while **John the Baptist** was preaching in the desert, he survived on "locusts and wild honey."

But over the millennia since John's head was put on a platter, scholars have argued about his diet. The idea that he ate grasshoppers was unpalatable for some highly civilized Christians, who wouldn't think of eating such creatures. Some have theorized that John instead ate the fruit of the locust tree, the carob. Others note that grasshopper eating was common in the region at the time. Even scholars who embrace the insect theory disagree over whether the locusts were boiled in butter or oil, or were cooked in a fire pit dug into the ground.

Even more contested is the honey issue. A modern audience might assume that John's honey came from bees, but the word *honey* also was used to describe tree sap as well as syrup that came from grapes, figs, and dates.

The **Venerable Bede,** an eighth-century English monk, wrote that John the Baptist ate insects that were "about the size of a finger." Bede also thought that John's honey came from trees, not bees: "In the same desert are trees, having broad round leaves of a white colour and sweet taste, naturally weak, and easily bruised by the hands for eating. This is said to be what is meant by . . . wild honey."

Mohandas Gandhi liked to joke that he was a "food missionary." He lived on only five food items a day, seeking to avoid a "pampered" lifestyle in which "I should find myself dying by inches."

Some of Gandhi's dietary views were quite progressive, such as his push for the consumption of fresh fruits and vegetables and his preference for homemade whole wheat bread over store-bought white bread. But occasionally his ideas seemed kooky. For example, Gandhi thought a diet of rice, lemons, and light fruit would help cure smallpox.

The French philosopher François-Marie Arouet, also known as **Voltaire,** preferred simple food, well prepared. He thought too many cooks ruined perfectly good food with an overabundance of nutmeg and pepper. Voltaire didn't care much for the fashionable food of his day, specifically denouncing a poultry-rabbit mince and *pigeon à la crapaudine,* a pigeon cooked spread-eagled, as a toad would be prepared.

He liked a glass of wine with his meal.

"I drink moderately," he wrote, "and I find very strange people who eat without drinking, and who do not even know what they are eating."

Voltaire was a lover of coffee as well as wine. When an acquaintance told Voltaire that coffee was a "slow poison," he replied, "You're right there, my friend: slow it is, and horribly slow, for I have been drinking it these seventy years, and it has not killed me yet."

The Bible was judgmental about lentils.

In the book of Genesis, **Esau** traded his birthright as the oldest male in his family to his younger brother **Jacob** in exchange for bread and a stew that included lentils. In another Old Testament story, **Ezekiel** was ordered by God to lie on his left side for 390 days to suffer for the sins of the house of Israel. During that time, he survived on bread made of wheat, barley, beans, millet, spelt—and lentils.

Karl Marx's daughter Jenny asked him to fill out a questionnaire listing his likes and dislikes in a variety of categories. His favorite color, not surprisingly, was red. And his favorite food was fish.

Pope Martin IV loved eels. He arranged for them to be fished out of a lake and dropped alive into a vat of wine, which killed and pickled the eels. Then they were roasted and served to the pontiff.

Martin so gorged on eels that they were blamed for his death in 1285. In Dante Alighieri's *Purgatorio*, the author imagines the pope loitering in purgatory because of his overindulgence. Dante's work includes this ditty:

> *The eels are glad that he is dead*
> *And lies interred in this low bed*
> *Who, as their doom for mortal sins,*
> *When living stripped them of their skins*

Philosopher **George Santayana** memorably declared, "Those who cannot remember the past are condemned to repeat it." But when it came to eating, Santayana remembered the past and *wanted* to repeat it. He left Spain as a young child but throughout his life retained a fondness for the simple dishes of his youth, such as gazpacho and potato omelets fried in oil.

As the prophet **Muhammad** conquered the Jews of Arabia, his new subjects were filled with hatred for him. A young Jewish woman named Zaynab, whose father, uncle, and husband had been killed, was ordered to cook roast lamb for Muhammad. She did so, seasoning the meat with poison.

One of Muhammad's companions swallowed the lamb and died. The Prophet took a single bite, thought it tasted strange, and spit it out.

Zaynab, questioned by Muhammad, said she figured that if he was truly a prophet, he would know about the poison. If he was not, he would die.

The Prophet granted her a pardon.

Some of Muhammad's followers nevertheless believed that Zaynab's poison lamb was responsible for his death—which occurred three years after he tasted the meat and refused to swallow it.

Desiderius Erasmus, the Dutch Renaissance scholar and theologian, wrote a pamphlet in 1530 with detailed advice on table manners, including how not to lick one's lips.

The **Supreme Buddha** was a gracious guest, even when he was served a meal that might have been fatal.

A blacksmith named Cunda invited the Buddha and his monks to have dinner at his home, and he served a dish called *sukaramaddava,* which can be translated as "pig's delight." The Buddha alone ate the dish, forbidding his companions to partake. This should have been a tip-off, since the Buddha was not usually a selfish guy.

Soon after eating, the Buddha fell violently ill but did not complain. He told a companion that the food was not to blame and Cunda should feel no guilt. In fact, the Buddha said, Cunda should be honored that he had served the Blessed One's final meal. Which indeed he had, because the Buddha soon died.

Religious scholars have long debated what "pig's delight" was. Some believe the dish was pork. Others say it was a food that would be delightful to pigs, such as truffles, roots, or mushrooms.

When the revolt known as the Fronde created chaos in his native France during the seventeenth century, **René Descartes** decided to remain in the Dutch town of Egmond. He wrote that although the town "does not have as much honey as God promised the Israelites, it is plausible to think that it has more milk."

Philosophers can be dodgy at dinner.

In 1829, composer Felix Mendelssohn sponsored a concert in Berlin of Johann Sebastian Bach's compositions. Afterward, at a celebratory dinner, Mendelssohn was seated next to Therese Devrient, the wife of a soloist. On her other side was a most unusual man who proved to be quite a nuisance.

Devrient later recalled the stranger's transgressions: "He continually tried to talk me into drinking some more wine. . . . He unrelentingly gripped my furthermost lace sleeve 'in order to protect it,' as he put it."

Devrient implored Mendelssohn, "Tell me who this dimwit beside me is."

Mendelssohn whispered back, "The dimwit there beside you is the famous philosopher, **Hegel**."

Mohandas Gandhi was famous for the food he didn't eat. He employed fasting to impose moral authority on matters large and small.

Hindu-Muslim violence in 1924 inspired a three-week fast by Gandhi in which he consumed only water. He ended the fast by drinking orange juice. The next year he fasted for a week because of a dispute among boys at his ashram school. He explained that to punish the boys directly would only harden them; instead, it was better for him to impose the suffering on himself.

Joseph Smith, founder of the Church of Jesus Christ of Latter-day Saints, had remarkable dreams about food.

Around 1811, the Mormon patriarch dreamed that he was escorted by a spirit guide through a desolate field of fallen timber. The spirit explained that this represented the world without religion and told him to eat the contents of a box in order to achieve wisdom and understanding. But suddenly all manner of beasts rose up and roared, prompting Smith to drop the box and flee.

In a later dream, Smith left the desolate field and encountered a fruit tree with branches spread "like an umbrella." Smith found the tree to be "white as snow, or if possible, whiter. . . . I drew near and began to eat of it, and I found it delicious beyond description. As I was eating, I said in my heart, 'I cannot eat this alone, I must bring my wife and children, that they may partake with me.' Accordingly, I went and brought my family . . . and we all commenced eating."

In the dream, Smith noticed that people in a tall building were watching them with scorn. Of course, no one likes to have strangers staring at them as they eat, and the people in the high-rise indeed faced punishment. "It is Babylon, and it must fall," the spirit explained.

The Bible depicts **Jesus Christ** as kind and forgiving, but its story about a fig tree seems to be an exception. A hungry Jesus entered Jerusalem, spotted a fig tree in the distance, and approached. But finding no fruit on the tree, he cursed it to remain fruitless forever, and the tree quickly withered. The tree appeared to be blameless: According to the Gospel of Mark, it wasn't even the season for figs.

Martin Luther, who would transform Christianity by initiating the Protestant Reformation, had to beg for food during his youth in Germany.

Luther's financially struggling parents sent him away to a school where students were expected to find food on their own. Luther and his fellow students went from house to house singing for bread. Ursula Cotta, daughter of a local burgher in the town of Eisenach, was impressed by Luther's singing and his manner. She and her husband offered him a place to eat and to live. Given a stable home, Luther received the education that would later help him to inspire millions.

Cotta was thereafter known as "the pious Shunamite," a reference to the woman who gave bread and shelter to the prophet Elisha in the Bible.

As a child growing up in Tibet, Lhamo Thondup savored his mother's homemade bread with thick cream, and also loved *tukpa*, a meat-and-noodle soup. Soon after he became the fourteenth **Dalai Lama,** his land was occupied by the Chinese army. The Dalai Lama recalled how his mother cried because family members and villagers were forbidden to give him food. Only Chinese cooks were allowed to prepare his meals.

In 1959, as Tibet erupted in rebellion, the Dalai Lama feared that the Chinese would kill him. He escaped on horseback, stopping to eat bread and drink hot water and condensed milk before crossing the last mountain pass to freedom in India.

The first rule of a Dutch dinner guest in the seventeenth century: Don't clown around while people are saying grace. Rationalist philosopher **Baruch Spinoza** was accused of that offense by a fellow diner, theologian Philippus van Limborch. The churchman wrote:

"During the prayer he showed signs of an irreligious soul by means of gesticulations by which he seemingly tried to demonstrate our stupidity in praying to God."

What "gesticulations"? By one account, Spinoza rolled his eyes.

In 732, **Pope Gregory II** banned the eating of horsemeat to differentiate Christians from barbarian invaders who sacrificed and ate horses in worship of Odin, a god who rode a horse with eight feet.

Swiss-born philosopher **Jean-Jacques Rousseau,** whose writings helped fuel the Age of Enlightenment, spent much of his twenties as an idler and hypochondriac who drained his inheritance and flirted with older women.

During a visit to the French city of Montpellier, he wrote to a paramour: "The food is worthless, it's worthless I tell you, and I'm not joking. The wine is too strong, and always unpleasant; the bread is passable, in truth, but there is no beef or butter. There is nothing to eat except bad mutton and lots of ocean fish, all cooked in stinking oil. You would find it impossible to taste the soup or the ragouts that they serve in my *pension* without throwing up."

You don't become a saint by eating angel food cake. Throughout history, many Christian heroes have refused the pleasure and nourishment of food:

- **Agnes of Montepulciano,** a Dominican nun born in thirteenth-century Italy, slept on the ground with a stone for her pillow and limited her diet to bread and water.
- **Catherine of Siena,** a fourteenth-century Italian who wore the

habit as a lay church official and campaigned for papal reform, hastened her death through fasting in which she rejected water as well as food.

- **Nicholas of Flue,** a fifteenth-century hermit who became the patron saint of Switzerland, was said to have survived on only the holy Eucharist for the last nineteen years of his life.

- **Rose of Lima,** a sixteenth-century Peruvian who was the first canonized saint in the Americas, combined piety with self-punishment, including self-flagellation, rubbing her face with pepper, and expelling her food after eating. In today's world, Rose would be diagnosed with a number of ailments, including bulimia.

- **Joseph of Cupertino,** a seventeenth-century Italian priest nicknamed the "Flying Friar" because of his reported ability to levitate, became the patron saint of pilots and air passengers. But apparently his colleagues didn't want him hovering over their dinner table, so he was banned from eating in the refectory for thirty-five years.

Some saints seemed more willing to be consumed than to eat:

- **Ignatius of Antioch,** who first wrote the phrase *Catholic Church,* was imprisoned by Rome and thrown to the lions in the year 107. Before his death, Ignatius described himself as "the wheat of God" whose fate was to be "ground by the teeth of wild beasts to become pure bread."

- **Lawrence** was martyred in the third century after running afoul of the pagan prefect of Rome.

According to legend, Lawrence was roasted alive on a slow fire over an iron grill, and at one point told his tormentors to turn him over so that both sides could be cooked.

During the civil rights movement in the American South in the 1950s and '60s, black activists held sit-ins at lunch counters—demanding to be either served or arrested. But the **Reverend Martin Luther King Jr.,** son of a prominent black minister in Atlanta, initially took a less confrontational path. Attempting to dine with a white acquaintance at an Atlanta airport restaurant, he was directed to sit behind a curtain while his companion was welcomed into the main dining area. King refused to sit where he was told and left. But he did not sit in.

Young activists finally persuaded King to join them in an October 1960 visit to Rich's department store in Atlanta. Demanding service at the store's restaurant, they were carted off to jail instead. King was jailed longer than any of the others.

While much attention was focused on blacks' efforts to eat at white restaurants, one tragedy of the civil rights movement involved whites eating at a black restaurant. A white Unitarian Universalist minister from Boston, James Reeb, joined King-led demonstrations in Selma, Alabama, in 1965. Reeb and other liberal white ministers dined on fried chicken and mashed potatoes and gravy at a black eatery called Walker's. Shortly after leaving the restaurant, they were ambushed by four white thugs. Reeb was smashed in the head with a stick and died two days later.

Confucius resolved not to eat more meat than rice, and he liked his meat fresh. He disapproved of dried meat sold by merchants, and he avoided eating any meat served more than three days after it was slaughtered, even if it was offered by nobles.

After Confucius's disciple Zilu was killed during a revolt at Wei, word came back that Zilu's enemies had turned his remains into pickled meat sauce. Confucius acted decisively, ordering that all the meat sauce in his house be thrown away.

Britain's **King James I,** who commissioned an authoritative translation of the Bible, found himself competing with a tasty fish for his legacy.

As mapmakers charted North America, some of them referred to the bay east of the Massachusetts Bay Colony as Cape James. But the name didn't stick. Instead, the bay took the name of its most popular fish. As preacher **Cotton Mather** wrote, New England had embraced the name Cape Cod and would not give it up "until shoals of cod be seen on its highest hills."

Life in Nazi-occupied Paris during World War II posed challenges for **Jean-Paul Sartre** and **Simone de Beauvoir,** who loved philosophy and each other. The two could no longer afford to eat at restaurants every day, and for the only time in her life Beauvoir did the cooking. She later said she felt constant hunger during the war and admitted decades later that she had purchased food on the black market despite Sartre's insistence that she not do so.

An out-of-town friend sent food parcels to them, but when the provisions were delayed in the mail, the contents often rotted before arrival. When Sartre got a whiff of one newly arrived rabbit, he threw it into a garbage can. But Beauvoir sneaked it out of the trash when he wasn't looking. She masked the smell by soaking the rabbit in vinegar and cooking it in herbs, then served it to Sartre, who ate it.

Aristotle praised camel's milk but found it strong, recommending that it be mixed with two or three parts water.

Bartolomeo Scappi, personal chef to **Pope Pius V** in the sixteenth century, liked his eggs experienced. He offered this omelet recipe: "Take eight two-day-old eggs and whisk them, as these are better for omelets than fresh ones are because the fresh ones make them tough and they don't turn out as yellow as the others."

He led his people out of slavery, walking with them across the miraculously parted Red Sea. He delivered the Ten Commandments. He made sure his followers were well protected and well fed. Yet despite all those accomplishments, **Moses** committed the ultimate sin of a host: serving bland food.

The Bible describes a restless group of Jews in the desert, surviving on manna that would fall from heaven with the dew overnight. For forty years they ate this, but they were not particularly happy about it. A colorful Bible-based biography of Moses by Oxford professor George Rawlinson in 1887 describes how "a disgust fell on the multitude at having nothing to eat but manna day after day—no change, no flesh, no fish, no high-flavoured vegetables, no luscious fruits, no cucumbers or melons, no onions, or garlic, or leeks. The people loathed the 'light food,' and cried out to Moses, 'Give us flesh, give us flesh, that we may eat!'"

According to the Bible, Moses brought this grievance to God, who delivered a flock of quail that fed the Jews for a month. But the quail came with a plague, and many of the Jews died. Presumably, the manna tasted a lot better after that.

What the heck was manna, anyway?

The Bible says it "was like coriander seed, and its appearance like that of bdellium [a gum resin from trees]. The people would go about and gather it and grind it between two millstones or beat it in the mortar, and boil it in the pot and make cakes with it; and its taste was as the taste of cakes baked with oil."

Which meant it wasn't as tasty as quail, but was a whole lot safer.

When **Mother Teresa** first established the Missionaries of Charity in the slums of Kolkata in 1950, she intended that she and the other nuns would eat the same meager food as those they served: only rice and salt. But experienced charity workers told her that such a diet would leave them too weak to perform their exhausting work. Teresa relented, and she and the nuns dined with religious fervor.

Teresa fed her nuns a regimented diet, sometimes more than they wanted. For breakfast, they consumed a glass of water, a glass of milk made from powder, and five chapatis (homemade bread without yeast) spread with clarified butter. Afterward, a vitamin pill. For lunch, the nuns ate five ladles of bulgur wheat and three bits of meat, if it was available. In the afternoon, two dry chapatis. Then for dinner, there was rice, tomatoes, onions, other vegetables, and a spicy lentil dish called dal.

When new recruits arrived at Motherhouse, they were surprised by the full plates of food. But Teresa told them to eat it all because God wants "obedience rather than victims."

Chicken soup's healing power has been preached for centuries.

Moses Maimonides, a Spanish rabbi and renowned Torah scholar who was born in the twelfth century, wrote that the soup produced by fat hens was effective in treating asthma.

But chicken soup was the weapon of a would-be assassin in 1916.

The new Roman Catholic archbishop of Chicago, **George**

Mundelein, was the guest of honor at a banquet attended by the Illinois governor, a former Chicago mayor, and many titans of industry. An anarchist cook named Jean Crones poisoned the chicken broth with arsenic, causing scores of the finest citizens of Chicago to vomit amid the splendor of the University Club. Mundelein claimed to be unaffected, telling the press, "You know it takes something stronger than soup to get me."

None of the victims died, reportedly because Crones over-poisoned his nefarious broth, causing them to eject the toxin rather than absorb it.

The anarchist escaped, and sightings were reported in a dozen cities. One helpful citizen told police that she had spotted Crones masquerading as a nun in Pittsburgh. He was never caught, and he died among friends in Connecticut nearly two decades after his arsenic attack. Mundelein outlived him by five years.

Was the Last Supper a traditional Jewish seder dinner? Many biblical scholars think so, but it may be a matter of believing the Gospels of Matthew, Mark, and Luke over the Gospel of John. According to John, the supper occurred too early in the year to be a seder.

If it was indeed a seder, does that mean that **Jesus Christ** and his disciples dined on the traditional dishes of horseradish, parsley, hard-boiled egg, celery leaves, lamb shank, and *haroset* (a mixture of nuts and chopped fruit)? Maybe not. The seder traditions underwent sweeping changes in the first and second centuries CE, after Christ's death.

It's clear from the Bible that the Last Supper included bread and wine because Christ breaks bread and says, "Take, eat; this is my body." Then he passes a cup of wine and tells them, "Drink from it, all of you; for this is my blood of the covenant, which is poured out for many for forgiveness of sins." But the rest of the menu—if there was anything else—remained unchronicled.

This crucial moment in the life of Christ has been re-created in centuries of art, with a variety of interpretations. Leonardo da Vinci's *The Last Supper* shows both lamb and fish on the table. Salvador Dalí's painting *The Sacrament of the Last Supper* includes only bread and wine. But, of course, neither Leonardo nor Dalí was painting from memory.

For Christians, the Last Supper led to the sacrament of the Eucharist. But the host that is eaten by believers has changed radically over the ages. In the first few centuries after the death of **Jesus Christ,** the host was large, with a hole in the middle. One food scholar compared its shape to a wreath. A single host might feed all or most of a congregation. The smaller, individually sized hosts, about the size of a coin, appeared in the eleventh century.

Circa 1250, **St. Thomas Aquinas** insisted that the host be made of wheat because Christ had compared himself to that grain, saying that "unless a grain of wheat falls into the earth and dies, it remains alone; but if it dies, it bears much fruit." Thomas was flexible in his demand, accepting "a moderate mingling of other flours" as long as wheat retained a majority.

Milarepa, an eleventh-century yogi venerated by Tibetan Buddhists, dwelled in Himalayan caves while seeking enlightenment. He wore a thin cotton robe in frigid temperatures, and he ate stinging nettles.

In Tibet today, some poor people eat nettles, but they mix them with potatoes and wheat, using the nettles as a sort of spice. Milarepa, on the other hand, elevated the noxious, prickly plant to the main course, eating nothing else for months at a time. Some said that Milarepa's skin took on a shade of green similar to that of the nettles.

German philosopher **Arthur Schopenhauer** objected to Dutch paintings featuring food, believing that they made viewers hungry and distracted them from contemplating the image. Schopenhauer made an exception for fruit because "it exhibits itself as a further development of the flower, and as a beautiful product of nature through form and color, without our being positively forced to think of its edibility." However, he believed it was wrong for paintings to depict the "deceptive naturalness" of "prepared and served-up dishes, oysters, herrings, crabs, bread and butter, beer, wine, and so on."

Because of secrecy and intrigue in the Renaissance-era Vatican, the death of a pontiff often raised suspicions of poisoning.

Some believe **Pope Clement VII** died after he was served poison mushrooms, perhaps intentionally. Others say the holy father succumbed in 1534 from a simple fever.

When **Pope Alexander VI,** of the notorious Borgia family, died suddenly in 1503, his face was described as "mulberry-colored and thickly covered with blue-black spots." According to one theory, God had punished the widely despised Alexander for his sins. But others believed that the pope's own perfidy was his undoing, and they told this story: Alexander informed Cardinal Arian da Corneto that he wished to visit him and would bring food. The cardinal, suspecting that the pope wanted to poison him, bribed a papal servant to reveal the plot. Alexander arrived with two boxes of confectionary, a poisoned one for the cardinal and an unpoisoned one for the pope. But the servant switched the boxes, and the church was soon in need of a new leader.

According to the Bible, when **Jesus Christ** was resurrected and appeared before amazed witnesses, he asked for something to eat and was given a piece of broiled fish. Some versions of the Bible say he also received a honeycomb.

The term *prison food* may inspire visions of tasteless or rancid slop. But when **Mohandas Gandhi** was arrested for leading public demonstrations against the British rule over India, his admirers made sure he had healthy fare.

At Yeravda prison from 1922 to 1924, he was allowed extra fruit sent by friends. When he defied the British salt tax in 1930, he was taken to Yeravda again, and friends sent more fruit. He gave away exotic items such as mangoes to the prison staff, but ate the humbler fruit himself. He also lived on vegetables, nuts, bread, bicarbonate of soda, curds, and goat's milk—never eating more than five food items a day. Because of the routine of prison life, some friends thought Gandhi was healthier in custody than when he was free.

Gandhi was always sensitive about his milk consumption, believing that he could keep a promise to his mother by avoiding cow's milk but drinking goat's milk instead. For that reason, when Gandhi was at Yeravda, he arranged for a goat to be brought regularly into his cell and milked in his presence.

The **Reverend Martin Luther King Jr.** worked on civil rights issues—and dinner—with activists Ralph Abernathy and the Reverend Fred Shuttlesworth.

As Shuttlesworth recalled, King was "lecturing young President Kennedy by phone on the necessity of non-violent 'creative tension' and he paused in mid-sentence to say, 'Wait a minute, Mr. President. Ralph, bring me a couple pieces of chicken, please, and bring some more of that bread. Fred, ain't this some great bread!'"

Pope Clement VII loved mustard and consumed it at virtually every meal. The pontiff's passion for mustard inspired many ordinary citizens to start eating it and develop new dishes using this papal-approved ingredient. Clement was asked to taste and assess many of these recipes, and he frequently granted favors to those who had brought him a mustard-laden recipe that he enjoyed. Any person who successfully courted Clement's assistance risked being tagged by rivals as "the pope's mustard maker."

Are rice and potatoes "gateway drugs"?

Friedrich Nietzsche apparently thought so. He wrote: "A diet consisting primarily of rice leads to the use of opium and narcotics, just as a diet consisting primarily of potatoes leads to the use of liquor."

CHAPTER 4

What Edvard Munched

Visual artists mixed palettes and palates

WHEN FRENCH ARTIST **Henri de Toulouse-Lautrec** compiled recipes, he spared few details. Along with providing his own illustrations, he added advice that is unlikely to appear in a modern cookbook, such as the size of the shot to use when killing a chicken and instructions that a cook should tenderize the chicken's meat by chasing it around the yard before shooting it.

Diego Rivera, the Mexican muralist of the early twentieth century, was an unreliable autobiographer. He claimed, for example, to have fought alongside revolutionary general Emiliano Zapata, though the evidence suggests otherwise.

Likewise, Rivera's claim that he was a cannibal is highly dubious. According to the painter, he made friends with medical students when he was a young man in Mexico City, and they dined on cadavers.

"I discovered that I liked to eat the legs and breasts of women," he said, adding, "Best of all, however, I relished women's brains in vinaigrette."

Biographers have found no sign that Rivera had friends who were medical students. But there is ample evidence that he liked women.

Norwegian painter **Edvard Munch** (pronounced "Moonk," not "Munch") once was tossed off a train in the middle of munching.

Aboard a train to Nice, France, the artist took the liberty of stretching out in a sleeping compartment that was not his. Then he reached into his pockets and took out his dinner—a piece of bread, four boiled eggs, and a bottle of wine. Just after Munch uncorked his wine, the couple who had reserved the compartment showed up, along with a conductor shouting at him, "Out! Out I say!"

Munch was removed from the train, and his possessions were tossed out after him. He stood on the train platform, fuming, with his dinner at his feet. A train window opened and a hand reached out, placing Munch's hat atop his head.

During the seven years that he worked on a painting of the hunter Ialysus and Ialysus's dog, the fourth-century Greek painter **Protogenes** reportedly lived entirely on lupin beans and water.

Pierre-Auguste Renoir's meals always took a back seat to his muse.

While some people have looked for chefs with a talent for soup or pastry making, the French impressionist told his wife to hire cooks whose skin retained the light.

"Renoir, as you know, always used his cooks as models," recalled sculptor Jacob Epstein. "Rodin once said: 'It is extraordinary how I can always get better onion soup at Renoir's than at home, though my own cook is a real one and Renoir's is a model.'"

No one knows whether **John Singer Sargent** was trying to flirt with his artistic subject or was simply in a prankish mood, but he painted his nose red and ate a cigar to get the attention of the Spanish dancer Carmencita when he was painting her portrait.

French artist **Henri Matisse** made it a rule never to eat any food after he had used it in a painting. A café waiter would come by in the morning and drop off oysters for Matisse to depict on canvas, and later the waiter would pick up the oysters to serve to customers for lunch.

"Although I savor their smell, it never occurred to me to have them for lunch—it was others who ate them," Matisse explained. "Posing had made them different for me from their equivalents on a restaurant table."

Katsushika Hokusai, the masterful Japanese artist of the 1700s and 1800s who created *The Great Wave at Kanagawa* and thousands of other works, was modest in his dining habits, sticking to the more common forms of tea and eating a bowl of noodle soup before bed. But he had a weakness for *daifuku-mochi,* a rice cake with a sweet filling.

According to reports, Hokusai feasted on fowl in an artistic sense. To demonstrate his versatility, he painted using chicken eggs in place of a brush. And in an exhibition for the shogun, he laid a large piece of paper on the floor, painted a sea of blue on it, and then pulled a rooster out of its cage, dipped its claws in vermilion and sent it scurrying across the paper. "Maple leaves on the Tatsuta River!" the great artist declared.

The Potato Eaters was **Vincent van Gogh**'s first great painting, but no one considered the Dutch artist to be a foodie.

His letters to his brother Theo included such cheery comments as "I breakfasted on a piece of dry bread and a glass of beer—that is what Dickens advises for those who are on the point of suicide."

Even when his hosts offered him lavish dishes, he often insisted on only bread and cheese, which he sometimes ate while sitting by himself in a chair, refusing to dine at the table with his hosts.

In his later days, when his demons held sway, he even tried to eat his paints to kill himself.

Andy Warhol was a pop artist—constantly popping sweets into his mouth.

He would visit pastry shops daily, sometimes bringing home an entire birthday cake and eating it by himself. At sumptuous meals, he would abstain, explaining, "Oh, I only eat candy." One time at an airport, his bag was searched at customs and found to be full of candy, chewing gum, and cookies.

He wrote: "I'll buy a huge piece of meat, cook it up for dinner, and then right before it's done I'll break down and have what I wanted for dinner in the first place—bread and jam. I'm only kidding myself when I go through the motions of cooking protein: All I ever really want is *sugar.*"

After his death, his collection of cookie jars was auctioned off for a quarter of a million dollars.

Marc Chagall longed to eat as well as his father did. "I always looked at him jealously when he was served dishes of meat with sauce, particularly roasts," the painter wrote when he was thirty-five years old. Chagall added that he hoped the day would come "when I myself will be a father, master of the house and can eat such a roast in a pot like that!"

When he wasn't dreaming of a meat roast, Chagall was dreading black kasha—a porridge usually made from buckwheat groats. There was "no more devilish food," he wrote, than black kasha. "The mere thought that the grains were in my mouth maddened me, as if my mouth were filled with buckshot," he complained. Chagall confessed that he sometimes fainted deliberately to avoid having to eat the kasha his family had prepared.

In their most desperate hours, some great painters tried to trade their canvases for cuisine. Charter members of the starving artists club included **Paul Cézanne, Edvard Munch, Vincent van Gogh,** and **Amedeo Modigliani.**

A restaurateur on Lake Annecy, near Geneva, Switzerland, had the bad judgment to reject Cézanne's offer to swap his artwork for a meal. On the other hand, a waiter at the Grand Café in the Norwegian city of Kristiania (now Oslo) developed quite a collection of Munch paintings simply by keeping the artist fed.

Modigliani often paid his restaurant bill with his work, but the Parisians who were providing the food seemed to act out of charity rather than savvy investing. One restaurateur stored Modigliani's paintings in his basement, where rats chewed them up. The operator of a potato stall accepted Modigliani's drawings and used them to wrap her fried chips.

Pablo Picasso, one of the richest artists in history, liked to talk about his days as a poor man. He especially enjoyed telling the sausage story.

As a struggling artist in Paris in 1902, Picasso shared an attic room with a friend, poet Max Jacob. Their flat was unheated and had only one bed. Jacob worked at a department store by day and claimed the bed at night. Picasso created artwork at night and slept during the day. At times, the two had to burn Picasso's drawings and watercolors to stay warm.

One day when Jacob and Picasso were especially destitute, they bought a sausage from a street stall. Bringing it home with great anticipation, they warmed it, and it grew bigger, and bigger, and bigger, and then it exploded into nothingness, leaving only a stinky smell.

Frank Lloyd Wright generally enjoyed good health, but during a bout of indigestion he decided he needed a gallbladder operation. The architect consulted G. I. Gurdjieff, a Greek-Armenian mystic who advised Wright's wife, Olgivanna.

Gurdjieff invited the Wrights to a meal that almost defied consumption: dish after dish of spicy food, plus a salad tossed with strange ingredients—all washed down with Armagnac brandy. Afterward, Wright felt miserable.

"Well, I guess that settles it," he told his wife. "You're a widow now."

He finally got to sleep, and when he awoke, he felt wonderful. He concluded that his anxieties had been "burned out" by the meal.

Claude Monet devoted a lot of time to painting the lush, green water lilies that flourished in his Giverny gardens. Another one of his favorite green sights was the cake that his cook, Marguerite, prepared each year for his birthday, November 14. The cake was called *vert-vert*. The recipe included three cups of spinach leaves to produce the natural green dye that gave the cake its distinctive color.

When Spanish surrealist **Salvador Dalí** and his wife, Gala, took an ocean voyage to the United States in 1934, Dalí persuaded the ship's cook to bake a baguette about eight feet long. Dalí waved the baguette around to impress the news media upon arrival in New York City.

As it turned out, reporters were more interested in why Dalí had painted a picture of his wife with a lamb chop on each shoulder. Dalí recalled answering, "I liked my wife, and I liked chops, and I saw no reason why I should not paint them together." At other times, he answered the same question differently, explaining that the Gala-and-lamb-chops painting was an "expression of my desire to devour her" and also calling it a reference to the William Tell myth in which the archer shoots an apple off his son's head.

Jackson Pollock was an abstract expressionist who created his most famous paintings by dripping paint on a canvas. In the kitchen, Pollock showed far more precision.

"He was very fastidious about his baking—marvelous bread and pies," said his wife, Lee Krasner. "He also made a great spaghetti sauce."

Henri Matisse could cook three different kinds of onion soup, a popular dish in northeastern France, where he grew up.

Georgia O'Keeffe got into a big hassle over pineapples.

In 1939, she accepted a trip to Hawaii from the company later known as Dole. In exchange, she agreed to paint two pictures in Hawaii for use in the company's advertisements. Things went badly soon after her arrival. She asked permission to live among the pineapple workers on the far side of Oahu but was told it was impossible because of the strict separation of classes at the time. An ad agency representative brought her a pineapple as a peace offering, but she rejected the fruit because it was "manhandled."

After three months, she returned to New York, submitting paintings of a red ginger flower and a green papaya tree—the latter unacceptable because a rival canning

operation handled that product. The company wanted a painting of a pineapple, and O'Keeffe didn't want to deliver. So the company delivered instead. In a shipping effort that was Herculean for 1939, the company sent a budding pineapple plant from Hawaii to O'Keeffe's Manhattan penthouse in only thirty-six hours.

She painted a picture of a pineapple bud, and all was well.

The fine artists who depicted shiny fruits and vegetables in brilliant still-life paintings over centuries had no idea that they were merely the opening acts for a publicity-grabbing puree of food and art: **Andy Warhol**'s Campbell's soup cans.

But Warhol wasn't being completely tongue-in-cheek in putting Campbell's on a pedestal. He really liked the soup.

"Many an afternoon at lunchtime Mom would open a can of Campbell's tomato soup for me, because that's all we could afford," Warhol said. "I love it to this day."

After a colleague suggested that Warhol paint soup cans, he sent his mother to an A&P grocery to buy all thirty-two varieties of Campbell's, and he produced works that became the totems of the pop art movement.

Not everyone in the art world was impressed. When Warhol's first soup-can exhibit opened in 1962, a competing gallery displayed Campbell's soup cans in its windows along with a sign reading, "Buy them cheaper here—sixty cents for three cans."

The avant-garde photographer **Man Ray**—born Emmanuel Radnitzky—adopted a bizarre fad diet while living in Paris in 1932. Practitioners could not eat potatoes or other starches on the same day they consumed fruit, nor could they eat fruit on the same day as meat. The diet required Man Ray to drink enormous amounts of mineral water and orange juice.

Food sometimes played a starring role in Man Ray's art. In one case, his creation was a loaf of bread, painted blue and then rested on a scale.

In 1926, a bronze piece from Romanian sculptor **Constantin Brâncuși**'s abstract series "Bird in Space" was challenged by U.S. customs officials, who wanted it classified as machinery instead of art.

But Brâncuși's friends didn't wonder whether his work was art. They just wanted to know, what's for dinner? That's because Brâncuși was a gourmet cook. He collected a variety of cheeses and maintained them at the proper temperature in his cellar, and he roasted chicken in the same kiln that had produced "Bird in Space."

Salvador Dalí was known for his ability to turn surrealism into serious cash. He received ten thousand dollars for a French television commercial in which he said, "I am mad, I am completely mad . . . over Lanvin chocolates." But he drew the line somewhere, rejecting an American businessman's proposal to open a chain of "Dalicatessens."

In the year 1500, **Michelangelo** complained that his side was swollen, and his father, Lodovico, wrote him a letter suggesting that the cause might be "bad, windy food." The father recommended a remedy that had worked for him: "I went for a few days eating only sops of bread, chicken and egg, and I took by the mouth a little cassia, and I made a poultice of thyme, which I put in a pan with rose oil, and chamomile oil, and when the poultice was ready I applied it to the front of my body, and in a few days was well again."

In the late nineteenth and early twentieth centuries, some artists in Paris were far more obsessed with what they drank than what they ate. Their beverage of choice was absinthe, also known as "the green fairy" or "bottled madness."

The drink put people into a dream state—just where the most experimental painters wanted to be.

Henri de Toulouse-Lautrec's only portrait of **Vincent van Gogh** shows him staring into space at Le Tambourin, a cabaret and restaurant known for its excellent Italian food. But there is no food in front of Van Gogh, only a glass of absinthe.

Toulouse-Lautrec was a great admirer of the green fairy. He was rumored to have kept his hollow cane filled with an emergency supply of the drink. He also created a combination of absinthe and cognac for dancer Yvette Guilbert that was dubbed "the Earthquake."

When he was in Paris, **Edvard Munch** drank absinthe. He wrote: "My own impression is that I am breathing sounds and hearing colors, that scents produce a sensation of lightness or of weight, roughness or smoothness, as if I were touching them with my fingers."

Munch created a painting depicting two men talking over glasses of absinthe. Originally named *The Absinthe Drinkers,* the painting was renamed *Une Confession* at the insistence of the American who bought it. The painting has since disappeared, perhaps hijacked by the green fairy.

France banned absinthe in 1915, and painters found inspiration elsewhere.

Michelangelo was often too busy to eat. During periods of intense labor, he would simply nibble on a piece of bread as he worked. When not on the job, he enjoyed a sweet white wine called Trebbiano, which he liked to share with friends.

In addition to his enthralling works of art that have survived to this day—including the sculptures *David* and the *Pietà,* and the ceiling of the Sistine Chapel—Michelangelo left behind three menus in his own hand. One of them, believed to have been intended for dining alone, called for two breads, wine, herring, and pasta. The menus included his drawings of the food, perhaps to guide a servant who couldn't read.

Coco Chanel, whose sense of style revolutionized the fashion industry in the early twentieth century, dined lavishly with Europe's rich and famous. But back home in her French Riviera villa, she preferred a simple baked potato and perhaps a fresh chestnut puree. Her cooks were told to avoid onions. "I don't like food that talks back to you after you've eaten," Chanel said.

By the last few years of her life, Chanel decided that there were too many fat women in Paris. "The important thing is not to eat," she told a fashion photographer. "It disgusts me to see the amount French people eat."

Acclaimed fashion designer **Karl Lagerfeld,** whose father made his money in the condensed-milk business, got tired of wearing tentlike clothes and went on a successful diet.

"I can hypnotize myself into only liking what I am allowed to eat," he said.

He also offered advice on pretending to eat without actually doing so: "At dinner parties, slide the food to the center of the dish and later squeeze it all together on the side of the plate. So as not to offend the host, occasionally put the fork to your mouth and make believe."

But discipline only goes so far.

"I do not smoke, drink alcohol or even coffee," he said, "but I would do anything for a good *bavaroise* chocolate cake and German whipped cream."

A friend of **Honoré Daumier** expressed concern about the French printmaker's shaky financial state.

"What more do I need?" Daumier said. "Two fried eggs in the morning, and in the evening a herring or a cutlet. To that add a glass of Beaujolais, some tobacco for my pipe, and anything more would be superfluous."

As a young artist in Paris, **Henri Matisse** ordered half portions at a cheap restaurant, and half a decade later was able to recall the bill of fare: "6 sous the half portion, 3 sous' worth of bread, 3 sous' worth of brie, and a coffee at 2 sous." He avoided ordering wine, which prompted his friend and fellow diner Emile Jean to share his carafe. "Watching you drink water like that makes me sick," Jean told him.

Try to imagine a waiter's worst nightmare. It might resemble **Vincent van Gogh.**

While staying at the Hotel-Restaurant Carrel in Arles, France, in 1888, Van Gogh wrote to his brother Theo:

You know, if I could only get really strong soup, it would do me good immediately: it's preposterous, but I never can get what I ask for, even the simplest things, from these people here. And it's the same everywhere in these little restaurants.

But is it so hard to bake potatoes?

Impossible.

Then rice, or macaroni? None left, or else it is all messed up in grease, or else they aren't cooking it today, and they'll explain that it's tomorrow's dish, there's no room on the stove, and so on. It's absurd, but that is the real reason why my health is low.

The painter's annoyance with the local accommodations may have hastened his move into the famed Yellow House, which he shared with **Paul Gauguin.** At first, this arrangement worked out, especially when Gauguin did the cooking. But then Van Gogh threatened Gauguin with a razor and cut off part of his own left ear, wrapped it in newspaper, and gave it to a prostitute.

Perhaps the Hotel-Restaurant Carrel's weak soup wasn't Van Gogh's main problem.

At **Edvard Munch**'s house in Aasgardstrand, Norway, he placed turnips on tall sticks in his garden, with each one symbolizing the head of one of his enemies. A visitor said Munch would shoot the turnips off the sticks "whenever he chose."

In 1907, **Pablo Picasso** played host to a bizarre banquet.

The young painter had become an admirer of **Henri Rousseau,** a self-taught artist in his midsixties whose naive style was ridiculed at the time but is now highly treasured. At a Paris studio, Picasso had noticed a Rousseau work amid a stack of ill-regarded paintings and offered five francs for it. The dealer told him that "the canvas is good and you may be able to use it," assuming that he would paint over Rousseau's work.

Instead, Picasso hung it in his studio and celebrated its creator by inviting him to a dinner in his honor. While biographers tend to believe that Picasso was sincere, the event in Picasso's studio was considered a farce by some of Picasso's more sophisticated and jaded friends. Gertrude Stein called it a "jokeful amusement."

Rousseau was placed on a kind of throne—a chair atop a packing case. Around him were lanterns, flags, and a banner reading HONNEUR À ROUSSEAU (Honor to Rousseau). Food was ordered from a caterer but arrived a day late. Picasso's merrymakers prepared some paella and scrounged enough other food to satisfy the guests. A pretty newcomer to the group named Marie Laurencin had overindulged in aperitifs at a nearby tavern, and upon arrival at the studio she fell into a tray of jam tarts. With booze on her brain and food on her clothes, she tried to hug and kiss her fellow guests.

Rousseau, meanwhile, enjoyed his place of honor, occasionally dozing off as the festivities progressed. Wax fell from one of the lanterns onto his head, and according to one guest it formed "a small pyramid like a clown's cap on his head." Even so, the elderly painter never lost face. He had brought his violin, and the party progressed in song late into the night, with Rousseau alternately playing and napping. He considered the banquet a highlight of his life.

Frank Lloyd Wright's wife, Olgivanna, carefully monitored her aging husband's diet. When a Philadelphia architects' organization invited Wright to accept an award in 1950, the group's president received a letter from Olgivanna with these dinner instructions: "One piece whitefish, and this is to be cooked not in the fire or on the fire or under the fire, but directly *over* the fire, dry without any butter or sauces or mishmash. Then maybe one baked potato but absolutely dry with no butter, and a little fresh peas, and then maybe a little raspberry Jello, and maybe a little coffee, and then you will go and buy one quart skimmed milk, Grade A, and bring it back and show this to me, so I am sure."

In case Mrs. Wright hadn't made herself clear, she reminded the group president that Wright's life was in his hands.

"I detest spinach because of its utterly amorphous character . . . ," wrote **Salvador Dalí.** "The very opposite of spinach is armor. That is why I like to eat armor so much, and especially the small varieties, namely, all shellfish."

When **Pierre-Auguste Renoir** was ill in 1882, **Paul Cézanne** and Cézanne's mother, Elizabeth, helped nurse him back to health with a puree of cod and potatoes.

"Mme. Cézanne made a brandade of cod for my lunch and I think I have rediscovered the Ambrosia of the gods," Renoir wrote, adding a strange comment for someone battling pneumonia: "One should eat it and die."

Renoir ate it but didn't die.

The elderly **Georgia O'Keeffe** settled in the New Mexico desert, creating a terraced orchard with apricot, apple, and peach trees. She also grew a variety of vegetables and herbs and used her basil and marjoram on homemade bread with butter. When grasshoppers invaded her garden, she skipped pesticides and brought in turkeys to evict the pests.

O'Keeffe's routine was to enjoy a hearty breakfast with some meat, then eat homemade yogurt or a health drink with skim milk at midmorning. For lunch, she would have a soufflé and something light, such as a salad. Her dinner was modest— fruit and cheese. In bed at night before she fell asleep, she read cookbooks.

J. M. W. Turner, the British painter known for audacious pictures of tempest-tossed ships and consuming fires, was a bit of a curmudgeon in real life. He earned a reputation as a poor host. The best hospitality that a visitor could expect at Turner's home was sherry and biscuits.

For some reason, writers tended to criticize Turner with food imagery. After seeing Turner's *Jessica,* poet William Wordsworth speculated that the artist had painted it after he "had indulged in raw liver when he was very unwell." Mark Twain endorsed the words of a Boston critic, who compared Turner's *The Slave Ship* to "a cat having a fit in a platter of tomatoes."

In a 1989 interview, celebrity fashion designer **Sonia Rykiel** confessed her addiction. "I am pursued by chocolate," she said, calling it "a drug and mystery you shouldn't try too hard to solve."

Like an illicit drug, Rykiel's chocolate is kept out of sight. "I keep chocolate hidden in a special place at home and it happens that sometimes I share it," she said, "but only with my sisters."

Sixteenth-century Chinese calligrapher-painter **Xu Wei** tried to use art to barter his way to better eating. He once gave a military official a painting of bamboo in exchange for bamboo shoots. In some cases, Xu presented food paintings—grapes, pears, and fish were among the featured comestibles—to people in hopes that his art would prompt a reciprocal gift of food. Xu even wrote a poem that laid bare his scheme:

At night by my window, guests and hosts talk
It's autumn on the river and the crabs and fish are fat
I don't have the money to buy crabs to go with the wine
I think I'll paint something to pay for it.

Andy Warhol once wrote: "I really like to eat alone. I want to start a chain of restaurants for other people who are like me called ANDY-MATS—'The Restaurant for the Lonely Person.' You get your food and then you take your tray into a booth and watch television."

Thomas Hart Benton painted scenes of vibrant and even wholesome Americana, but he could be naughty and crude at times.

While dining at a friend's house, he got into a discussion about St. Augustine. As his friend's maid, who was deeply religious, passed the mashed potatoes, Benton said, "You know what happened to St. Augustine, don't you? They chopped off his balls!"

The maid threw the platter of potatoes into the air and stomped into the kitchen, slamming the door behind her.

Maya Lin, designer of the Vietnam Veterans Memorial in Washington, D.C., came up with her concept as an undergraduate at Yale. Sitting in a university dining hall, she fashioned a model out of mashed potatoes.

Unfortunately, that model doesn't exist today. Lin ate it.

CHAPTER 5

Hail to the Beef

Dining was drama from Washington to Obama

PRESIDENTS AND PRESIDENTIAL aspirants frequently have used food as a prop or metaphor to mock adversaries, project confidence, or clarify positions.

President William McKinley was attacked for having "no more backbone than a chocolate éclair." Presidential hopeful Walter Mondale lampooned fellow candidate Gary Hart's substance—or lack thereof—by asking, "Where's the beef?" **President George H. W. Bush** insisted his requests of the Democratic Congress had been reasonable: "I wasn't asking the Congress to deliver a hot pizza in less than 30 minutes." However, one of the most memorable food-oriented expressions ever attributed to a president is a myth. **Herbert Hoover** didn't promise "a chicken in every pot"—a group of Republican businessmen did.

During **Richard Nixon**'s first official trip to London as president, there were some clumsy moments, such as when he knocked over an inkwell on an antique table. According to Roger Morris, a National Security Council staffer under Nixon, these embarrassing incidents may have shaped a presidential decree.

"On his return to the White House," wrote Morris, "he would

soon ban any soup being served at state dinners, since he almost invariably dribbled it on himself or the table."

Thomas Jefferson may have been America's original foodie. Here's why:

- He introduced eggplant to the United States.
- The first American recipe for ice cream was written by Jefferson and is housed in a collection at the Library of Congress.
- He was planting and eating tomatoes at a time when many Americans feared they were poisonous.
- Jefferson's presidential dinners set new standards for culinary excellence.
- More than 180 years after his death, *Gourmet* magazine named him one of the twenty-five people "who changed food in America."

Ronald Reagan felt close enough to Mikhail Gorbachev to inform the Soviet leader of his strategy for encouraging his son Ron, an atheist, to believe in God.

According to official notes taken by the president's aides, Reagan told Gorbachev "he had long yearned . . . to serve his son the perfect gourmet dinner, to have him enjoy the meal, and then to ask him if he believed there was a cook."

In November 1963, **John F. Kennedy** was the guest of honor at a Fort Worth, Texas, breakfast featuring soft-boiled eggs, bacon, toast and marmalade, orange juice, and coffee. As history would sadly record, it was the last meal the president would ever eat.

Soon before the inauguration of **Bill Clinton,** the *New York Times* offered this blunt assessment of his diet: "President-elect Clinton prefers the stuff with fat in it."

As Clinton's body weight rose during his initial campaign for president, his wife, Hillary, decided that the real culprit was portion size. "If you'd just be careful about the amount," she used to chide him.

Yet Mrs. Clinton had her own indulgent moments. Robert Reich, who served as labor secretary under President Clinton, recalled going to the movies with Hillary in the 1960s. "The only thing I remember," said Reich, "is that she wanted what seemed to me to be an extraordinary amount of butter on her popcorn."

The month before the Clintons moved into 1600 Pennsylvania Avenue, they were urged by a group of American chefs—led by Alice Waters, owner of the highly touted Chez Panisse in Berkeley, California—to appoint a White House chef who would promote American-style cooking, stressing local and organic ingredients. The Clintons followed this advice, moving away from a menu based on classical French cuisine.

Archibald Butts, an aide to **President Theodore Roosevelt,** once raved about a meal served at the Roosevelt family's estate in Oyster Bay, New York. The fried chicken "was covered with white gravy, and oh, so good!" Butts recalled. "The president said that his mother had always said it was the only way to serve fried chicken; that it gave the gravy time to soak into the meat...." Breakfast at the Oyster Bay home was equally rich: generous helpings of peaches and cream, fried liver, bacon, and hominy grits with salt and butter. "Why, Mr. President, this is a Southern breakfast," exclaimed Butts, a native Georgian.

Not all of Roosevelt's decisions delighted Southerners. In

October 1901, Roosevelt invited Booker T. Washington to dinner at the White House—the first time a black American had received such an invitation. Newspapers and politicians in Dixie were enraged. The *Memphis Scimitar* called Roosevelt's invitation the "most damnable outrage which has ever been perpetrated by any citizen of the United States." One angry headline proclaimed, ROOSEVELT DINES A DARKEY.

Roosevelt was undaunted. "I shall have him to dine as often as I please," he told a friend. Roosevelt's hospitality may have spurred a group of black admirers to present the president with an unusual gift for his forty-third birthday: a possum. Teddy vowed to eat the possum "well browned, and with sweet potatoes on the side."

Visitors invited to dinner with **President George Washington** quickly learned that the nation's first president was not good at small talk, and his table manners could be downright annoying.

"The President seemed to bear in his countenance a settled aspect of melancholy," Pennsylvania senator William Maclay wrote of a dinner hosted by Washington. "No cheering ray of convivial sunshine broke through the cloudy gloom of settled seriousness. At every interval of eating or drinking he played on the table with a knife or fork like a drumstick." Author John Dos Passos put it more bluntly: "His dinners were excruciating."

As a boy in Abilene, Kansas, **Dwight Eisenhower** helped bolster his family's income by selling hot tamales on the street—three tamales for five cents. Ike's mother taught him how to sew and cook, and the family's Sunday dinner became his assignment, including the apple pie.

Cooking was therapeutic for Eisenhower, and the dishes he prepared—even as president—were pleasing to others. According to Ike speechwriter William Bragg Ewald Jr., "Many Secret Service men [could] vouch for his breakfasts." Leonard Bernstein dismissed the food in Eisenhower's White House as "ordinary," but the dishes probably suited Ike's simple tastes.

Thomas Jefferson once advised other Americans traveling to Europe to observe the lives of the common people, including "what they eat." As the U.S. minister to France during the 1780s, Jefferson did a lot of observing—and eating.

In Marseilles, he marveled at "the most delicate figs" on the continent. He tasted green peas in the Italian city of Pavia. He learned that Germans believed "the small hog makes the sweetest meat." In Holland, Jefferson ate waffles for the first time and found them so delicious that he purchased a waffle iron. He watched a farmer make Parmesan cheese and described the process in his journal with more than five hundred words of meticulous detail. His journal provided no information on Germany's red wines, other than his opinion that they were "absolutely worthless."

After a national magazine asked **Barack Obama** to "get personal and tell us what he wants for his children," the soon-to-be-inaugurated president wrote a letter that began by telling what he did *not* want for his daughters. In the first sentence, Obama acknowledged that the two years Malia and Sasha spent with him during the presidential campaign meant they were "eating all sorts of junk food your mother and I probably shouldn't have let you have."

Ronald Reagan was a self-described "dessert man." The president's ideal meal was steak, macaroni and cheese, and chocolate mousse, but this was served to Reagan only when his wife, Nancy, was out of town. White House pastry chef Roland Mesnier said, "We would have been shot if ever she found out!"

Nancy was a take-charge first lady who wanted the menu to feature a wide variety of desserts. Mrs. Reagan once inspected a dessert of raspberry mousse with fresh fruits around it. "Quite characteristically," lamented the pastry chef, "the first lady took the trouble to rearrange the fruit on the plate herself with her bare hands."

Andrew Jackson's inauguration in 1829 was a raucous event. A stampede of citizens descended upon the White House and ravaged trays of food "as if these people hadn't eaten for days," complained one observer. To coax revelers to leave the premises, White House staffers were forced to haul tubs of punch out onto the lawn.

When he was governor of Arkansas, **Bill Clinton**'s giant-sized appetite was so well known among the state's press corps that journalists would crack jokes, such as, "Is the forklift with the governor's lunch here yet?" The governor's staffers went to extraordinary lengths to try to contain their boss's eating. During one meeting, a Clinton staffer literally snatched a cupcake out of the governor's hand.

Millard Fillmore's last words before dying in 1874 assessed the food he had been served earlier that evening. "The nourishment is palatable," he said.

During the few years that **John F. Kennedy** was president, just about everything seemed more lavish, including the food. Official state dinners were accompanied by menus printed completely in French, a departure for the White House.

According to one guest, the first private dinner that the Kennedys hosted in the White House featured "an enormous gold bucket, as big as a milk pail, and this was waiting for us in the oval sitting room upstairs filled almost to the brim with ten pounds of caviar. . . . I had never seen ten pounds of caviar—much less fresh caviar—in one bucket before."

Jackie Kennedy's decision to hire French chef René Verdon was a hit. "People talk about what Mrs. Kennedy has done redecorating and restoring the White House, but they should talk more about how she has improved the food," said one dinner guest.

The sophisticated dining reflected Jackie's tastes, not her husband's. When he was single, JFK's food and drink choices reflected his bachelor status: no wine and no fussy appetizers. As a bachelor, he once hosted a dinner for three that consisted basically of chicken with Scotch drunk before, during, and after the meal. One of Kennedy's friends acknowledged that before he married Jackie, JFK "certainly had no great feeling about good food or good wine."

Ronald Reagan reportedly went seventy years without eating a tomato. According to a chef at the White House, Reagan's disdain for tomatoes sprang from a childhood prank when he was offered what he had been told was an apple, bit into it, and then realized he had been deceived.

Martin Van Buren caught criticism from all corners. The lack of refreshments at Van Buren's presidential receptions prompted one visitor to lament "the shabby court of Martin the First." At the same time, Van Buren's gourmet lifestyle was denounced on the floor of the U.S. House of Representatives. During an 1840 floor speech, Representative Charles Ogle mocked Van Buren's dining habits, saying that it must be exquisite "to sip with a golden spoon his soupe à la Reine from a silver tureen."

In March 1990, **George H. W. Bush** was in no mood to compromise. "I do not like broccoli," the president declared with Dr. Seuss–like clarity. He explained his decision to ban the veggie from Air Force One and the White House: "I haven't liked it since I was a little kid and my mother made me eat it. And I'm president of the United States, and I'm not going to eat any more broccoli!"

Bush liked to be awakened at 5 a.m. by White House staff with breakfast in bed. The president loved eating the kind of food found at a snack counter, on a picnic table, or in a fast-food restaurant—hamburgers, nachos, beef jerky, tacos, guacamole, chili, barbecued ribs, candy, hot dogs, popcorn, and ice cream. A former aide to Bush summed it up: "Junk food is his lifestyle."

French food, wrote one biographer, sent **Thomas Jefferson** "into raptures." But his passion for French and other foreign foods led Patrick Henry to denounce him as "a man unfaithful to his native victuals."

When Jefferson sought to hire a French cook, he enlisted the help of the Chevalier d'Yrugo, Spain's minister to the United States. The chevalier recommended a cook, and Jefferson authorized the minister to offer the man up to twenty-five dollars per month—significantly more than the going rate for an accomplished French cook.

The fine dining during Jefferson's presidency did not come cheaply. In an era when a whole turkey could be bought for only seventy-five cents, Jefferson's food bill was exorbitant—frequently fifty dollars a day. Most guests left raving about the food, but one dinner guest in 1802 complained of eating "a pie called macaroni" that "tasted very strong, and not agreeable."

Jefferson also had some down-home tastes. He summoned his Monticello cook, Annette, to the White House specifically to prepare eggs, batter cakes, and the other hearty breakfast foods he loved.

While attending Duke University's law school in the 1930s, **Richard Nixon**'s standard breakfast was a Milky Way candy bar. In 1937, while working in California for the law firm of Wingert and Bewley, Nixon rarely left the office for lunch; he frequently subsisted on a chocolate bar.

Calvin Coolidge must have been relieved that someone other than his wife was doing the baking in the White House.

After his wife, Grace, made biscuits, Coolidge would drop one on the floor and stomp his foot to mimic the considerable noise it made. Once, after his wife baked an apple pie, the tough crust reportedly prompted Coolidge to ask friends, "Don't you think the road commissioner would be willing to pay my wife something for her recipe for pie crust?"

The mass media have long enjoyed taking playful jabs at White House dining habits.

In 1909, *Harper's Weekly* magazine published a cartoon of **William Howard Taft** as a fat man in golf attire with several restaurant menus stuffed in the pockets of his jacket.

Woodrow Wilson's secretary of state, William Jennings Bryan, was ridiculed in 1913 for serving Welch's grape juice instead of wine at a dinner honoring the British ambassador. For Welch's, there was a silver lining: The publicity helped to turn Welch's into a household word.

After Britain's Parliament enacted special taxes on tea and other imported materials, **John Adams**—who loved tea—decided his drinking habits would have to change. "Tea must be universally renounced," Adams wrote to his wife, Abigail. "I myself must be weaned, and the sooner the better."

Lyndon B. Johnson, a notorious food scavenger, ate like a man who had a plane to catch. "He wolfed his food," said former Texas Governor John Connally. "Most of the time, he had no manners. He'd eat off of the plate of either person on either side of him. If he ate something that he liked and they hadn't finished theirs, he'd reach over with his fork and eat off of their plate."

Bobby Baker, an aide to Johnson, said LBJ would eat his dessert, then his wife's, and then move on to other plates. Baker said his boss ate "like a starving dog," gorging himself on "God-awful platters of the heavy Southern cooking he preferred."

After taking the oath of office, **George Washington** ate lunch alone.

The first president was especially fond of fish and nuts—"He eats an enormous quantity of nuts," reported a Frenchman who dined with him. Washington, who blamed his dental problems on years of cracking walnut shells with his teeth, found something softer to eat: ice cream. Records show he spent about two hundred dollars for ice cream during the summer of 1790.

A few months before he was elected president, **Barack Obama** traveled to his native Hawaii for a brief vacation. "I'm going to get a plate lunch," he announced moments after his arrival in Honolulu.

For Hawaiians, the term *plate lunch* has a specific meaning. As an Associated Press reporter explained, "It should be called: heaping pile of rice and meat crammed into a plastic foam container that could feed a small family, costs about $6, will require a couple of Rolaids, and induce a two-hour nap."

The most noteworthy meal served at the White House during the presidency of **James Madison** was the one that he and Dolley Madison never finished. The president and first lady were preparing to entertain forty guests in the executive mansion on the evening of August 24, 1814. But news of approaching British soldiers spurred the Madisons to flee the premises, leaving behind an assortment of prepared foods and wines.

The British troops who entered the White House were rude patrons—they ate the food, left no tip, and burned the president's mansion before leaving town.

If the creators of the "Got Milk?" advertising campaign had been recruiting spokespersons in the 1830s, **Andrew Jackson** would have been perfect. He was a war hero who loved fresh milk, so much so that he kept a cow on the White House grounds.

An interest in reptiles and a mischievous streak sometimes led young **Theodore Roosevelt** to place snakes in the water glasses on his family's dinner table.

For lunch, **John F. Kennedy** nearly always had soup. True to his New England roots, chowder was a favorite. JFK's preference for dinner entrées was ecumenical: steak, lamb, chicken, and turkey—preferably white meat. If he had dessert, it was usually something chocolate.

Kennedy's appetite was generally small, and even when he was hungry, his celebrity status sometimes interfered with mealtime. One day when Kennedy was a U.S. senator, his secretary brought him a lunch tray in the committee room where he was seated. As he tried to eat his lunch, a crowd of reporters surrounded him, and JFK had to escape the mob by carrying his food tray into a nearby telephone booth.

The first stove was installed in the White House during the presidency of **Millard Fillmore.** (Until then, food had always been cooked in the kitchen hearth.) Unfortunately, the stove arrived with no instructions, and Fillmore's cook couldn't figure out how to operate it. The resourceful Fillmore walked to the U.S. Patent Office, read the patent application filed by the stove's manufacturer, and returned to the White House able to show his cook how to fire up the stove.

Did journalist David Frost and **Richard Nixon** have a 1977 telephone conversation whose opening topic was cheeseburgers? In a scene from the motion picture *Frost/Nixon,* Frost answers the phone in his hotel room and assumes the caller is his girlfriend wishing to know what he wants for dinner.

"I'll have a cheeseburger," Frost quips. But the caller is former President Richard Nixon, who tells Frost, "I used to love cheeseburgers."

In the scene, Nixon says that his personal physician instructed him to stop eating cheeseburgers and switch to "cottage cheese and pineapple instead. He calls them my Hawaiian Burgers."

Although the Nixon-Frost "cheeseburger" conversation never happened, at least one detail from this fictional chat accurately reflected Nixon's dietary habits. Cottage cheese was Nixon's typical lunch meal during his presidency. And his cottage cheese—flown to Washington, D.C., weekly from Knudsen's Dairy in California—was served with a ring of pineapple.

One of the **Ronald Reagan** administration's most controversial decisions was its ill-fated proposal to reclassify ketchup as a vegetable in the federal school lunch program. Senator H. John Heinz III, whose family founded the H. J. Heinz Company, criticized the plan. "This is one of the most ridiculous regulations I ever heard of," said Heinz, "and I suppose I need not add that I do know something about ketchup and relish, or did at one time."

When it came to presidential appetites, **William Howard Taft** probably had the heftiest. He often skipped lunch, but this did little to lessen his girth because he ate such gigantic dinners. Taft, who reportedly weighed 332 pounds by the time of his inauguration, gained 55 pounds during his first year in office. Periodic diets trimmed his size, but he nevertheless left office in 1913 weighing 340 pounds.

Physicians and his wife, Nellie, regularly pressured Taft to reduce his eating. As he began one of his diets, he complained to his housekeeper, "It's a terrible sentence the doctor has imposed on me." The president himself was deeply frustrated by his dietary struggles. "I tell you," Taft once said, "it's a sad state of affairs when a man can't even call his gizzard his own."

Taft's tremendous girth rendered him unable to tie his own shoes—his valet had to perform this task. When Taft became stuck in his bathtub, it reportedly took several men to pull him free. Taft promptly ordered a new tub that was seven feet long, forty-one inches wide, and weighed a ton. When news of the tub mishap leaked out, the president became the butt of jokes: "Taft was the most polite man in Washington. One day he gave up his seat on a streetcar to three women."

Presidents are role models, and that extends to food, too. After **George H. W. Bush** publicly expressed a fondness for pork rinds, sales reportedly climbed by 11 percent.

George Washington praised his first cook, Samuel Fraunces, for preparing "genteel dinners." When Fraunces left, he had raised expectations so high that Washington sought a replacement with a newspaper ad that declared: "No one need apply who is not perfect in the business" of cooking.

At one point when the president was living in Philadelphia, he handed these duties to his slave Hercules, who had cooked for him at his Mount Vernon estate in Virginia. But Pennsylvania law required a slave to be freed after six consecutive months of residence. To evade the law, Washington sent Hercules back to Mount Vernon just before the six-month threshold. Later, Hercules returned north to resume cooking for him.

In the end, Washington was one of the few Founding Fathers whose will freed all of his slaves.

Abraham Lincoln's eating habits were as unpretentious as his public image. A woman who knew the Lincolns in Illinois called Abe "a hearty eater" who told her he "could eat corn cakes as fast as two women could make them." He enjoyed vegetables, and he appreciated a cup of coffee first thing in the morning.

The president's bodyguard wrote that Lincoln was especially fond of bacon. Yet his favorite food was probably the apple, and lunch was often just an apple with a glass of milk. His law partner, William Herndon, found it strange that Lincoln would "begin eating [an apple] at the blossom end. When he was done he had eaten his way over and through rather than around and into it. . . . I never saw an apple thus disposed of by any one else."

The stresses of a wartime presidency left Lincoln feeling increasingly indifferent toward food. John Hay, one of Lincoln's secretaries, said, "He ate less than anyone I know."

As the Senate majority leader, **Lyndon Johnson**'s hectic schedule and horrific eating habits drove his body weight up to 225 pounds. In 1955, Johnson suffered a heart attack that he mistook as indigestion from an oversize lunch of hot dogs and beans.

While recuperating from his heart attack, LBJ began eating a lot of cantaloupe, and tapioca pudding helped to ease his craving for sweets.

Johnson began to take regular walks, and soon healthy eating became his obsession. "He became the goddamndest diet fanatic that ever lived," recalled George Reedy, who served on LBJ's Senate staff. But LBJ's self-control didn't always last very long, especially when it came to desserts.

In 1965, the birthday cake presented to Johnson on his fifty-seventh birthday was decorated with plastic facsimiles of objects saluting the president's successes. A hypodermic needle symbolized the passage of the Medicare Act, and miniature houses represented the housing assistance bill that Johnson had championed.

In **Thomas Jefferson**'s day, the American diet was less meat-heavy than it is today. Yet even for his era, Jefferson ate a small amount of meat, which he called "a condiment to the vegetables which constitute my principal diet." Of all of the vegetables grown in Jefferson's garden, English peas were among his favorites—he grew thirty-nine varieties of peas.

As his 270-pound frame attested, **Grover Cleveland** loved to eat. Unfortunately, the kind of comfort food that Cleveland adored was not within the repertoire of the French chef he inherited from outgoing president Chester Arthur. A frustrated Cleveland wrote a friend: "I must go to dinner, but I wish it was to eat pickled herring, Swiss cheese, and a chop at Louis' instead of the French stuff I shall find." Awaiting dinner on another night, President Cleveland caught the aromas of corned beef and cabbage coming from the servants' quarters. Cleveland ordered his valet to take the dinner prepared for him "down to the servants and bring their dinner to me."

In 1912, food helped **Woodrow Wilson** score a public relations coup. His two leading foes for the presidency—Roosevelt and Taft—were known for their appetites for rich food. Candidate Wilson strolled into New York City's Penn Station, where, reported the *New York Times,* the traveling public saw "Democracy's candidate" bypass "the well-appointed dining room to his right." Wilson opted instead for a stool at the lunch counter, where he consumed a "simple dinner" consisting of a sandwich and a glass of buttermilk.

In the years before he became president, **Calvin Coolidge** presided over the U.S. Senate as vice president, and lunchtime was nutritional but not social: Coolidge usually ate lunch by himself at a corner table in the Senate dining hall. The constant sight of Coolidge eating alone prompted someone to ask Republican Senator Edwin Ladd, "Is that how you treat your presiding officer?"

Coolidge's odd table manners may have repelled would-be lunch companions. Even when others joined him for a meal, "Silent Cal" would sit quietly, eating crackers and nuts and not engaging others in conversation.

Joining **Thomas Jefferson** for a meal was typically a pleasant gastronomic experience. But at least one dinner with Jefferson was blamed for hastening a man's death. The unlucky diner was James Hutchinson, who had served as Pennsylvania's surgeon general.

During Philadelphia's yellow fever epidemic in 1793, physician Benjamin Rush wrote a letter to his wife, asserting that there were many cases in which the fever "was brought on after a full meal. This was the case in Dr. Hutchinson after dining with Mr. Jefferson in the open air on the Banks of Shuilkill [River]."

Richard Nixon had a "life-long revulsion" for string beans, writes a biographer, owing to the time he spent during the 1920s picking beans to supplement the family's income.

William Howard Taft's breakfasts were gargantuan. According to one report, Taft ate a twelve-ounce steak for breakfast almost every morning, as well as two oranges and several pieces of buttered toast. He washed them all down with ample amounts of coffee with cream and sugar. Oddly, the only breakfast food Taft wouldn't eat was eggs.

Decades before fast-food restaurants introduced "value menus," **Franklin D. Roosevelt** and his wife, Eleanor, were demonstrating how consumers could squeeze more out of their food dollar. Shortly after the Roosevelts moved into the White House, Eleanor prepared the "Depression lunch" for her husband that had been recommended by Cornell University's Farm and Home Week: hot stuffed eggs with tomato sauce, mashed potatoes, prune pudding, bread, and coffee—all for the affordable cost of 7½ cents. The president cleaned his plate.

During **John F. Kennedy**'s childhood, mealtime was a carefully regulated event. The family was so large that his mother, Rose, scheduled two separate mealtimes: one for the younger children and another for the older children and adults. On some days, the Kennedy family drank its way through twenty quarts of milk.

JFK frequently arrived late to the dinner table, and the penalty for tardiness was the forfeiture of any food or courses that had already been served. But, according to Rose, the penalty meant little because young John would "slip into the kitchen and charm the cook" into providing him with more food.

In June 1939, only months before Europe erupted in war, **Franklin** and **Eleanor Roosevelt** hosted King George VI and Queen Elizabeth of Great Britain for a picnic at which the royals ate their first hot dogs. The king bit into his hot dog with fervor, but the queen was perplexed at how to eat one. President Roosevelt urged her to push the frankfurter into her mouth, but the queen chose to use a fork and knife.

Nearly seventy years after the Roosevelts feted British royalty with hot dogs, another U.S. president welcomed Britain's prime minister—with hamburgers. In 2008, **President George W. Bush** hosted Prime Minister Gordon Brown at the White House, where Bush stressed the two nations' "very special" relationship. To underscore his point, the president quipped, "Look, if there wasn't a personal relationship, I wouldn't be inviting the man to [have] a nice hamburger. Well done, I might add."

Thomas Jefferson on death row? Fourteen years before he became president, it could have happened. During a visit to Italy in 1787, Jefferson was so taken with the rice of its Piedmont region that he hired a laborer to help him smuggle two sacks of the grain out of the country—a crime that carried the death penalty. Jefferson even filled his coat pockets with the Piedmont rice.

After he returned to the United States, Jefferson shared the rice grains with Edward Rutledge, a fellow signer of the Declaration of Independence who lived in rice-growing South Carolina. But the state's farmers never took a fancy to Piedmont rice.

When **Calvin Coolidge** wasn't at his desk, there was a good chance he was snacking in a White House storeroom that contained pickles, jams, and jellies. Perhaps this explains why one detractor said Coolidge looked like he had been "weaned on a pickle."

The Vermont-born Coolidge projected an image of Yankee frugality, but the thirtieth president of the United States sometimes enjoyed eating his breakfast—often a porridge of wheat and rye—while someone massaged his scalp with Vaseline.

Another strange trait of Coolidge's: He called every meal "supper" whether it was a breakfast, lunch, or a formal state dinner.

Ronald Reagan's best-known indulgence was jelly beans. He started eating them soon after he became the governor of California in 1967, supposedly to help him break a pipe-smoking habit. His favorite jelly bean flavor was licorice.

The Jelly Belly Candy Company, based in Fairfield, California, shipped more than three tons of jelly beans to the nation's capital for Reagan's inaugural events. The company introduced its blueberry-flavored jelly bean specifically for the occasion so that red, white, and blue jelly beans could be displayed together at the events. More than forty million jelly beans were consumed during Reagan's inaugural parties.

A portrait of Reagan made from ten thousand jelly beans is displayed at the Ronald Reagan Presidential Library.

Once, while aboard an evening train en route to Ohio, **William Howard Taft** requested a snack but was told there was no dining car. The response infuriated the president. His secretary, Charles Norton, reminded him that he had eaten dinner at the White House shortly before the train's departure and that a breakfast meal would be prepared. Taft was not placated.

"Where's the next stop, damnit?" the president demanded. When the reply was Harrisburg, Pennsylvania, Taft stared at Norton. "I am president of the United States," he snarled, "and I want a diner attached to this train at Harrisburg. I want it well-stocked with food, including filet mignon. You see that I get a diner."

When Norton tried to dissuade him, Taft shot back, "What's the use of being president if you can't have a train with a diner on it!"

On New Year's Day 1802, **Thomas Jefferson** was the Big Cheese: The president stood in the doorway of the White House to receive the mammoth gift of a Cheshire cheese that weighed 1,235 pounds and measured more than four feet in diameter. It took roughly three weeks to transport the block of cheese from western Massachusetts to the White House.

Thirty-five years later, it was **President Andrew Jackson**'s turn to be feted with *fromage*. Jackson scheduled an 1837 reception to allow the public to taste a fourteen-hundred-pound block of cheddar that a farmer in Oswego County, New York, had created in his honor.

By the time of the reception, the huge block of cheese had been stored in the White House lobby for two years. The odor of the fully ripened cheese could be smelled several blocks away, creating what one observer called "an evil-smelling horror." Entire families arrived by train to see and taste the giant cheese. Some Washington shops closed their doors for the event. Hungry visitors at the White House dropped small crumbs of cheese, and the steady foot traffic ground these morsels into carpets.

President Jackson avoided this mayhem by remaining downstairs. In roughly two hours, the entire block of cheese was devoured.

In 1954, when Winston Churchill was visiting, White House staff informed **President Dwight Eisenhower** that the British prime minister always ate a large lunch on Sundays. But Ike was in no mood to change his own habits. "I suppose we have enough food in the White House to give Churchill his huge luncheon," the president said, "but I'll be damned if I'm going to change my habits for the Prime Minister—I'll have a light luncheon."

The most famous dinner of **George H. W. Bush**'s administration took place nearly seven thousand miles away from the White House, and it presaged the president's declining political fortunes. In January 1992, President Bush suddenly became ill and vomited during a dinner hosted by Japan's prime minister. News clips of the incident were shown repeatedly on television.

A presidential spokesperson cited intestinal flu as the cause and became frustrated by the media's interest. "The president is human; he gets sick," said the spokesperson.

In 1944, as **Franklin Roosevelt**'s health deteriorated, the president's staff did its best to engage in positive spin. Vice President **Harry Truman** played along. After eating lunch with the president one day in August, Truman told reporters that Roosevelt "looked fine and ate a bigger lunch than I did." Out of earshot of the press, Truman confessed to his military aide, "I had no idea he was in such feeble condition." Truman had just watched Roosevelt pour more cream into his saucer than into his coffee cup.

Lyndon Johnson could be petty and belligerent, and those who prepared his food were sometimes in the line of fire. Once when he brought Speaker of the House Sam Rayburn home for a meal, he berated his wife, Lady Bird, in front of Rayburn. "Can't you serve the speaker of the house anything better than turkey hash?" he asked. Rayburn came to Lady Bird's defense by assuring Johnson that he loved turkey hash.

On another occasion, LBJ berated a secretary who brought him a lackluster cup of coffee. "No wonder you don't have a husband," he snapped. "You can't make a simple cup of coffee."

For **Woodrow Wilson,** a typical breakfast was two raw eggs in fruit juice, served with oatmeal and coffee.

As the nation entered war in 1917, Wilson worried about domestic food shortages and hoped to set an example for the nation by declaring "Meatless Mondays" and "Wheatless Wednesdays" at the White House.

A pretzel nearly ended the presidency of **George W. Bush.** On January 13, 2002, the second President Bush was watching a football game on television when a pretzel he was eating became lodged in his throat. Moments later, he fainted and fell to the floor, leaving a nasty red bruise on his cheek.

Afterward, Bush promised to take his mother's advice to heart: "When you're eating pretzels, chew before you swallow."

In 1997, **Bill Clinton** hosted a summit in Denver of the Group of Eight member nations, and several members of the White House kitchen staff traveled there to fulfill the president's request for a dinner that was distinctly American. The resulting menu, which included both bison and rattlesnake, received a mixed review from the foreign heads of state.

On another night of the G-8 summit, Madeleine Albright, Clinton's secretary of state, took her Russian counterpart to dinner at a restaurant featuring "Rocky Mountain oysters"—deep-fried bull's testicles.

After he retired to Monticello, **Thomas Jefferson** received a steady stream of uninvited admirers. Some were friends, but many were complete strangers.

The tranquillity of a family dinner sometimes was disturbed by an unannounced audience of strangers pressing their faces against the windows to observe their hero. Jefferson often welcomed these visitors to his table, prompting Monticello's overseer to complain that Jefferson's hospitality was exploited by guests who arrived "in gangs" and "almost ate him out of house and home."

Abraham Lincoln once tasted a hot beverage that a waiter had brought to his table and then told the waiter, "If this is coffee, then please bring me some tea. But if this is tea, please bring me some coffee."

CHAPTER 6

Dinner Theater

Stage and screen stars were showy eaters

$\mathcal{W}$HEN **JOAN CRAWFORD** was cast in the 1942 movie *Reunion in France,* she initially had romantic designs on costar **John Wayne.** But the chemistry was never there. "We hit it off like filet mignon and ketchup!" she snapped.

Before he embarked on an acting career, **Errol Flynn** tried to make his fortune by raising tobacco in New Guinea, where he had purchased a female concubine. One day, she killed a crocodile with a spear, and the two of them proceeded to cook and eat it. Flynn called the crocodile "delicious, like a young tender lobster or crayfish."

Kirk Douglas's Jewish roots led him to believe during his youth that he would be struck down by God if he ever ate ham or bacon. One day, however, much to his surprise, "I bit into a ham sandwich and nothing happened to me," he said. "It tasted delicious, and I didn't even throw up."

By 1946, hot pastrami sandwiches were on Douglas's mind. He bought one each night after concluding his performance in a

Broadway play. However, one evening when Frank Sinatra opened at the Paramount Theater, hundreds of women descended on the theater, hoping to catch a glimpse of Ol' Blue Eyes. This crowd blocked Douglas's normal route to the subway and delayed his arrival home with his sandwich.

"[Sinatra] pissed me off before I even met him," said Douglas. "Because of him my hot pastrami sandwich got cold."

One of the best-known **Katharine Hepburn–Spencer Tracy** films is *Guess Who's Coming to Dinner*. But it wasn't tough to guess the menu when the couple dined in real life. The typical centerpiece of Hepburn's meal was a salad, and she usually cooked Tracy a dinner that featured roast beef and potatoes.

"Spencer was like a baked potato," Hepburn said years later. "He looked like that, and he gave good value."

After he decided not to attend the 2008 Cannes Film Festival, film director **Pedro Almodóvar** felt nostalgic. He recalled an earlier trip to Cannes, including a visit to La Mère Besson, a restaurant with "the best anchovies, fish soups, and bouillabaisse." And he remembered breakfasts at the Martinez Hotel with coffee, croissants, and orange juice—"which really disagrees with me."

Eating the scrumptious Seville orange jam at a restaurant called Tetou, wrote Almodóvar, "compensates for the trip to Cannes, even if you fail and the critics don't give you even one miserable little star."

Soon after **Robert Downey Jr.** kicked his illegal drug habit, he gave credit to the fast-food chain Burger King. According to Downey, he was driving a car with a lot of "dope" one day in 2003 when he decided to stop for a hamburger at a Burger King outlet.

"It was such a disgusting burger I ordered," he said. "I had that, and this big soda, and I thought something really bad was going to happen." Downey viewed his lousy meal as an omen, and he threw all of his drugs into the ocean, deciding then and there to get clean.

Jimmy Stewart recalled his mother's attempt to put more meat on his skinny frame by making him eat "huge portions of oatmeal every morning." The onslaught of oatmeal didn't raise young Stewart's weight, but it did have one impact—Stewart grew to despise oatmeal and refused to eat it as an adult.

In November 1940, when Stewart tried to enlist in the army, a physical exam found him ten pounds underweight. He adopted a high-fat diet. But he didn't gain an ounce.

A few days after winning the Oscar for his starring role in *The Philadelphia Story,* Stewart reported for another physical. This time, he pleaded with the officer in charge to examine him but to skip the weigh-in. Stewart's request was honored, and he reported for duty in March 1941.

Hollywood is obsessed with physical beauty, but actors who are serious about their craft can earn points by gaining weight for their roles. Some examples of force-feeding:

- **Robert De Niro** packed on at least fifty pounds to play boxer Jake LaMotta in the 1980 film *Raging Bull*. "It was very easy," De Niro said. "I just had to get up at 6:30 in the morning and eat breakfast at seven in order to digest my food to eat lunch at twelve or one in order to digest my food to eat a nice dinner at seven at night. So it was three square meals a day, that's all. You know, pancakes, milk, beer."

- **Charlize Theron** gained thirty pounds to portray a serial killer in the 2003 film *Monster*. "My diet consisted mainly of Krispy Kreme doughnuts and anything that was swimming in cream or had cheese on top of it," she said. "I would also eat really late at night and not exercise at all."

- **Matt Damon**, who dropped forty pounds to play a heroin addict in the 1996 film *Courage Under Fire*, gained thirty pounds for a role more than a decade later as a whistleblowing executive in *The Insider*. "The gaining weight was alarmingly easy— just drinking beer, a lot of beer, even dark beer, and eating pizza and burgers, all the stuff you would normally tell yourself not to eat—and it came right on," Damon said.

- **Renee Zellweger** added about twenty pounds after being cast as a lovelorn British working girl in the 2001 film *Bridget Jones's Diary*. Fattening up became annoying, she said: "It got to the point where I begged people on the set, 'Please, please, don't bring me one more Snickers bar!'"

In 1925, **Tallulah Bankhead** had a leading role in the play *Fallen Angels*. She and her male costar did just as the script instructed— eating a five-course meal onstage during each performance. Unbeknownst to the audience, nearly every item that made up these courses was created from bananas. Bankhead struggled to speak clearly as she was chewing constantly.

Mike Nichols, who directed *The Graduate* and other films, was born in Berlin with a much less WASPy name: Michael Igor Peschkowsky. In 1939, the seven-year-old Jewish immigrant arrived in New York City, where he was pleasantly surprised to see a delicatessen displaying Hebrew letters on its neon sign.

"This was only the beginning of our excitement in the U.S.," Nichols recalled. "Next were Rice Krispies and Coca-Cola: we had never had food that made noise. It was great."

Kabuki actor **Bando Mitsugoro VIII** was beloved in Japan. And blowfish was beloved to Bando.

The fish is considered a delicacy in Japan but requires careful preparation to avoid tetrodotoxin poisoning, which can paralyze and kill the diner. In western Japan, blowfish is called *teppou*—meaning "gun"—signifying its peril.

Japan's emperor is legally forbidden to eat blowfish because of its danger, but there was no law standing in the way of Bando when he ordered the fish at a Kyoto restaurant in 1975. A chef initially denied the great actor's request, but finally relented and served his meal. Which was the last he ever ate.

To entice the rats to attack **Ernest Borgnine** in the 1971 movie *Willard,* the producers hired an animal trainer who smeared the actor with peanut butter. One of the rats bit Borgnine, forcing him to get a tetanus shot.

Although **Sidney Poitier** smoked moderately and had a hearty appetite, he maintained some healthy habits. He sometimes drank shakes made with asparagus and spinach juice. Even when he played poker, Poitier made wholesome choices. While the other cardplayers smoked heavily and swilled whiskey, Poitier munched on hard-boiled eggs and drank milk.

Film director **Michael Curtiz** complained about "lunch bums"—actors or actresses who left the set, ate a heavy lunch, and then re-turned without sufficient energy to perform their parts. But when he directed *Casablanca,* Curtiz had little to gripe about.

Humphrey Bogart rarely ate such heavy, slow-paced meals. **Claude Rains** usually lunched on two or three apples. **Ingrid Bergman** loved sweets, but she heeded warnings to watch her calories.

Charlie Chaplin's cleanliness and eating habits left much to be desired. During the filming of the 1914 movie *Tillie's Punctured Romance,* actress Marie Dressler finally rebelled after seeing the same piece of rancid banana resting on Chaplin's collar for sixteen consecutive days. Dressler informed director **Mack Sennett** that "if the banana is not removed, I shall enact you the goddamnedest vomiting scene" in the history of drama.

A couple of months before filming was to begin for *The Ugly Amer-ican,* **Marlon Brando** was given an assignment: lose at least fifteen pounds.

At a Hollywood party, the film's producer was impressed at Brando's initial restraint but stumbled upon the actor later in a dark kitchen, holding a whole pie in one hand and a quart of milk in the other. The producer pleaded with Brando to stop eating the pie, but Brando stalled until he had washed down the last bite of pie with milk.

French film director **Louis Malle** is known as a man who enjoys good food, but his movie *My Dinner with Andre* infuriated food and wine critic Daniel Rogov, who called Malle "the director most consistently traitorous to the gastronomic cause." Malle's crime, according to Rogov, was that his film made it difficult for moviegoers to appreciate the dining experience shared by two friends at a restaurant.

"The two eat completely different dinners," wrote Rogov, "both complemented by ill-suited wines and both made up of courses that no gourmet would consider appropriate one after the other."

When **Marilyn Monroe** was introduced to the parents of her fiancé, Arthur Miller, they welcomed her warmly. Mrs. Miller offered to teach Monroe how to prepare chopped liver, gefilte fish, chicken soup, and borscht. Monroe must have taken the offer seriously. On their wedding night a few weeks later, she promised her new husband she would "cook noodles like your mother."

The comic actor **Buster Keaton**'s favorite dish of all was called Lobster Joseph. Keaton secured the recipe from a Paris restaurant. It was not an entrée for the calorically timid: Its rich sauce was fashioned from sour cream, butter, sherry, and brandy.

Keaton hosted barbecues at his home, but he was not one of those clean-while-you-cook individuals. According to a biographer, "Keaton used every utensil whenever possible. If a recipe called for two bowls, he would dirty seven. Afterward the [kitchen] would look like the Red Army had passed through."

When traveling in foreign countries, actress **Angelina Jolie** prefers to live and eat like the natives. In a remote part of Ecuador, Jolie tasted a corn stalk and declared it "sweet." In Cambodia, Jolie encouraged her son, Maddox, to follow her lead—"We'll take our shoes off and walk across the rocks and go eat a cricket." She sampled bee larvae, which she didn't like, but she was rather fond of cockroaches, a Cambodian delicacy that Jolie called a "meaty . . . high-protein snack food." One drawback of eating cockroaches, she explained, was that "there's this very pointy bit on their stomach you just can't eat. You have to kind of pop that off."

In the early 1930s, **Henry Fonda** and **Jimmy Stewart** rented a speakeasy in New York City and colaunched the Thursday Night Beer Club. Fonda and Stewart charged their guests—mostly aspiring actors like themselves—two dollars for a beer and a steak. The steaks were usually cooked by Fonda.

Béla Lugosi's wife had a beef about lamb. When Beatrice Weeks sought to end her marriage to the actor, she cited his "violent temper" in her divorce papers. According to Weeks, Lugosi once slapped her face for eating a lamb chop that he had stored in the icebox. "If you want lamb chops—buy your own," Lugosi allegedly told her.

When it came to dietary matters, Lugosi was fairly health conscious. He liked his vegetables raw, and he sometimes drank beet juice and other vegetable extracts. Yet Lugosi also enjoyed delicacies like Roquefort cheese and goose liver, imported from his native Hungary.

It's deliciously fitting that the man who played Count Dracula on the big screen preferred his meat "blood rare" (in the words of his second wife, Lillian) and enjoyed drinking a Hungarian red wine called Egri Bikaver—translated as "bull's blood of Eger."

Broadway actress **Ethel Merman** was a woman of simple tastes.

In 1951, she and the rest of the cast celebrated the one-year anniversary of *Call Me Madam* on Broadway with a party at the trendy New York City restaurant L'Aiglon. Merman had been so busy talking with reporters and mingling with theater devotees that she had little chance to eat the food. So when the party ended, she left L'Aiglon and went for a bite at Hamburger Heaven.

While staying at New York City's Plaza Hotel, **Cary Grant** ordered two English muffins from room service, but he only received three halves. Grant was irate, and he confronted the hotel's staff. "What did you do with the fourth half?" Grant demanded. The Plaza's custom back then was to serve only three halves and keep the fourth half for use as the base for orders of eggs benedict.

Grant was so furious about the room-service incident that he talked about forming an "English muffin-lovers society." Grant even placed international phone calls to complain to his friend Conrad Hilton, who then was the Plaza's owner. From then on, Grant always received his fourth half at the Plaza.

Ava Gardner liked to eat meals at a leisurely pace, and she was known for cleaning her plate. "She would join us for dinner some nights at the café," a film producer recalled, "and she could eat twice as much as anyone and drink three times as much."

At times, Gardner behaved like a scavenger. British actor Donald Sinden recalled a cast dinner during the filming of *Mogambo* when Gardner "suddenly darted her fork across the table and took something off my plate. I said, 'Please don't do that.' She said, 'What's the matter, honey?' I said, 'I do dislike people mucking around with other people's food.' And she laughed."

Al Pacino doesn't read when he eats. And he doesn't like to watch others do both at the same time. During an interview at a hotel restaurant, Pacino told a journalist, "That guy there, reading and eating, annoys the hell out of me. He's not tasting his food, I can tell you that right now."

In 1957, the aspiring actress **Barbra Streisand** worked as an apprentice at a summer stock theater, but she was not making many friends. At the theater's dining hall, she frequently cut in line and shoved fellow apprentices out of the way. A would-be actress branded her a "little Brooklyn brat."

Streisand blamed her uncouth eating and social habits on her upbringing. "I wasn't taught manners," she said. "My family never had meals together. We never had conversations. I would eat over a pot."

On the set of his martial-arts movies, **Bruce Lee** was a democratic diner. The man who helped create a global kung fu craze insisted on eating with the rest of the cast and crew. But it was a different story off the set in Hong Kong, where Lee chose private dining rooms in restaurants to avoid mobs of fans. His favorite dish was beef with oyster sauce.

The restaurant industry periodically intersected Lee's life— and not just when he was hungry. Lee took his first kung fu class at Hong Kong's Restaurant Workers Union Hall. During the years he lived in Seattle, he worked nights as a waiter at a Chinese restaurant.

Each morning, **Gary Cooper** consumed an entire can of sauerkraut to help keep his digestive tract regular.

"I was always hungry," said **Bette Davis,** recalling the years before she became a screen star. Once her career took off, Davis quickly got used to eating hearty meals made from the finest ingredients. Her contract for the 1951 film *Another Man's Poison* required that she be provided with high-quality steak every day. This was a challenge in postwar London, where food rationing remained in effect.

"Because fine beef wasn't plentiful, we had to have it flown over," explained **Douglas Fairbanks Jr.,** who was one of the picture's executives. "We really didn't mind the expense, but it wasn't very good for morale on the set, especially when she and [costar] Gary Merrill ate their steaks in front of the others."

Katharine Hepburn ate her meals like an Olympic sprinter. As fellow diners finished their bowls of soup, she would be moving on to dessert.

During the filming of the movie *Indochine,* **Catherine Deneuve** noticed that rats in her dressing room were eating her yogurt. But the French actress was amused, not frightened. "I like all these little animals that run and eat and hide all the time," she explained.

By 1936, Dave Chasen's career in vaudeville had run its course, so he opened a restaurant in Beverly Hills. But before he welcomed diners, Chasen needed a place to hone his cooking. So he used the fireplace at the home of film director **Frank Capra** to perfect his recipe for barbecue spare ribs. "For weeks he knelt, sweaty and sooty, in front of hot coals," Capra recalled. "We ate spare ribs till they came out of our ears."

Yet during Chasen's more than sixty years in operation, it was the chili that gave the restaurant a loyal following among movie stars.

W. C. Fields loved the chili, which cost a quarter in the early days. Right before **Clark Gable** succumbed to lung cancer, he reportedly enjoyed Chasen's chili for his last meal. In 1963, when **Richard Burton** was wooing **Elizabeth Taylor,** he ordered Chasen's chili packaged and flown to her on the movie set of *Cleopatra*. The *Los Angeles Times* wrote that there was "no more fabled food in L.A." than Chasen's chili.

Banana shortcake was another Chasen's specialty. In **Groucho Marx**'s opinion, the reason to eat dinner at Chasen's was "to get to the shortcake." Marx once requested that a half-dozen banana shortcakes be sent to the diners at a nearby table. But five of those six diners were either dieting or uninterested—so all six shortcakes were served to **Gregory Peck.**

In a 1977 interview, **Elizabeth Taylor** was amazingly candid. "I can hardly get into any of my clothes," she admitted, "but I eat out of enjoyment." For years, she resisted appeals from friends to diet.

"When anyone tried to help me," said Taylor, "I'd say, 'Look, I know what I'm doing. I'm going through a phase. I can't diet until I'm ready, and if you push me, the minute you finish your lecture I will go in and have some hot fudge.' "

The first time **Tony Curtis** used a charcoal grill to cook dinner was also memorable for another reason. "I bought a couple of steaks from the market," Curtis recalled, and he picked up his date from her hotel. Curtis was pleasantly surprised that he'd succeeded in lighting the charcoal—"and that it stayed lit." He cooked the steaks and served them with string beans, tomatoes, and a bottle of wine.

"I knew something was going to happen that night, and so did she," Curtis said.

At about two o'clock in the morning, he and Marilyn Monroe retreated into the bedroom and made love.

Movie magnate **Louis B. Mayer** took his corn on the cob very seriously. He would go to a field within walking distance of his Metro-Goldwyn-Mayer studio, peel back the husks to examine the kernels, and carefully choose each ear of corn to purchase. He had his personal driver transport the corn to Mayer's home.

Later, as his family tasted the corn, Mayer would pepper them with questions to confirm that he'd chosen correctly—"How do you like it?" and "How does it compare to the corn from a week ago?"

Marlene Dietrich's favorite foods reflected her German heritage: pork knuckles with sauerkraut, beef broth, salted potatoes, turnips, and Berlin pea soup. When she traveled between America and her native Germany, she preferred to book passage on German passenger ships because she knew traditional German foods would be served.

Dietrich did not think highly of American cooking. "Judging by the vast amount of cookbooks printed and sold in the United States," she wrote in 1962, "one would think the American woman a fanatical cook. She isn't."

Film director **Alfred Hitchcock** had a giant-sized refrigerator at his home in Southern California. He and his wife had fresh lamb and Dover sole flown in weekly from England. "This food is our luxury," Hitchcock once explained. "We don't have a swimming pool or a tennis court."

During his first visit to the United States, Hitchcock told journalist H. Allen Smith that America was famous for steak and ice cream. Hitchcock devoured both of them in copious amounts. Once for breakfast, he ate vanilla ice cream drizzled with brandy.

One evening at New York City's '21' Club restaurant, Hitchcock ate a déjà vu dinner. He had a steak for his meal and an ice-cream parfait for dessert. Then he devoured a second steak with yet another serving of ice cream—only to order a third round of steak and ice cream. After eating his third dinner, Hitchcock concluded the evening with a cup of tea.

Long before he gained fame as a bodybuilder, actor, and politician, **Arnold Schwarzenegger** served as a tank driver in the Austrian army. The military's meals were a welcome sight to Schwarzenegger, whose family rarely had meat for dinner more than once a week.

"In the army, you could have meat every day," he recalled. "And then, if you screwed up, they would put you in the kitchen at night to peel potatoes and do preparation work for the chef the next day. That was no punishment to me; it was the ideal situation, to go and eat everything you wanted."

Mae West credited chocolate for her glittering stage presence. "I always feel my best when I eat chocolate," she said, "and when you feel your best, it shows."

The Academy Award–winning director **George Cukor** hosted dinner parties, and then he and his friends would drive along Sunset Boulevard in search of "after-dinner mints"—the term Cukor, who was gay, used to refer to young men.

In the mid-1960s, a huge mishap in the kitchen deprived **Dustin Hoffman** of his first major Broadway role and almost ended his career before it began.

After the first day of rehearsals for the Pulitzer Prize–winning play *The Subject Was Roses,* Hoffman went to his girlfriend's house, where the two prepared beef fondue.

When the fondue pot exploded, Hoffman was drenched with hot cooking oil, and a small fire started in the kitchen. The actor tried to snuff out the flames with his bare hands. He delayed having his third-degree burns examined by a physician, and they became seriously infected. Hoffman spent about a month in the hospital.

Meanwhile, Hoffman's understudy assumed his starring role in *The Subject Was Roses.* Dejected, Hoffman seriously considered going back to college and abandoning his quest for an acting career. But he soldiered on.

There was a reason female costars occasionally complained about **Clark Gable**'s breath. The food he was most passionate about was raw onions, which Gable would eat with or without bread.

Before they make it big, most actors and actresses must survive on a shoestring budget.

During the 1920s, **George Burns** and **Bette Davis** often ate at automats—low-cost, self-serve establishments where patrons used coin-operated vending machines to open small doors and retrieve foods and drinks. At the automat located in Times Square, the most expensive item cost fifteen cents. Burns sometimes used one of his sister's hairpins to open the doors and grab food for free.

When she first arrived in New York City, **Lucille Ball** survived partly by hanging out near the counter of a diner where she would look, in her words, for a "one-doughnut man." This person would order a couple of doughnuts and a coffee, drink the coffee, eat one of the doughnuts, and then leave a nickel tip before exiting the diner. Immediately after such a man stepped away from his stool, Ball would insert herself there, use the nickel to order a cup of coffee, and eat the leftover doughnut.

Billy Wilder fondly recalled the chocolate of his youth in Europe. But those memories were entangled with the ensuing war. "I remembered how delicious the chocolate was in Berlin when I got there, before Mr. Hitler destroyed the chocolate, and the buildings, and the people."

In the late 1930s, **Harpo Marx** hosted a dinner party that quickly turned into mayhem. One guest knocked over a tray of hors d'oeuvres. Then another guest—author Aldous Huxley, who suffered from poor vision—accidentally stuck his hand deep into a platter of fish and mayonnaise. Throughout the meal, guests could hear the sounds of dishes breaking in the kitchen.

By the late 1970s, **Gloria Swanson** had no room in her diet for sugar—except for natural sugars found in raw fruit. When she met a companion who had brought cookies from a fashionable bakery, Swanson voiced her stern disapproval: "Cookies like that are poison."

Ice cream cones played a crucial role in **Clint Eastwood**'s successful foray into politics. The actor was irked after his hometown adopted an ordinance banning the storefront sale of ice cream cones. (City officials considered the street-side eating of ice cream cones to be undignified.) Eastwood's libertarian attitudes and fondness for ice cream prompted him to launch a campaign for mayor of Carmel-by-the-Sea, California. But one term as mayor was enough for Eastwood. As a biographer summed up, "Eating ice cream in public somehow wasn't enough of a victory to motivate him to continue."

Joan Crawford considered **Spencer Tracy** to be a talented actor, but during the filming of the 1937 movie *Mannequin,* she found it tough to perform the costars' romantic scenes. According to Crawford, Tracy would show up for these scenes with "beer and onion breath." The actress complained, "I was supposed to act all lovey-dovey with him when I wanted to gag."

In the 1967 movie *Cool Hand Luke,* **Paul Newman** plays a prisoner who wins a bet among his fellow inmates by eating fifty hard-boiled eggs.

Whenever he found the time, **George C. Scott** liked to cook. Orange pancakes and hamburgers with crumbled blue cheese were among his favorite foods to prepare.

One Thanksgiving morning at his thirty-acre estate in Westchester County, New York, Scott was alarmed to discover Gogo, his female German shepherd, preparing to engage in canine coitus with a Dalmatian. (Scott wanted purebred puppies—nothing else.) Desperate to interfere with Gogo's plans, Scott and his family hastily grabbed food items that were intended for Thanksgiving dinner and hurled them at the two dogs. Four pies were ruined in the chaos, and one of Scott's children was bitten by the greatly perturbed Gogo. These events forced the Scott family to eat a modest and unconventional Thanksgiving dinner: scrambled eggs and bacon.

Ginger Rogers once ate her entire dinner at a ritzy New York City restaurant, including the soufflé, while wearing a pair of dark sunglasses. Rogers told the restaurant owner that she wore dark glasses so that she wouldn't see other diners beyond her own table.

If it looked like much of the cast for the movie *Goodfellas* could have been recruited from an Italian restaurant in New York City, there was a good reason why. The film's director, **Martin Scorsese,** cast many actors for the movie while he was having dinner at Rao's Restaurant in New York City. The cast included at least ten actors from the restaurant visit, including Johnny "Roast Beef" Williams.

One of **Bette Davis**'s favorite foods was potatoes. "If all other food disappeared and there was a famine and they left me only potatoes, I could live forever," she said. By the time her theatrical career blossomed, Davis's love of potatoes had earned her the nickname of "Spuds."

Davis was particular about how her potatoes were served. Davis loved them mashed, cut into hash browns, or formed into pancakes. But french fries were her least favorite way to eat them because "you really can't taste the potatoes as well." And she strongly preferred her potatoes with the skins left on. "Can you imagine," she once said, "there are people who don't eat their potato skins! I could never get along with that kind of person."

Laurence Olivier loved "kippers"—the term his fellow Brits used for cured seafood. In 1970, he drafted a petition calling for kippers to be restored to the breakfast menu of the Brighton Belle, a passenger train that traveled between London and the city of Brighton.

It wasn't the only time Olivier was in a fishy state of mind. He once wrote that the time he spent apart from his second wife, **Vivien Leigh,** made him "feel like a half cooked codfish thrown back into the sea."

One evening in 1982—about fifteen years after Leigh's death—Olivier went to Gallagher's, a New York City restaurant where the couple had dined numerous times. Olivier ordered the meal that Leigh supposedly ordered many times at Gallagher's: steak, salad, home fries, and a baked potato. The dessert Olivier ordered was also believed to have been Leigh's favorite: scoops of vanilla ice cream covered with crème de menthe. Olivier only picked at the dinner and never touched the dessert as it slowly melted.

Married in 1964, **Elizabeth Taylor** and **Richard Burton** were probably Hollywood's ultimate "power couple." Gossip columnist Liz Smith felt certain she knew what made them tick. "Food was their reason for living," she wrote.

Smith accompanied them soon after their wedding to a glamorous Parisian restaurant where she witnessed "an orgy of ordering, feasting, sending back, seizing tidbits from one another's plates, and the quaffing of much fine wine and champagne." Once when Smith heard that Taylor was ill in Mexico, the columnist sent a cable expressing her concern.

Taylor replied by telegram: "Elizabeth Taylor Burton is alive and eating tacos in Mexico."

Even when Taylor and Burton were far from the fifty states, their thoughts often drifted to American food. "When we're in Europe," said Burton, "we never talk of our friends in America, or

plays we want to see, or films. We only talk about the food here—
pancakes, fried eggs, hamburgers, ice cream sodas."

Ingrid Bergman loved to eat, especially sweets, which is why movie
director **George Cukor** called the actress "a refrigerator-raider."
When it came to maintaining a svelte figure, Bergman called ice
cream with chocolate sauce the "greatest danger." "I could get fat
thinking about it," she said.

Bergman adored London's Harrods department store, especially its food hall. When she looked for a home in the city, she
stipulated that it had to be near Harrods.

When Bergman was chosen to costar in *Casablanca* with **Humphrey Bogart,** she went to lunch with Bogie, intent on getting better acquainted with him. But the two did not click. "We didn't have
the same taste in food, and certainly not the same interest in it," she
recalled. "He ate very little and ate it very fast."

In the mid-1960s, Bergman prepared a crayfish dinner for director **Alfred Hitchcock.** "Totally revolting!" was Hitchcock's terse
reaction to Bergman's surprise entrée. A steak was hastily prepared
to placate the director.

It came as no surprise to actress **Joanne Woodward** that salad
dressing was the first of many upscale foods that her husband, **Paul
Newman,** sold under the label of Newman's Own. During a 1950s
dinner date with Newman at a stylish restaurant, Woodward witnessed his obsession with the perfect salad.

"He took an already oiled salad to the men's room, washed it
clean," recalled Woodward, "and returned to the table to do things
right, with oil cut by a dash of water."

While studying acting at Miller's Theater Studio, **Barbra Streisand** and each of her fellow students were asked to portray an inanimate object. Streisand chose to be a chocolate chip cookie. What was going through her mind as she portrayed one?

"I was stuck into a sticky batter, put into an oven, where I swelled and started to melt and burn," Streisand imagined. "I was taken out of the oven, where the air congealed my outer layer, leaving my insides mushy. My head started to droop when someone ate me."

Streisand said chocolate chip cookies never tasted the same to her after that.

As a teenager trying to launch a Broadway career during the 1920s, **Ginger Rogers** was chaperoned by her mother, Lela Rogers, who also served as her business manager and cook. The two traveled with a suitcase that contained a virtual kitchenette: a percolator, a hot plate, a toaster, eating utensils, and salt and pepper. Her mother's simple cooking was no hardship for young Ginger.

"Believe me, nothing tasted as good as the toast and coffee Mother made each morning in our hotel room," she recalled. Lela would heat up soup, canned chili, or a toasted cheese sandwich before or after a performance. During winter months, the Rogerses kept a bottle of milk outside on the window ledge of their hotel room.

Pot roast à la mode? At a cafeteria in Newark, New Jersey, **Jackie Gleason** would order pot roast and sometimes ask the server to drop a scoop of ice cream onto it.

Charlton Heston told a radio interviewer in 1987 that peanut butter is "a valuable creative contribution to American society, as important as mom and sliced bread." Heston once sent a jar of his favorite peanut butter to conservative columnist William F. Buckley Jr., and Buckley sent Heston a jar of his favorite.

Heston's conservative philosophy was reflected in how he ate peanut butter: plain on bread or on an English muffin. After hearing of someone who placed dill pickles on her peanut butter, Heston shuddered and said "that's probably a KGB plot."

The breakfasts that **Julie Andrews** ate during the early 1940s were memorable but for the wrong reason. Owing to England's wartime rations, her family ate a lot of Spam, usually accompanied by potatoes or a vegetable. Sometimes they ate powdered eggs.

In the 1954 play *Mountain Fire,* Andrews struggled to speak in the Tennessee drawl of her character. Yet her biggest challenge was performing love scenes with a male costar who constantly munched on garlic for health reasons.

"Someone told me that if you eat garlic in self-defense, you don't notice it on someone else," Andrews recalled, "so I began to eat a lot of garlic myself. It didn't make the slightest difference, except to make other members of the company keep their distance from us both."

After the New York *Daily News* referred to "the plump **Judy Garland,**" MGM Studios pulled a tighter rein on the teen actress's diet. "From the time I was thirteen," she recalled, "there was a constant struggle between MGM and me—whether or not to eat, how much to eat, what to eat. I remember this more vividly than anything else about my childhood."

No matter what Garland requested for lunch at the MGM Studios cafeteria, waitresses were instructed to serve her only chicken soup with matzo balls. Garland called it a "prisoner's menu."

"My idea of a good time," Garland reminisced, "was a caramel sundae at Wil Wright's ice cream parlor in Hollywood—oodles of sauce and whipped cream."

Marlon Brando was easily distracted while dining out. Some of the fancier Japanese restaurants in the Los Angeles area—including one that Brando patronized—requested that diners remove their shoes.

According to his first wife, "it was not unusual for him to forget his shoes when leaving; he could drive home, walk across the yard into his house, and not notice his stockinged feet until he sat on the bed to remove his shoes. Once he left a Japanese restaurant wearing an unfamiliar pair of shoes. He never became aware of the switch—I later exchanged the shoes without disturbing him."

Both **Joan Crawford**'s 1955 marriage to Pepsi-Cola president Alfred Steele and her later service on Pepsi's board of directors made her a vigorous partisan for the soft drink company.

While Crawford was filming the 1962 movie *What Ever Happened to Baby Jane?* she ordered a cooler stocked with Pepsi beverages delivered to the set for the cast and crew. Soon afterward, a Coca-Cola dispenser appeared on the set too. It was rumored that actress **Bette Davis** requested the Coca-Cola dispenser just to get under Crawford's skin. Another possibility is that the Coca-Cola cooler was ordered by the film's director, **Robert Aldrich,** who both drank the soft drink and had friends at the company.

When Crawford heard that the lead character in **Billy Wilder**'s 1961 movie *One, Two, Three* was a Coca-Cola promoter working in Europe, she urged Wilder to change the product to Pepsi. Her pressure may have backfired; Wilder refused to alter the lead character's affiliation and even added a scene in which the character sees a Pepsi cooler in an airport and kicks it.

Bette Davis was an excellent cook, and she preferred a home-cooked dinner to one ordered in a restaurant. But Davis's most memorable dinner occurred onscreen: a large rat on a platter served to costar **Joan Crawford** in *What Ever Happened to Baby Jane?* After the film opened in theaters, Davis hosted a cocktail party at New York City's Plaza Hotel. At her instruction, the Plaza's chef prepared a pâté in the shape of a rat.

CHAPTER 7

General Foods

For history's warriors, rations were sometimes irrational

*A*FTER DEFEATING THE Russians and Austrians at Austerlitz, French **Emperor Napoléon Bonaparte** was welcomed home with festivities that included a rabbit hunt. But the rabbits didn't follow the battle plan. A thousand were released from cages, and instead of fleeing, they charged toward Napoléon's party. The emperor ordered his aides to grab sticks and stem the onslaught but to no avail. The rabbit horde reached Napoléon, with some of them running between his legs and even jumping into his arms as he tried to swat them with his riding crop. Fleeing into his coach, he escaped unharmed.

The fault was with the rabbit suppliers. Instead of trapping wild beasts, they had gone to farmers and bought tame animals that were being raised to produce pâté. The rabbits apparently charged at Napoléon because they thought he would feed them.

Alexander the Great banned his soldiers from chewing on mint leaves, fearing that they would become sexually excited and unable to fight effectively.

In the final months of World War I, German **General Erich Ludendorff** was disheartened to watch the steady deterioration of his army's positions on the western front. But that was only part of his frustration.

Back home, critics complained that German officers were eating much better than their frontline troops. By October 1918, Ludendorff had grown tired of this criticism, and he proposed a deal to Prince Max, the imperial chancellor. Ludendorff said he and his officers would live on the same rations as ordinary soldiers so long as the government and all of Berlin did the same. Prince Max didn't take the general up on his offer.

Thomas "Stonewall" Jackson's image as an eccentric genius made it easy to accept the myth that he spent the American Civil War sucking lemons. The rather imaginative General Richard Taylor wrote that Jackson "was rarely without one," but that view was not shared by Stonewall's staff, friends, or wife. A Virginia military colleague said a lemon was a "rare treat" for Jackson "whenever it could be obtained from the enemy's camp."

In fact, Jackson liked all kinds of fruit, including apples, oranges, watermelons, grapes, and berries. Peaches—not lemons—were his favorite.

As warrior king of the Ashanti tribe, **Osei Bonsu** presided over a complex and brutal society in the part of West Africa that is now Ghana. During the early 1800s, the king enforced a system of slavery, public executions, and warfare. And he ate royally.

An Englishman who visited the Ashanti city of Kumasi said he never dined better than at Osei Bonsu's table. The meal featured soups, stews, plantains, yams, rice, oranges, roast pig, roast duck, and chicken. The royal beverages included port, Madeira, gin, and

Dutch cordials, reflecting the Ashanti's enthusiasm for trade with Europeans, from whom they also bought rifles.

A favorite drink of Osei Bonsu was palm wine, which he quaffed while greeting followers, allowing much of it to spill through his beard and onto the ground, as was customary.

In the warrior state of Sparta, bad food was a point of pride. A Spartan king named **Agesilaus II** boasted of the "contempt for luxury." Whether a Spartan was a king or a follower, the meal was the same: black porridge and barley bread. A guest who sampled the grim fare remarked, "Now I understand why the Spartans do not fear death."

Frederick the Great, the Prussian king and military leader, thought coffee made women barren and men effeminate. Beer, on the other hand, was the beverage of victory.

Frederick was raised on beer soup, which featured beer, sugar, salt, cream, flour, egg yolks, and a spice such as allspice or cinnamon. In a 1777 proclamation, he called on his subjects to drop their "disgusting" coffee habits and turn to beer soup.

"Many battles have been fought and won by soldiers nourished on beer," the proclamation read, "and the king does not believe that coffee-drinking soldiers can be depended upon to endure hardship or beat his enemies in the case of the occurrence of another war."

But even the king's decree could not curb the growing evil. Four years later, Frederick imposed a royal monopoly on coffee beans. If he couldn't stop his subjects from drinking the stuff, at least he could make a fortune from it.

To **Napoléon Bonaparte,** food was fuel, not fun.

The French emperor had his favorites—such as roast chicken, black cherries, fried potatoes with onions, and Chambertin wine—but in general he just wanted to get through his meals and on to the business of conquering. Those who dined with him said he ate silently and rapidly, always finishing in less than twenty minutes.

Even so, Napoléon ate well, which could not be said of his troops. During an expedition to Egypt, he planned for his troops to "live off the land," even though many were stationed in the desert and suffered terribly from hunger and thirst. In later Napoleonic wars, his desperate soldiers killed their horses and cooked them in pots that they fashioned from the armor of dead soldiers. The eating of horses became so commonplace that France legalized the practice in 1811.

While serving as supreme allied commander in Europe, **General Dwight Eisenhower** vowed that his soldiers "would fight for Coke, a wholesome symbol of the American way." Ike ordered three million bottles of the beverage for delivery to the European front in 1943. No wonder Coca-Cola president Bob Woodruff was a close friend of Ike's.

If **Gavrilo Princip** hadn't been a coffee drinker, would World War I have happened?

The Serbian firebrand's plot to kill Austria's Archduke Franz Ferdinand was hatched in a Belgrade coffeehouse in April 1914. Two months later, when Ferdinand visited the Bosnia-Herzegovina city of Sarajevo, Princip and his coconspirators were ready. A comrade threw a bomb at Ferdinand's car, but the archduke escaped unharmed. Princip, hearing the bomb blast and thinking the archduke dead, neglected to shoot at the motorcade as it passed. When he realized that the archduke was still alive and that he had missed his opportunity, Princip retired to a coffeehouse to drown his sorrows. Meanwhile, the archduke made a speech and returned to his car, which took a wrong turn and stopped to turn around—in front of the very coffeehouse where Princip was drinking. Princip seized this improbable second chance and fatally shot Ferdinand, setting off a war that would kill ten million people.

By the time they marched into Savannah, Georgia, in December 1864, **Major General William Tecumseh Sherman**'s Union troops were tired and hungry. But the area's rice mills, warehouses, and farms were nearly bare. To satisfy their stomachs during the city's occupation, soldiers had to get their feet wet.

"There [are] a hundred and twenty men detailed out of the brigade to go to Thunder Bay to rake oysters for us," reported one Wisconsin soldier.

In his diary, a Union officer from Illinois recorded the menu of an officers' dinner on New Year's Day 1865—and oysters were the star: oyster soup, oysters on the half shell, fried oysters, and roasted oysters. "A little top-heavy as to oysters," wrote the officer, "but we don't complain."

At harvest time, **Osei Bonsu,** king of the Ashanti tribe in western Africa, held a yam festival. The tribe paraded the skulls of conquered chiefs and sacrificed slaves, then poured the slaves' blood into the holes where the yams were dug up in order to ensure the continued fertility of its crops.

Osei Bonsu's death—and the beginning of his tribe's decline—occurred in the early nineteenth century as war erupted between the Ashanti and another nation with a history of cruel conquest: the British. In one clash, the Ashanti overran a force led by Sir Charles

MacCarthy. The British leader was beheaded, and his heart was eaten by Ashanti commanders. (Osei Bonsu likely died in the days before the battle and did not share in this "heart-healthy" meal.)

In a later battle, the British believed they had recovered Mac-Carthy's skull. But it turned out to be the skull of a tribal elder—perhaps even Osei Bonsu. The Ashanti kept MacCarthy's skull under wraps, except when they displayed it once a year as a highlight of the yam festival.

Woquini, also known as Roman Nose, was chief of the southern Cheyenne when the U.S. Army was conquering the West. A spiritual man, Woquini once lay on a raft floating on a lake without food or water for four days.

During a meal with his Sioux allies in 1868, he ate fried bread, only to discover afterward that the Sioux woman preparing his food had used an iron fork. This violated the dietary rules that he thought protected him against the white man's bullets. Woquini went into a lengthy purification ritual, forcing his fellow warriors to attack the bluecoats without him.

Eventually, Woquini heeded his comrades' pleas and joined the battle, but he seemed resigned to his fate. And indeed, as he led a charge, he was shot in the spine. He died hours later, a victim of bluecoats and fried bread.

As evidence that **Attila the Hun** was a regular guy, historians note that he drank his beer from a wooden bowl instead of a golden cup.

Napoléon Bonaparte was an early aficionado of the banana, a fruit that didn't travel well and was slow to reach Europe. His empress,

Joséphine, asked her mother to ship some from the island of Martinique, but it's unclear whether they ever reached Napoléon's table. If so, the emperor might have been one of the first people to eat a banana in Europe. Even if not, Napoléon helped peel away the mysteries of the banana for Europeans. While in exile on the island of St. Helena, he enjoyed banana fritters soaked in rum.

"Cooking in the enemy camp at unusual times suggests that he is about to move," wrote Prussian strategist **Carl von Clausewitz.**

When **Genghis Khan** was twelve, his father was poisoned by his enemies at a banquet. Years later, he wreaked a terrible revenge on that group of adversaries, slaying every member who stood taller than the hub of a cart's wheel.

Even among family members, Khan tolerated no nonsense when it came to meals. As a youth, he killed a half brother who had stolen his fish.

General Bernard Montgomery, the top British commander in World War II, sat down to dinner at a Brighton hotel with **Winston Churchill.** The prime minister, holding a cigar in one hand

and a glass of whiskey in the other, asked Monty what he'd have to drink. "Water" was the answer, and the general went on to explain that he neither smoked nor drank and was 100 percent fit. The annoyed Churchill responded that he smoked and drank and was 200 percent fit.

Later, after Monty won the battle of El Alamein in North Africa, he invited a captured German opponent, General Ritter von Thoma, to dine with him and discuss tactics. Such fraternization did not sit well with some members of Parliament, who brought it up with Churchill. The prime minister also objected to the meal.

"Poor von Thoma," Churchill quipped. "I, too, have dined with Montgomery."

Saladin, the Islamic hero who captured Jerusalem in the twelfth century, followed the rules of hospitality. After the battle of Hattin, two captured Crusader leaders, Reynauld of Châtillon and King Guy, were brought before him. Saladin gave Guy a beaker of cold water, a gesture that spared him from execution because of a Middle Eastern custom that a host could not kill a person to whom he had given food or drink. Guy shared his water with Reynauld, who had twice broken truces. Saladin declared that he had not given the drink to Reynauld and promptly beheaded him.

A soldier's meal during the American Civil War sometimes consisted of green corn, tainted beef, or hardtack. The officers ate better, but not by much. Confederate **General Robert E. Lee** enjoyed a rare exception to these poor meals in February 1865 after a well-wisher gave him a turkey. Lee spent days fattening it up on rice in anticipation of a visit by Confederate **President Jefferson Davis.** When Davis didn't show up, Lee's headquarters staff enjoyed the meal, and one diner called it "the largest turkey I ever saw."

As a rule, though, Lee set an example for his troops with his modest lifestyle, so much so that his staff sarcastically referred to him as "the Tycoon."

When Irish rebels attempted to shake off British occupation during the Easter Rising of 1916, one of their leaders was **James Connolly,** a socialist from a poor background. After helping lead the takeover of the General Post Office in Dublin, Connolly was wounded in the ankle. He asked for a cup of tea, but none could be found, so a rebel offered a cup of Bovril beef soup instead. Connolly refused it because the soup was the product of "scab labor." Connolly was captured and later executed.

Vitamin deficiencies are most often associated with the poor and powerless. But in Japan during the 1800s, the affluent were racked with beriberi—a deficiency of thiamine, or vitamin B_1—because of their diet of polished white rice. The illness was so common in the city of Edo (now Tokyo) that it was called "the Edo disease." One prominent victim was **Tokugawa Iemochi,** the fourteenth Tokugawa shogun, or hereditary military leader. His death at age twenty was a key event in the demise of the shogun system.

To relax after warfare, American **General George Patton** went hunting.

Patton and his comrades enjoyed a boar hunt in Morocco in 1942, with the commander bringing down two boars and a jackal. Then the hunting party had lunch under tents, hosted by the sultan of Morocco. The feast was a test of endurance and stomach capacity. First came an entire barbecued sheep for each table of six. Forks and plates were unnecessary; Patton and his fellow diners used one hand to put the meat into their mouths and the other hand to shoo away flies. Next, the sultan's minions delivered six chickens to each table, one per person. A serving of barley with meat and turnips followed, and Patton tried to ball it up and throw it into his mouth.

Afterward, the Americans were offered the boars and jackal they had killed but declined, apparently feeling less carnivorous than when the day began.

Mata Hari, the Dutchwoman who became an exotic dancer and pretended to be from India, enjoyed bathing in milk. After the French arrested her as a German spy during World War I, she was said to have demanded milk baths in prison, even though some French children had no milk to drink. But that rumor of her callousness appears to be false—as was the idea that she was a legitimate spy in the first place. She was executed nevertheless.

Shaka became the general and ruler of the Zulus in the early nineteenth century, at a time when shifting patterns of food production were transforming his southern African tribe. The introduction of maize increased the Zulu population, and the tribe's growing herds of cattle demanded new grazing land. Shaka launched a campaign of conquest, introducing new tactics. Previously, the Zulu had thrown their spears, which not only disarmed them but also delivered a weapon to their foes. Instead, Shaka equipped his army with a new stabbing spear called the *iklwa,* named after the sound that it made when pulled out of a victim. After a Zulu warrior killed an enemy soldier with the *iklwa,* he would cry, *"Ngadla!"*—meaning "I have eaten!"

Genghis Khan's Mongols lived off their horses. Each fighter had three mounts so that he could ride one horse and let the other two rest while they traveled long distances in conquest.

The Mongols preferred mares because they also provided milk for a fermented drink called koumiss. And when hunger was rampant, the Mongols would cut into the vein of their weakest horse and drink its blood for sustenance, without killing the animal.

In the years following the French Revolution, **Maximilien Robespierre** was a driving force behind the "Reign of Terror" that was carried out by the ironically named Committee of Public Safety. Although he played such a pivotal role in his country's history, he was an atypical Frenchman. Not only did he water down his wine, but he also was indifferent to what he ate.

"Many times I asked him what he would like to eat at dinner," said his sister Charlotte, "and he would reply that he had no idea."

During the sixteenth century, the emperor **Babur** of India led his forces on a successful invasion of the central Asian city of Nasukh. Although his army tasted victory, the most significant thing that the emperor tasted that day was a melon.

In his chronicles, Babur noted that his empire had captured Nasukh during "the season when the melons were ripe." He praised them for being "wonderful, delicate, and toothsome." In the final years of his life, he longed to return to this region. Once, while day-dreaming about this distant region, he was served a melon.

"To cut it and eat it affected me strangely," he wrote. "I was all tears."

In 1822, **Denmark Vesey** led the largest slave rebellion plot in American history. A free black man, he worked as a carpenter in Charleston, South Carolina. With dozens of coconspirators, he planned the mass murder of white people and the torching of the city. He and a mystical colleague, "Gullah Jack" Pritchard, gave recruits parched corn and ground nuts, along with instructions that they eat nothing but that on the morning of the insurrection. They were told that when the uprising began, they would be given a crab's claw, to place in their mouth and guard them from harm. But the plot was exposed by slaves loyal to their masters. Vesey and Pritchard were among three dozen plotters put to death.

Manius Curius Dentatus, a Roman military genius, was approached by a delegation of the Samnites in the third century BCE with the idea of bribing him. But according to legend, they found him sitting by the hearth humbly roasting turnips—demonstrating that an offer of gold would not impress him.

British **General Charles Cornwallis** wrote letters stating that he so enjoyed the salt pork in New York that he dreaded leaving the city to pursue George Washington's army during the Revolutionary War. Indeed, he might have been better off pigging out in the Big Apple instead of being sandwiched by Washington's army and the French fleet at Yorktown. Claiming illness, Cornwallis sent a subordinate to surrender in his place.

Prussia's **Frederick the Great,** who had several horses shot out from under him in battle, sometimes found his fights during peacetime more challenging. Recognizing the potato as a practical food for his people, Frederick launched a crusade to gain public acceptance of the tuber in the mid-1700s. But when he shipped potatoes to the city of Kolberg, he received a defiant message declaring that "not even the dogs will eat them." The king dispatched troops to stand over his subjects in the fields and make sure they planted potatoes, at the risk of having their ears and noses cut off if they refused.

Potatoes gained their current prominent role in German cuisine only after Frederick was seen eating them on the balcony of his palace.

General George Patton liked to recall the year that his grandmother's olives were particularly delicious. When the family got to the bottom of the barrel, they discovered, floating in the brine, an enormous skunk.

General Ulysses Grant, the leader of the Union forces who had once served as a commissary officer, told his superiors during the Civil War: "I will not move my army without onions." The next day, three trainloads of onions were dispatched.

General John Nicholson, who helped quash India's attempt to shake off British occupation in 1857, provided a shocking bit of dinner theater one evening. Tipped by a cook's assistant that the British officers' soup was poisoned, Nicholson confronted the cooks. He challenged one of them to sip the soup, but the cook refused, citing caste restrictions. Then Nicholson had the soup poured down a monkey's throat, and the animal was soon in lethal distress. Nicholson ordered the perpetrators hanged from a tree and then strode into the officers' mess hall to report, "I am sorry, gentlemen, to have kept you waiting for your dinner, but I have been hanging your cooks."

In December 1941, when **General Dwight Eisenhower** heard the news that the Japanese had bombed Pearl Harbor, his reaction was to make a batch of vegetable soup—a cathartic ritual that, his son wrote, "allowed him to pull his thoughts together."

If not for the Turkish leader **Suleiman II,** would we have the croissant?

Suleiman and his Ottoman army marched on the Austrian capital of Vienna in 1529, laying siege to the city. Austrian bakers, working in the wee hours, detected the army tunneling under the city walls and raised the alarm, thwarting the attack. When Suleiman's army was forced to retreat, Vienna's bakers celebrated by creating a pastry in the shape of a crescent—the symbol on the Ottomans' flag.

When **Alexander the Great** conquered Persia in 334 BCE, he also conquered the peach. The fruit was unknown in Europe until Alexander sent a few peach pits back to Greece. Alexander called it a Persian apple.

What Alexander did for the peach, the Roman general **Lucullus** did for the cherry. The military leader took over lands to the east, such as Armenia, and brought back a cherry tree, whose fruit soon spread far and wide in western Europe. It wasn't the region's first cherry, but it was a superior and highly prized variety.

The British people made impressive sacrifices during World War II. But **Winston Churchill** and his aides didn't let their stiff upper lips prevent them from tasting fine food and drink. No mere war could keep Churchill from champagne, caviar, and oysters. The diary of Churchill's secretary, John Colville, offers a bizarrely blithe account of society lunches and fancy restaurant dinners at the height of the Blitz, when German bombs were raining on London. One entry reads: "At dinner, fortified by 1911 champagne, the P.M. talked brilliantly, though less epigrammatically than usual."

But dining for the privileged few was not always ducky. Diplomat Harold Nicholson was forced to eat at the Ministry of Information's restaurant and declared: "It is absolutely foul. It is run on the cafeteria system and we have got to queue up with trays with the messenger boys."

Mitsuo Fuchida, the leader of the first wave of Japanese pilots at Pearl Harbor, gained fame by uttering the words "Tora! Tora! Tora!" as a signal to his commanders that they had achieved complete surprise. But the period after World War II was quite a comedown. Fuchida raised chickens and supplied eggs for an

American artillery unit that was part of the postwar force occupying Japan.

In some cases, **Napoléon Bonaparte**'s culinary influence has been overrated.

According to a widely told story, chicken Marengo was invented during the battle of Marengo in Italy when Napoléon's chef could not locate the provision wagon and had to cook with the ingredients he could find. The dish includes chicken, crayfish, tomatoes, garlic, and olive oil, and it may also feature fried eggs and either cognac or brandy. But researchers say the battlefield story appears to be a myth cooked up by a restaurant owner seeking to profit from Napoléon's cachet.

And then there's the pastry called the Napoleon, with alternating layers of puff pastry and filling. Also known as *mille feuilles,* the pastry got its nickname from its creators in Naples, Italy, who called it a Napolitain. The name Napoleon is simply a corruption of that term, but food fabulists have invented their own mythology, including a ridiculous story that the emperor carried the pastry in his breast pocket as he marched on Russia.

Arthur Wellesley, known as the **Duke of Wellington,** ate only two meals a day, breakfast and dinner. His lack of indulgence is demonstrated by a story from the battle of Salamanca in Spain in 1812. Wellington ate breakfast that morning on horseback, munching on a chicken drumstick. Told that the French had left a gap in their lines, Wellington tossed the drumstick into the air and launched the decisive attack.

The duke wasn't the only warrior whose breakfast was spoiled by history.

Ulysses S. Grant was enjoying his first meal of the day on

April 6, 1862, when a surprise Confederate attack brought his army to the brink of disaster in the battle of Shiloh.

The Japanese air raid on Pearl Harbor on December 7, 1941, occurred at breakfast time for many of the Americans who were attacked. One hundred fifty miles away from the harbor, U.S. **Vice Admiral William "Bull" Halsey** was sipping his second cup of coffee aboard the aircraft carrier *Enterprise* when he heard of the raid. Some of the Japanese pilots bombing Pearl had begun their day with a breakfast of *seki-han,* a dish of rice and red beans that is reserved for special occasions.

Steak tartare, a dish featuring raw beef, got its name from **Genghis Khan**'s Mongol hordes, who were labeled Tartars by the Europeans. According to legend, the Mongols spent so much time on horseback that the best way to tenderize their beef was to put it under their saddles as they rode. German cooks of the Middle Ages, aware of this tale, attached the "tartar" name to a dish of minced but uncooked meat with pepper, onion, and salt.

Where does the term *tartar sauce* come from? Some say the sauce was so named because it had similar seasonings as steak tartare. Others say it got that name because it was served with steak tartare. Still others say it may have been called tartar simply because, like Genghis Khan's hordes, it had a potent effect.

J. Edgar Hoover, the most famous domestic warrior in American history, ate lunch in the same hotel with the same person every workday for twenty years.

The director of the Federal Bureau of Investigation was accompanied by assistant Clyde Tolson for midday dining at Washington, D.C.'s Mayflower Hotel. Hoover tended to order the same lunch each day: chicken soup, grapefruit, cottage cheese, white buttered toast, and a salad of iceberg lettuce. He brought his own diet dressing for the salad.

Reporters soon learned Hoover and Tolson's habits and would stake out the lobby of the Mayflower, prompting the much-feared lawmen to sneak out through the kitchen.

Their nightly meal was also routine. For more than forty years, the FBI honchos ate at Harvey's Restaurant, except for a time when Hoover had a feud with a new owner. Hoover often enjoyed a medium-rare steak and green turtle soup and also participated in Harvey's oyster-eating contests. The restaurant would give Hoover a bag of ham and turkey to take home for his dogs.

Even though Islamic leader **Saladin** and England's **Richard the Lionheart** ordered the mass execution of each other's captured soldiers during the Crusades, they maintained a chivalric, long-distance admiration for each other. Hearing that Richard was ill, Saladin once sent him a gift of fruit, along with snow to cool his drinks.

The current U.S. field ration, known as meals ready to eat (MREs), has received mixed reviews. The smoked frankfurters, for example, are nicknamed "the four fingers of death."

But **General Tommy Franks,** commander of the American-led invasion of Iraq in 2003, liked to eat MREs while on plane trips. And an MRE played a big part in a story he told about inadequate vehicle armor putting soldiers at risk: "One of my platoon leaders told me that his soldier was eating an MRE and the pound cake had a hole in it, and there was a bullet buried right in the middle like a little chocolate surprise."

Baron Friedrich von Steuben, the German drillmaster whose military discipline may have saved George Washington's army at Valley Forge, hated to dine alone. To make light of the army's shabby clothing, he organized a dinner at which all participants wore torn pants. The diners "clubbed their rations"—put them together—for a meal of beef and potatoes, with hickory nuts for dessert. Lacking wine, they acquired cheap whiskey and made "salamanders," a drink that was set afire and imbibed while it was still aflame.

By 1864, the American Civil War had turned in the favor of the North, especially in places such as Virginia's once lush Shenandoah Valley. Union **General Philip Sheridan**'s command there received six thousand turkeys for Thanksgiving.

Meanwhile, the Shenandoah's farmers had to cope with constant Yankee raiding. One farmwife was exhorted to hide her bacon because the Yankees were coming. Instead, she piled it in her front yard and dusted it with flour. When the Yankees asked why it was white, she explained that retreating rebels had left it there, laughing as they did so. The Yankees rode on without the bacon, thinking it was rotten or poisoned.

The **Duke of Wellington** is best known for defeating Napoléon at Waterloo, a victory that inspired the joyous villagers of Denby Dale in west Yorkshire to bake a giant meat pie in celebration in 1815. It was their second such meat pie celebration, the first occurring twenty-seven years earlier when King George III reportedly recovered from his madness. Contents of each pie were thought to include about two sheep and twenty fowl.

Wellington's greatest culinary honor was beef Wellington. The origin of the dish is claimed by Ireland, France, Australia, and New

Zealand. But there's a consensus that the dish took on Wellington's name after his triumph at Waterloo.

One of Wellington's chief officers at Waterloo had an even more meaningful link between his military exploits and his meals. In the waning hours of the battle, **Henry William Paget,** the Earl of Uxbridge, was struck by cannon fire in the right knee, forcing him to have his leg amputated. Years later, he brought his sons back to the scene of the battle. Finding the table on which his leg was removed, he and his sons enjoyed a dinner on that very surface.

General Tso's Chicken, which is found on the menus of most Chinese restaurants in North America, is named for a man who never tasted it: nineteenth-century **General Tso Tsung-t'ang,** who helped put down China's bloody Taiping Rebellion. A twentieth-century rebellion—by **Mao Ze-dong**'s communists—prompted chef Peng Chang-kuei to flee China and settle in New York City, where he invented the entrée in the 1970s. Peng named the dish after Tso, a hero of his Hunan province, even though such sweet and savory dishes are almost unheard of in Hunan.

The fuel for modern warfare?

Pizza.

In the run-up to the 2003 invasion of Iraq, pizza was delivered to Central Intelligence Agency headquarters as U.S. Secretary of State **Colin Powell** and CIA Director **George Tenet** held four days of meetings to prepare their case that Iraq had weapons of mass destruction. As it turned out, the pizza was more genuine than the intelligence.

A few years earlier, after Middle Eastern suicide hijackers killed nearly three thousand Americans in the September 11, 2001, attacks, one of the terrorists' Florida neighbors recalled, "From their trash, you could see that they shopped at Wal-Mart and ate a lot of pizza."

In America's first war with Iraq, the launch of the air offensive in January 1991 was tipped off by Frank Meeks, owner of sixty Domino's pizza franchises in the Washington area. Meeks told the news media that key government offices were placing large orders at odd hours, including more than fifty to the White House be-tween 10 p.m. and 2 a.m. as the U.S. prepared its attack.

But pizza also can be an instrument of peace. In 2000, Powell noted that his former Soviet enemy, Mikhail Gorbachev, had ap-peared in a Pizza Hut commercial.

"The former head of the evil empire is selling Pizza Hut," Powell said. "Is capitalism great or is capitalism great?"

The Roman general **Lucullus** was an indulgent eater and a gener-ous host. Once when the general ate without guests, his chef cut back on the fare, earning Lucullus's rebuke. "On those days when I am alone, you must make a special effort," he said, "for that is when Lucullus dines with Lucullus."

CHAPTER 8

Experiments in Dining

Food was a stimulus to the scientific method

Pʏᴛʜᴀɢᴏʀᴀѕ, ᴛʜᴇ ꜰᴀᴍᴇᴅ Greek mathematician, limited his diet to bread, honey, greens, and occasionally fish. Wine was permitted, but only after dark. Pythagoras and his followers looked down upon meat eating, and they also had an aversion to fava beans.

History has not recorded why Pythagoras abhorred fava beans. Some believe he had a rare inherited deficiency called favism in which consumption of fava beans can cause destruction of red blood cells, leading to illness or death. Others think the objection to the beans reflected his view that they were akin to meat, or even that they were a resting place for the souls of the dead. Still others think Pythagoras's opposition was more practical—that he believed the beans increased male sexuality, inspired bad dreams, or simply led to flatulence.

According to legend, the beans proved fatal to Pythagoras even though he didn't eat them. Pursued by Syracusan soldiers around 490 BCE, he could have escaped across a field of fava beans but chose not to, stopping at the edge of the field, where he was killed.

Percy Spencer, an engineer at Raytheon Company, was testing a tube used in radar in 1946 when he noticed that a candy bar in his pocket had melted. Realizing that some strange heating phenomenon was at work, he placed popcorn kernels near the tube and watched them pop. Next, he put an egg nearby and it exploded, depositing its contents on a co-worker's face. The idea of the microwave oven was born.

William Buckland, the British geologist and paleontologist who pioneered the discovery of dinosaurs, wasn't content with examining dry bones. As a career-long hobby in the first half of the nineteenth century, he set out to eat the meat of as many different animals as possible.

Buckland was joined in this quest by his zoologist son **Francis,** who persuaded the London Zoo to give him a cut of meat from any animal that died there. The Bucklands' bill of fare included insects, hedgehog, snake, crocodile, porpoise, mole, mouse, bear, puppy, snail, elephant, rhinoceros, kangaroo, and panther.

But the father really went over the edge when a friend showed him a snuffbox containing the embalmed heart of Louis XIV, or at least a piece of it. William Buckland grabbed the morsel, tossed it in his mouth, and swallowed it.

That might not even have been William Buckland's most amazing exploit. While taking a carriage ride one day, the geologist realized he was lost. Stepping out of his carriage, he scooped up a handful of dirt and ate it. Using his geological knowledge and his fine sense of taste, Buckland concluded that he was in Uxbridge, on the fringes of London.

After Columbia University professor **Tsung-Dao Lee** was named co-winner of the 1957 Nobel Prize in physics, a sign went up in the window of his favorite Chinese restaurant in New York. It read: EAT HERE, WIN NOBEL PRIZE.

Thomas Edison, who would later invent the world's first practical electric lightbulb and phonograph, moved from Boston to New York in 1869, arriving by steamboat with a full imagination and an empty wallet. Hungry, he passed a wholesale teahouse, saw a man tasting the tea, asked for a drink, and was given one. He considered that to be his first breakfast in New York.

That same day, Edison tracked down a friend who was a telegraph operator and borrowed a dollar from him, using it to buy apple dumplings and a cup of coffee at Smith & McNell's restaurant in Lower Manhattan. Edison remembered it as one of his favorite meals ever. Years later, when the rich and famous inventor ate regularly in such dining meccas as Delmonico's and Sherry's, he would sometimes take detours to Smith & McNell's to savor the apple dumplings and coffee.

When Polish scientist **Maria Sklodowska** married French scientist **Pierre Curie,** she thenceforth became Marie Curie, or Madame Curie. As a wife of that time, it was her duty to assume all domestic tasks. She handled grocery shopping and recipes with the same precision and sense of purpose that would later win her two Nobel Prizes. But she had to ask her sister to explain a less-than-scientific kitchen concept: How much precisely is a "pinch"?

Actually, food mattered little to the Curies. Pierre sometimes could not remember what he had for dinner or even *if* he'd had dinner.

A friend, scientist Georges Sagnac, wrote to him: "You hardly eat at all, either of you. More than once I have seen Mme. Curie nibble two slices of sausage and swallow a cup of tea with it."

Sagnac added: "You must not read or talk physics while you eat."

The world paid little attention when **Orville Wright** and **Wilbur Wright** achieved the first controlled human flight on a powered, heavier-than-air machine on December 17, 1903. Proper recognition was still years away. But the Wright family proudly held a welcome-home dinner featuring porterhouse steaks when the brothers arrived in Dayton, Ohio, after their exploits in the sand dunes of Kitty Hawk, North Carolina.

Orville's main desire was milk, and plenty of it. He drank so much of it that a housekeeper began watering it down, thinking he wouldn't notice. He did, accusing her of "dairying the milk."

Justus von Liebig, a German chemist whose contributions to agriculture earned him the title of "father of the fertilizer industry," provided the straight poop that rescued the English beer industry.

In 1852, two English brewers, Allsopp's and Bass, battled false rumors that they had enhanced the bitterness of their beverages by inserting strychnine, a poison. The beer makers hired the highly respected Liebig for a considerable sum to attest to their beers' safety, and he did so enthusiastically, but perhaps not scientifically. As he wrote at the time: "The main test consisted in drinking a bottle with great enjoyment."

As a young man, **Charles Darwin** served as naturalist on HMS *Beagle* during a five-year, round-the-world voyage that helped shape his scientific views—and eventually transformed the world's understanding of evolution. Darwin's adventure also allowed him to make a natural selection of interesting food.

He was eating ripe tamarinds and biscuits as he sat on the beach

at Quail Island off Africa's western coast and made the fateful decision to write a book about his observations. Later, he helped the
crew hunt for game, including deer, cavia, and guanaco. The naturalist also chewed on the hallucinogenic ava plant, and dined on
ostrich, armadillo, tuna, turtle, and shark. Yet another menu item
was barracuda—which Darwin spelled as "Barrow Cooter" in his
diary.

Henry Cavendish, the Londoner who figured out the chemical
composition of air and water and accurately calculated the mass
of the world, didn't devote much thought to food. For that reason, he often ate only mutton. When he had guests, he would serve
a single leg of mutton, with nothing to accompany it. Before one
such dinner, his housekeeper complained that a leg of mutton was
inadequate, and he responded, "Well then, get two."

Television was invented because of the potato. Sort of.

Philo Farnsworth, a fourteen-year-old Idaho prodigy who was
already an award-winning inventor, worked with a horse-drawn
harrow on his family's farm in 1921. Harvesting potatoes one row
after another led him to conclude that an image could be scanned
and reproduced line by line—one row after another. He later described this as the key insight that led to his groundbreaking work
on television.

George Washington Carver, the African American botanist and
food developer, appeared before a congressional committee in
1921 to testify in favor of tariff protection for the peanut industry. Allotted ten minutes to speak, Carver spent several minutes

taking out samples of his various peanut products. Committee chairman Joseph Fordney joked in reference to Prohibition, "If you have anything to drink, don't put it under the table." Carver told him the drinks would "come later if my ten minutes are extended." The remark charmed the lawmakers, who gave him extra time and showed great support—though one Connecticut representative made an unfortunate watermelon joke.

Before Carver left, he had shown an amazing array of products made from peanuts, including flour, milk, coffee, Worcestershire sauce, cheese, and oil. He also had eaten a cereal made of sweet potatoes and peanuts as part of his testimony. And he got his tariff.

Years before **Galileo Galilei** clashed with the Roman Catholic Church over whether the earth revolves around the sun, the Italian physicist got into an egg fight with a church-affiliated scholar, Jesuit priest Orazio Grassi.

The issue was whether a projectile heats up or cools off in flight. Grassi believed that friction made a projectile hotter, and he cited tenth-century Greek historian Suidas's tale of the Babylonians whirling eggs in slings to cook them.

The skeptical Galileo and his assistants put the story to the test. They took turns whirling a raw egg, and the egg stayed raw. Then Galileo tried it with a newly boiled egg, and the egg cooled off, leading him to conclude incorrectly that friction cools a projectile.

In fact, there are competing factors: Friction would indeed heat the egg, as Grassi surmised, but the heat would be dissipated by convection, just as blowing on a hot object cools it. Though Galileo was wrong, his mockery of Grassi's argument was devastating:

"If we do not achieve an effect which others formerly achieved, it must be that in our operations we lack something which was the cause of this effect succeeding, and if we lack but one single thing, then this alone can be the cause. Now we do not lack eggs, or slings, or sturdy fellows to whirl them; and still they do not cook, but rather they cool down faster if hot. And since nothing is lacking to us except being Babylonians, then being Babylonians is the cause of the eggs hardening."

American molecular biologist **James Watson** found a stimulating intellectual environment in Britain and a research partnership with Englishman Francis Crick in which they unraveled the structure of DNA. But Watson hated British cuisine. His memoir *The Double Helix* is infused with references to "tasteless meat, boiled potatoes, colorless greens, and typical trifles," as well as "brown soup, stringy meat, and heavy pudding." Trying to avoid the native fare, he sometimes "took in the poison put out by the local Indian and Cypriote establishments."

In the late 1890s, most people would have been reluctant to step aboard a flying contraption of any kind. But Brazilian aviation pioneer **Alberto Santos-Dumont** was determined to give society's elite a flavor of what they were missing. He hosted "aerial dinner parties" at his high-ceilinged Paris apartment, and invited such guests as jeweler Louis Cartier and Empress Eugénie, wife of the French sovereign.

Initially, these aerial dinners were achieved by suspending a table and chairs from the ceiling of his dining room. On one occasion, the weight of the guests caused the ceiling to collapse. Plan B was more practical: Dinner guests were instructed to climb ladders that led to extremely tall chairs.

Nobel Prize winner **Paul Dirac,** a British physicist who moved to Florida, was asked what he liked best in America. "Potatoes" was his answer.

Isaac Newton devised his theory of gravity after seeing an apple fall from a tree at his mother's home. But he was sometimes so busy thinking that he forgot about eating.

A maid recalled finding Newton in his kitchen standing over a boiling pot with his watch plunged in the water, while he stared at an egg in his hand, baffled.

For dinner one night, a friend was invited to Newton's house, but found the genius in deep reverie when he arrived. Deciding not to disturb him, the guest ate by himself. When Newton rejoined the world, he saw the dirty dishes and remarked, "Well, really, if it wasn't for the proof before my eyes, I could have sworn that I had not yet dined."

Physicist **George Gamow,** who was the chief proponent of the "big bang" theory of the universe, was a scientific skeptic from the start.

As a child in the Russian Empire city of Odessa (now in Ukraine), Gamow decided to test whether the Russian Orthodox Church was correct in teaching that the Eucharist was the body of Christ. Instead of swallowing the Eucharist in church one day, Gamow held it behind his cheek, went home, and examined it under a microscope his father had bought for him. Comparing the

Eucharist to a piece of regular bread and to a sliver of his own skin, Gamow concluded that it resembled the former, not the latter.

"It was just bread, so I think I changed my religious attitude," he said.

At precisely 1 p.m., **Sigmund Freud**'s family would assemble for midday dinner, the big meal of the day. The Vienna psychiatrist's wife and children would be seated at the table as Freud entered from his study and the maid simultaneously arrived with the soup.

Freud concentrated on his food—displaying an oral fixation of sorts—and generally remained silent while eating, a habit that disappointed any guests who might be in attendance.

His favorite dish was boiled beef, known as *Rindfleisch*. The family ate it three or four times a week, but the Freuds' cook created variety by serving it with at least seven different sauces. They also dined on asparagus, corn on the cob, and Italian artichokes, which Freud especially enjoyed. But cauliflower was verboten, and Freud also disliked eating chicken.

"One should not kill chickens," he said. "Let them stay alive and lay eggs."

Louis Pasteur demanded solid answers to even the most mundane questions. When it seemed that his children were always dropping their toast on the carpet with the buttered side down, he didn't just laugh it off. He investigated thoroughly and found the answer: His children were buttering both sides of their bread.

Thomas Edison was too much of a workaholic to be a gastronome and too much of an American to understand the French.

He summarized an 1889 visit to Paris this way: "Dinners, dinners, dinners, all the time. . . . I could never get used to so many dinners. At noon I would sit down to what they called *déjeuner*. That would last until nearly three o'clock, and a few hours later would come a big dinner. It was terrible."

The **Comte de Buffon,** aka Georges Louis Leclerc, was an eighteenth-century French scholar and writer who inspired generations of naturalists. He produced forty-four volumes of *Histoire Naturelle* by keeping a strict schedule of work and dining. A servant would get him out of bed by physical force or by throwing ice water at him, earning a bonus if Buffon was awake by 6 a.m. Then Buffon worked until breakfasting at 9 a.m. on two glasses of wine and a roll. Next came more work, a leisurely and social lunch at 2 p.m., a nap, a walk, more work, and bedtime at 9 p.m.—with no supper.

When anthropologist **Margaret Mead,** author of the groundbreaking *Growing Up in New Guinea,* returned to the South Pacific islands in the 1950s, she maintained her professional distance. For example, she wouldn't eat with the locals.

"When she ate, all the people of the village had to leave her house," recalled colleague Lenora Schwartz. "She insisted on ceremony; she'd have a tablecloth and nice dishes. She trained everyone to leave when the tablecloth and dishes came out."

Years later when a student was leaving on a field trip, Mead asked her how she would bake bread.

"I don't like bread, so maybe I won't bake it at all," the student said.

"But you must," Mead said, "to keep up white prestige!"

Physicist **Richard Feynman** found inspiration in a Cornell University cafeteria when a fellow diner tossed a plate. "As the plate went up in the air I saw it wobble, and I noticed the red medallion of Cornell on the plate going around," he later wrote. "It was pretty obvious to me that the medallion went around faster than the wobbling." Feynman set out to explain why, and his observations led to new theories in quantum electrodynamics—and ultimately a Nobel Prize.

The title of Feynman's memoir *Surely You're Joking, Mr. Feynman* came from a hostess's response when she asked the young physics professor whether he wanted cream or lemon in his tea, and he absentmindedly answered, "I'll have both, thank you," not considering that lemon juice would cause the cream to curdle.

Pliny the Elder, the Roman whose encyclopedia *Natural History* was a key reference for centuries of scholars, condemned artichokes as one of "the earth's monstrosities."

Alexander Graham Bell, inventor of the first practical telephone, kept late hours and sometimes slept until noon. A breakfast tray would be left beside his bed, and he sometimes would eat the food at room temperature, long after it was delivered.

Even in old age, when Bell's diabetes led to dietary restrictions, he remained a night owl who raided the refrigerator.

After one such kitchen expedition, a doctor was summoned to treat him for indigestion and reportedly said: "To go downstairs at three in the morning, load up on Smithfield ham, cold potatoes, macaroni and cheese, and then go right to bed is the most ridiculous thing imaginable. That meal might have put an end to you, sir."

Bell responded that "it was the best meal I've enjoyed in an age" and well worth the trouble.

It may come as little surprise that **Robert Oppenheimer,** "the father of the atomic bomb," liked his food spicy. A fellow physicist once complained that Oppenheimer took him to a Mexican restaurant "with food so hot that I could swallow only a few bites." The complainer was **Edward Teller,** known as the "father" of an even hotter weapon than Oppenheimer's—the hydrogen bomb.

A Druid who lived near Manchester, England, advanced the fields of archaeology and anthropology without ever taking a college course. He lived before the birth of Christ, and when his remains were found amid peat in 1984, he was called **Lindow Man.**

The ancient Druids held ceremonies in which a ground barley cake would be baked, with one section badly scorched. Then the cake would be broken into pieces and placed in a leather bag. Each participant would take a piece, and the one with the scorched piece would be put to death in a bizarrely cruel rite that might include bludgeoning, drowning, windpipe crushing, and throat cutting.

Scientists who examined Lindow Man's well-preserved but badly abused corpse found traces of scorched cake in his stomach and his intestines—and a serene expression on his face.

Nikola Tesla, the Serbian American genius who achieved world-changing advances in both electricity and radio, was neither plugged in nor tuned in to normal human behavior. At the height of his career, he often dined alone at one of New York's finest restaurants—either Delmonico's or the Waldorf-Astoria. He ordered thick steaks, and sometimes more than one per meal, though he migrated toward vegetarianism as the years passed. He welcomed whiskey and wine in moderate amounts, but banished coffee and tea.

No matter what he was eating and drinking, he did so under very exacting conditions:

- The tablecloth had to be fresh, with a stack of clean cloth napkins on the table's left side. The supply of napkins reflected Tesla's obsession with numbers divisible by three, but reports vary on whether he required two dozen napkins or only eighteen.
- He would wipe each dish and each piece of silverware with a napkin and then would drop the napkin to the floor.
- His table could not be used by anyone else when he was not there.
- Plates and bowls had to be oval.
- Nearby diners could not wear pearls.
- If a fly landed on his table, he considered it fair cause to have the entire table stripped of its contents and the meal begun anew.

During **Benjamin Franklin**'s salad days, long before he established himself as an inventor by developing bifocal glasses and a lightning rod, he embraced vegetarianism.

Working for his brother James in Boston as a teenager, Franklin's no-meat diet was driven in part by his need to save money. He subsisted largely on biscuits and raisins.

After a falling out with James, Franklin left Boston for Philadelphia, taking a ship as far as New York. Watching the crew cook cod, his newfound vegetarianism was strongly challenged.

"I balanced some time between principle and inclination," he later wrote, "until I recollected that when the fish were opened, I saw smaller fish taken out of their stomachs. Then, thought I, 'If you eat one another, I don't see why we may not eat you.' So I dined upon cod very heartily and have since continued to eat as other people, returning only now and then occasionally to a vegetable diet."

Rita Levi-Montalcini, an Italian neurologist who shared the 1986 Nobel Prize in medicine for her study of nerve growth factors, was banned from university work during World War II because she was Jewish. Undaunted, she turned her family's Turin kitchen into a secret laboratory, conducting embryology with fertilized hen's eggs from a nearby farm. When the experiments were done, the eggs became omelets that fed her family.

Two-time Nobelist **Linus Pauling,** who took megadoses of vitamin C and became a promoter of the practice in his later years, held a variety of food-related jobs as a young student in Oregon.

He was a milkman for a month, and also cut up beef to feed residents of a girls dormitory. While in high school, Pauling and a friend set up a basement lab and offered butterfat-testing services to local dairies. But the dairies thought they were too young to be trusted, and the business flopped.

As a pioneer in food production, **George Washington Carver** was in demand as a visiting speaker, and his automobile tours were well remembered by those accompanying him. Sometimes there was no time to stop and eat, and a participant sent Carver a letter fondly remembering "our sandwich lunches in the Buick at 50 mi. per hour . . . you yelling for sardine sandwiches and me struggling in the backseat trying to spread the butter."

Oliver Heaviside, the eccentric British electrical engineer of the late 1800s and early 1900s who offered pioneering theories in radio transmission and long-distance telephone service, salted his personal letters with discourses about food, such as:

- "Made several discoveries. Parsnips cook easily. Carrots don't."
- "It is fat (real animal fat) that is needed in cold weather, rather than sugar. Ask the Greenlanders."
- "The great lentil question popped up yesterday. Never! . . . Lentils are High-Church. Always eaten in Lent by the stricter sort, as a penance, accompanied in private by hair-shirts and beads."
- "Pork. Awful at night."
- "I am not fit for a cook. I forget. Then it all goes to cinder, to be discovered hours later. Or if I boil an egg, I am startled by a loud report, either I did not put any water in or else it has all boiled away."

Albert Einstein welcomed young physicist L. L. Whyte to his Berlin home for a chat, and after twenty minutes, Einstein's maid came in with a huge bowl of soup. Whyte later recalled that he considered leaving so that Einstein could eat, but the master physicist whispered, "That's a trick. If I am bored talking to somebody, when the maid comes in, I don't push the bowl of soup away and the girl takes whomever I am with away and I am free." Whyte was flattered that he had passed the soup test and could talk longer with Einstein.

Another story about Einstein and soup is sometimes described as apocryphal. As a child, Einstein was a late talker. But one night at supper, he is said to have declared, "The soup is too hot." His parents were relieved but curious. They asked him why he hadn't talked before. His answer: "Because up to now everything was in order."

Benjamin Thompson might have become an American hero if he hadn't become an American villain. When the Revolutionary War broke out, the Massachusetts native sided with the British, abandoned his wife, and served as an officer in the occupying army.

After the Revolutionary War, he left his native Massachusetts and spent much of his remaining life in Europe. He became an impressive scientist—the leading expert of his day on thermodynamics and a pioneer in understanding ocean currents. The Germans liked him so much that they gave him the title of **Count Rumford,** the name by which he is best known today.

Rumford designed the first enclosed kitchen range, invented a drip coffeemaker, and promoted "Rumford soup," an inexpensive mixture of potatoes, barley, and peas intended to improve the diet of the unwashed masses. He even wrote instructions for the best way to eat pudding.

Yet his scientific and culinary innovations were not celebrated in the United States, and Rumford's decision to serve in the British army was only one of the reasons why.

It was an act related to cooking that poisoned American attitudes toward him. During the war, his troops built a fort in Huntington, New York, in the middle of the local cemetery—pulling up headstones to construct ovens to feed his soldiers. Local citizens reportedly saw the names of their friends and family members burned in reverse on loaves of bread from the ovens.

Austrian monk **Gregor Mendel** grew a variety of vegetables, including cabbage, carrots, and pumpkins, to feed the residents of his monastery. He also grew thirty thousand pea plants to feed his own scientific curiosity. His creation of hybrids established the laws of heredity, although his legacy was appreciated only after his death.

Despite the part that peas played in his life, Mendel was more fond of cucumbers.

When the wife of **Robert Goddard** wrote that he had been eating "gargantuan meals at night," she was relieved, not distressed. Esther Goddard knew all too well that her husband—a pioneer of rocket design—rarely took his mind off of his work long enough to eat a sit-down meal. She noted, "Fifteen minutes after dinner, he could not have told what he had eaten."

During World War II, Goddard served as a paid consultant to Curtiss-Wright, a rocket manufacturer in New Jersey. After a Curtiss-Wright executive reviewed the expense vouchers submitted by Goddard, he was dumbfounded. "Upon seeing how much you spent for meals," he wrote the scientist, "I greatly wonder how you exist on so little food."

Swedish chemist **Karl Scheele** is now considered the first scientist to have discovered oxygen and several other elements, but he wasn't credited at the time because others published first or were more prominent. Another impediment to Scheele's fame was his premature death at age forty-three, which was attributed to his foolish habit of tasting the chemicals he worked with, including such toxic substances as mercury and hydrogen cyanide. He was found dead at his workbench in 1786, the suspected victim of accidental self-poisoning, though the exact chemical culprit was not determined.

Breakfast is Nobel time.

John Bardeen of the University of Illinois was frying eggs when he heard that he had shared the 1956 Nobel Prize in physics. He got so flustered that he dropped the pan and the eggs on the floor.

Microbiologist **Salvador Luria** was washing his breakfast dishes when a neighbor shared a radio report that Luria had won the 1969 Nobel in medicine. **George Olah** got a phone call during breakfast informing him that he would receive the 1994 Nobel for chemistry. **Maria Goeppert-Mayer,** a 1963 winner in physics, celebrated her good news with champagne, bacon, and eggs.

Three months after World War II ended, German physicist **Otto Hahn** was in a British detention facility and had just finished breakfast when one of his fellow detainees who was reading the *London Daily Telegraph* told him that he had won the Nobel Prize.

But perhaps the weirdest breakfast experience related to the Nobels happened to the founder of the prizes himself. **Alfred Nobel** was eating breakfast and reading a French newspaper in 1888 when he ran across a headline reading THE MERCHANT OF DEATH IS DEAD. It was his own obituary. The newspaper had erroneously reported the death of the inventor of dynamite when in fact it was Nobel's brother who had died. Some believe that this sneak peek at his legacy inspired Nobel to create prizes dedicated to peaceful human achievement.

By the early 1930s, **George Washington Carver** began to think that peanut-oil massages had a special ability to restore the muscles of polio victims. In an interview with the Associated Press, Carver cautioned that he had not found a cure, but the article's description of "the tissue-building properties of the oil" caused a sensation. Thousands wrote to Carver seeking the "miracle oil" to treat polio, Parkinson's disease, leprosy, multiple sclerosis, and baldness. One entrepreneur asked Carver to endorse the oil's use as a bust developer. But soon it became clear that the massage, not the peanut oil, was the key to the treatment.

In his later days, the cash-strapped and eccentric **Nikola Tesla** survived on warm milk and Nabisco crackers. He would meticulously number the empty cracker tins and stack them on his shelves to store various objects.

Thomas Edison once invited his friends to a steak dinner but instead served them cut-up pieces of leather that had been heated and bathed in gravy. After his guests tried in vain to carve their food, Edison admitted his prank and ordered the cook to bring in the real steaks.

Sigmund Freud believed that the rooms of a house were generally female—because of their hollow space—and that the kitchen was the most female room in a house.

Constantin Fahlberg, a chemist at a Johns Hopkins University lab working on derivatives of coal tar, was eating dinner after work one evening in the late 1870s and noticed that his bread tasted sweet. Not only that, but his hands and arms had a sweet taste as well. He went back to his lab and tested everything he had worked on that day. His accidental discovery: an artificial sweetener that he later called saccharine.

CHAPTER 9

Singing for Their Supper

Musicians kept their cooking in concert

*W*HEN **ELVIS PRESLEY** left the building, he was probably going for a snack.

The king of rock 'n' roll was born into poverty in Mississippi, and his father was in prison for part of his youth. During Presley's hardscrabble upbringing, his family's idea of meat for dinner was fried squirrel, if a relative got lucky while hunting. Most of the time, the Presleys survived on greens, bread, and peanut butter.

A person coming from such circumstances might be understandably indulgent about food, but Presley took eating to more absurd heights than anyone could possibly justify. He snacked constantly—on Hostess cupcakes, Eskimo Pies, Krispy Kreme doughnuts. He was known to consume five hot-fudge sundaes for breakfast. When he ate pie or cake, that didn't mean just one piece. He often ate the whole thing.

Psychologists have theorized that Presley's personality was influenced by the fact that he was a "twinless twin." His brother, Jesse, was stillborn, with the baby Elvis arriving about a half hour later. Thus, Presley joined an exclusive group of famously creative "twinless twins," a fraternity that included painter Diego Rivera, pianist Liberace, and playwright Thornton Wilder.

The effect of being a surviving twin is not fully understood. But when it came to food, it's possible that Presley was simply taking double portions.

German composer **Ludwig van Beethoven** was sometimes so absorbed in his work that he neglected to eat. Suddenly inspired on the streets of Vienna one day, he ducked into a hotel restaurant and took a table at dinnertime. When a waiter asked him what he wanted, Beethoven rudely shooed him away. Two hours later, the dinner guests had come and gone, with a clatter of plates all around him, yet the composer was still putting pen to paper. Finally, he rolled up his composition and asked what he owed. Told he hadn't eaten anything and owed nothing, the master declared himself satisfied and left.

The favorite food of 1990s grunge rocker **Kurt Cobain** was macaroni and cheese. And not just any macaroni and cheese—Kraft brand macaroni and cheese.

German composer **Richard Wagner** was a tyrannical mentor to philosopher Friedrich Nietzsche, and Wagner's wife, Cosima, would send Nietzsche on humiliating quests for prized foods such as Dutch herring and Russian caviar. One note from Cosima ordered the groundbreaking existentialist to pick up "several pounds of caramels, a similar amount of pate d'abricots, a box of candied fruit (not the ones in bottles with syrup, but crystallized), and a bag of glace oranges." Wagner's wife added that she would "very much like to have these provisions by early August."

When Nietzsche advocated vegetarianism, Wagner called him an "ass." But later in life, Wagner became a vocal proponent of meatless meals, arguing that "eating the bodies of murdered animals" had debased the Aryan race.

Wagner wasn't satisfied to control his own food; he came up

with a new world order of dining. He praised the Japanese for their vegetable diet, ignoring the fact that many ate fish. He rejected the idea that man might be a natural carnivore, asserting that "on the swampy margins of Canadian lakes animal species allied to the panther and tiger still live as fruit-eaters." While conceding that humans in the most northerly regions might need "flesh-food," he thought that everyone else could do without. His solution: a mass migration of the earth's people to the more temperate parts of the globe, with the northern regions to be "abandoned to the undivided possession of hunters of boars and big game, who could give a very good account of themselves as destroyers of the somewhat too prolific beasts of prey in the deserted districts."

Wagner allowed himself a high level of hypocrisy. All his life—even when he was advocating vegetarianism—he loved a good steak.

French composer **Hector Berlioz** had little respect for either Italian melodies or meals.

"Music for the Italians is a sensual pleasure and nothing more," Berlioz sniffed. "For this noble expression of the mind they have hardly more respect than for the art of cooking. They want a score that, like a plate of macaroni, can be assimilated immediately without their having to think about it, or even pay attention to it."

Indeed, Italy's **Giuseppe Verdi** embodied Berlioz's stereotype. He made both his own music and his own pasta. And whenever he needed inspiration, he would eat a bowl of noodle soup.

Ray Charles said he grew up so poor that his family "ate everything on the pig but the oink."

Composer **Giacomo Puccini** and conductor **Arturo Toscanini** had an on-again-off-again friendship. One Christmas, Puccini sent Toscanini a panettone, an Italian sweet bread often given as a holiday gift. After dispatching the panettone, Puccini remembered that he and Toscanini were currently on bad terms, and he followed up the gift with a telegram reading: "Panettone sent by mistake. Puccini." The next day, he got a telegram back: "Panettone eaten by mistake. Toscanini."

Weeks before he wrote the lyrics for the smash hit "I Got Rhythm," **Ira Gershwin** created dummy lyrics as placeholders for the melody:

> *Roly-poly*
> *Eating solely*
> *Ravioli*
> *Better watch your diet or bust!*

No other composer could match forks with Italy's **Gioacchino Rossini,** who turned dining into a grand symphony.

"To eat, to sing, to digest, and to love are the four acts of the comic opera that is life," declared Rossini, who wrote such stirring operas as *The Barber of Seville.*

The aria *"Di tanti palpiti"* from Rossini's first successful opera, *Tancredi*, was nicknamed the "rice aria" because he was said to have written it in a hurry while his risotto cooked.

Rossini's career arc was unusual. His first major opera was performed in Venice in 1813, before he was twenty-one, and he wrote thirty-four more before composing his last at age thirty-seven. Rossini spent the last four decades of his life on other matters, such as fine dining.

He loved foie gras and adored truffles, which he called "the Mozart of mushrooms." Rossini claimed to have cried only three times in his life: when *Tancredi* was booed on opening night, when he heard Nicolo Paganini play the violin, and when a truffle-stuffed turkey fell out of a boat while he was having a picnic.

Jazz great **Louis Armstrong** often ended his letters to fans with the phrase "Red beans and ricely yours, Louis Armstrong."

Indeed, that was the New Orleans native's favorite dish, but there was plenty of competition. Armstrong loved to eat. In fact, the only foods he wouldn't touch were cucumbers and bananas.

Food held a central place in the trumpet virtuoso's universe, as reflected in the songs he recorded: "Big Butter and Egg Man," "Cheesecake," "Cornet Chop Suey," "All That Meat and No Potatoes," "Life Is Just a Bowl of Cherries," "Clarinet Marmalade," "Steak Face," "Tea for Two," "Coca-Cola Fanfare," and "Struttin' with Some Barbecue."

Classical music lovers owe a debt to female writer George Sand, whose real name was Aurore Dupin.

Composer **Frédéric Chopin** was chronically ill and died when he was thirty-nine years old. Yet he might have died at an even younger age if Sand hadn't nursed him and supervised his diet while the two resided in Majorca. Chopin couldn't tolerate the olive oil that was pervasive in Spanish food. To make matters worse, the cooking of pork—the staple meat of Majorca—produced a smell that nauseated the composer.

Before long, Sand was personally selecting and cooking Chopin's food. She never allowed Chopin to begin a day of composing or playing until he drank some chocolate or hot broth.

Johannes Brahms was looking forward to dinner with fellow German composer **Johann Strauss.** Beforehand, the sickly Brahms had to visit his doctor, who ordered him to limit his diet.

"But this evening I am dining with Strauss and we shall have chicken paprika," Brahms protested.

Out of the question, the doctor said.

"Very well then," Brahms replied. "Please consider that I did not come to consult you until tomorrow."

Celebrated tenor **Luciano Pavarotti,** a pasta lover, was estimated to have gained and lost more than five thousand pounds in his career. He once theorized that fat people were happy because their nerves were "well protected."

But the quest for happiness is only one reason many opera stars have had grand waistlines.

Some seem to believe the myth—apparently unsupported by science—that heft makes them sing better. And then there's the hectic lifestyle, with frequent travel that makes exercise difficult. There's also the common practice of eating a big meal after an evening performance, thereby packing on the calories when there's no time to burn them off. And there's a mentality that mezzo-soprano **Marilyn Horne** noted: "Ours is a very lonely profession. Eating is company."

But the role of the "fat lady" in opera is being rewritten. In 2004, **Deborah Voigt** was fired at London's Covent Garden for being too large to fit into the cocktail dress designed for her character in Strauss's *Ariadne auf Naxos.* Voigt later underwent gastric bypass surgery and was rehired for the same role at the same venue.

Maria Callas found a natural method of losing weight: the tapeworm.

Callas, a Greek soprano who was the most famous opera star of the post–World War II era, was often overweight when she was young. Even while living in Nazi-occupied Athens, her weight soared as she supplemented war rations with black-market food, stuffing herself with dried figs, nuts, and ersatz sausage. One critic ridiculed her physical appearance in the opera *Aïda,* complaining that "it was difficult to discern Callas's ankles from those of the elephant in the scene."

The soprano's transformation into an international beauty began in 1953 after she saw Audrey Hepburn in the film *Roman Holiday* and resolved to become slim. And indeed she did, dropping nearly seventy pounds.

Her method was a matter of controversy and rumor. Officially, a no-pasta, no-bread, raw-meat diet was credited. When an Italian food company called Pantanella Mills advertised that its "dietetic" pasta made the soprano svelte, Callas sued. Pantanella Mills was run by a nephew of Pope Pius XII, and the pope himself appealed for Callas to drop the lawsuit. She refused and won.

It was eventually discovered that the cause of Callas's weight loss was neither pasta nor the lack of it. In fact, she had swallowed a tapeworm. Callas explained that she must have consumed the worm in either a salad or raw meat, but friends later said it was no accident. One friend, Giulietta Simionato, said Callas told her, "Look, there are many stories about this, but it's true that I ingested a tapeworm. I took it voluntarily and that's how I lost thirty kilos."

Elvis Presley turned his Memphis mansion, Graceland, into a gourmand's theme park.

He kept odd hours, sometimes rising at 5 p.m. and not retiring until 8 a.m. He had cooks on staff twenty-four hours a day, and breakfast food was served at all hours. A closed-circuit television camera was trained on the kitchen so that Elvis could monitor the pie baking and banana pudding making from his bedroom, where he took many of his meals.

Even in the 1960s, when sirloin steak was only a dollar a pound, Presley's grocery bill was five hundred dollars a week. But his staff didn't have to go shopping for his favorite beverage, Pepsi, because Graceland was a regular stop on the delivery truck's route.

Composer and pianist **Igor Stravinsky** sometimes adopted a diet of raw vegetables. While eating a meal of tomatoes and potatoes with composer Nicholas Nabokov one day, Stravinsky noticed that his dining partner had left a slice of cutlet on his plate. He asked if he could have it, and Nabokov agreed. Stravinsky ate it with sour cream, explaining, "I want to astonish the raw potato in my stomach."

Stravinsky was no dining eccentric, but he hung around with a British food freak named Gerald Hugh Tyrwhitt-Wilson, also known as Lord Berners.

Without a doubt, Lord Berners was a minor composer and a major loon.

Stravinsky recalled that "if Lord Berners' mood was pink, lunch might consist of beet soup, lobster, tomatoes, strawberries." He even used pink dye to color the pigeons outside his home so that they would match the meal. On a different occasion, Stravinsky's wife sent Berners a powder so that he could turn mayonnaise blue.

Italian tenor **Enrico Caruso** once declared: "Watermelon—it's a good fruit. You eat, you drink, you wash your face."

The most distinctive aspect of **Louis Armstrong**'s approach to dining was what he did afterward. Beginning in his youth, he was a dedicated user of laxatives, which he called physics. His mother insisted on it, perhaps because the impoverished family often ate rotten food.

Armstrong explained his mother's view: "Mayann used to tell me always stay physic-minded. You may not get rich, but you won't ever have those terrible ailments such as cancer, etc. And she would go out by the railroad tracks and pick a lot of peppers—grasses, dandelions, etc., and she'd bring it home and boil that stuff and give us kids a big dose of it. And, my gawd—we'd make sprints to the toilet and afterwards feel 'oh, so good,' all cleaned out 'n' stuff."

As an adult, Armstrong used laxatives to battle a weight problem as well as to support his overall health, and he became an evangelist for laxatives. He employed products such as Bisma-Rex and Pluto Water, but his favorite was Swiss Kriss, a collection of herbs promoted by nutritionist Gayelord Hauser.

So dedicated was Armstrong to his favorite laxative that when he was writing a letter, he sometimes dropped his signature "Red beans and ricely yours" and instead used "Swiss Krissly yours."

Swiss Kriss came in small envelopes, which Armstrong gave away in person and through the mail. The product looked a bit like marijuana, and some fans reportedly were disappointed when it turned out to be only a laxative.

Armstrong would talk about laxatives with anyone he met, even bringing up the subject during a visit with the British royal family. Once while conversing with an elderly woman, Armstrong pulled out a packet and handed it to her. She asked what was in it, and he replied in his New Orleans jazzman accent: "Oibs, mama, oibs!"

Some musicians have sustained long careers through careful attention to their diet.

Jazz trumpeter **Dizzy Gillespie** gave up meat around age sixty, explaining: "My intestines wrote me a letter."

Jazz pianist **Dave Brubeck** also made a late-career, low-cholesterol commitment heavy on fruit and vegetables. Brubeck recalled his healthy kinship with Gillespie: "He had his own juicer and I had mine and we'd take them on the road. We'd laugh about it. I'd get carrots by the bushel. . . . Carrot juice is good for you."

Duke Ellington, the brilliant jazz composer and pianist, was an improvisational eater. According to a trombonist in his band, he once ate thirty-two sandwiches during a dance intermission. When he wasn't able to finish breakfast before rushing to a train, he would take his meal with him. A famous story has him on a train discussing his similarities to Bach—and pulling a piece of greasy meat out of his pocket in the middle of the conversation.

Ellington attempted to rein in his diet—but only occasionally and often incompetently. A *New Yorker* article in 1944 described a typical mealtime struggle in which he would try to consume only Shredded Wheat and black tea. But then he would see a colleague enjoy a steak and would eat one himself. He would attempt to hold the line there but to no avail. "Then he really begins to eat," the article said. "He has another steak, smothered in onions, a double portion of fried potatoes, a salad, a bowl of sliced tomatoes, a giant lobster and melted butter, coffee, and an Ellington dessert—perhaps a combination of pie, cake, ice cream, custard, pastry, jello, fruit, and cheese. His appetite really whetted, he may order ham and eggs, a half-dozen pancakes, waffles and syrup, and some hot biscuits. Then, determined to get back on his diet, he will finish, as he began, with Shredded Wheat and black tea."

At age seventeen, **Frank Sinatra** had a fight with his father, who wanted him to get a regular job instead of trying to become a singer. The confrontation, which caused Sinatra to leave home, occurred over breakfast. "I think the egg was stuck [in my throat] for about 20 minutes, and I couldn't swallow it or get rid of it," Sinatra recalled. After moving from his parents' Hoboken, New Jersey, home to a struggling existence in New York City, he survived on cream-cheese-and-nut sandwiches.

Decades later, Sinatra was wealthy enough to order room service, but an incident at Miami Beach's Fontainebleau hotel must have caused him to lose his appetite. Sinatra had befriended both the Kennedy family and Chicago mobsters and was suspected of helping the mob donate to John F. Kennedy's presidential run in 1960. After Kennedy was elected, he allowed his brother Bobby to crack down on organized crime, and Sinatra fell into the mob's disfavor. Staying at the Fontainebleau in 1961, Sinatra accepted a room-service meal. But when the silver top of a tray was lifted, it revealed only the skinned head of a lamb resting on a plate— presumably an indication of the mob's displeasure. For years afterward, a Sinatra staffer recalled, Ol' Blue Eyes hated the smell of roasted lamb.

In the rock 'n' roll era, food often was more of a message than a meal.

The playful and twisted outlook of rock stars is perhaps best exemplified by the cover of the Who's album *The Who Sell Out,* featuring singer **Roger Daltrey** in a bathtub full of baked beans.

There have been plenty of groups named after food: Cream, Strawberry Alarm Clock, Smashing Pumpkins, Red Hot Chili Peppers, Wild Cherry.

And there have been lots of songs about food: **The Beatles'** "Strawberry Fields Forever," **Frank Zappa's** "Call Any Vegetable" and "Peaches en Regalia," **Booker T & the MGs'** "Green Onions," **Van Morrison's** "Tupelo Honey," **Jimmy Buffett's** "Cheeseburger in Paradise," **Harry Nilsson's** "Coconut," **Beck's** "Satan Gave Me a Taco," and **Richard Harris's** "MacArthur Park," with the strange lyric about the cake left out in the rain.

Even **Paul Simon's** "Mother and Child Reunion" is food-inspired. Simon got the title from the name of a chicken-and-egg dish at a Chinese restaurant.

Perhaps **Elvis Presley's** favorite meal was something he called a "peanut butter and 'nanner sandwich." Two pieces of white bread were toasted lightly, with peanut butter spread on one piece and a mashed-up banana spread on the other. The pieces of bread were put together and the sandwich was fried in a skillet in butter. Presley ate it with a knife and fork.

But the most impressive sandwich on Elvis's menu was something called the Fool's Gold. He once flew more than eight hundred miles to eat one.

On February 1, 1976, Presley was at Graceland, entertaining two Colorado police officers. They got to talking about the Fool's Gold, a $49.95 menu item at a restaurant called the Colorado Gold Mine Company in Glendale, Colorado, outside of Denver. Presley had eaten one before, but the officers had not. One of them uttered the fateful words: "Boy, I wish I had me one of them now!"

Under Presley's code of hospitality, anything a guest requested should be granted. So he led the officers and members of his entourage into his stretch Mercedes, and they sped to the Memphis airport and boarded his personal jet. Presley's people called ahead to Denver, and the restaurant flew into action.

The Fool's Gold was no ordinary sandwich. A cook would warm an entire loaf of Italian bread, hollow it out, and then stuff it with peanut butter, grape jelly, and a pound of bacon. The restaurant prepared twenty-two of the sandwiches and rushed them to the Denver airport, meeting Presley and his group as they arrived after their two-hour flight. A hangar was turned into a dining hall, and the guests feasted on Fool's Gold and champagne. Presley, who seldom drank alcohol, washed his dinner down with Perrier.

The Beatles—whose record label was named after a fruit, Apple—recorded a song about food called "Savoy Truffle." **George Harrison** wrote it about his friend, guitarist **Eric Clapton,** who was eating copious amounts of chocolate. The song's lyric about "good news" refers to a brand of assorted chocolates called Mackintosh's Good News, which featured such selections as ginger sling and creme tangerine.

The song's refrain warns of Clapton's inevitable trip to the dentist when his teeth rot:

Yes, you'll have to have them all pulled out
After the Savoy truffle!

For **Ludwig van Beethoven,** food often was something to argue over. One fellow diner recalled a meal at which Beethoven "dickered with the waiter about every roll." Once, he threw a stew at a waiter. Another time, he tossed eggs at a cook.

On his deathbed, he accepted pastry and wine from a parade of well-wishers. But the arrival of a case of Rudesheimer Berg wine prompted his last words: "Pity, pity—too late!"

Food has often contributed to the mythology of rock music, with some of the stories true and others patently false.

Punk rock icon **Iggy Pop** really did smear his torso with peanut butter at the Cincinnati Pop Festival in 1970. And he did subsist in Berlin for a year on a diet of red wine, German sausages, and Bavarian black bread.

Cass Elliot, on the other hand, did not choke to death on a ham sandwich, as is widely believed. Elliot, the melodious singer for the Mamas and the Papas, died in 1974 in a London apartment—the same apartment where The Who drummer **Keith Moon** would later die. The first doctor to examine Mama Cass noticed a ham sandwich beside her body and reached a hasty conclusion that was accepted by the public because of her well-known struggles with weight. But as it turned out, the sandwich beside Elliot was untouched, and she had died from a heart attack, not from choking.

When he became a celebrity, **Elvis Presley** stopped cutting up his own food. Before his plate was presented to him, the food was sliced into bite-sized pieces by his cooks or his wife, Priscilla.

The King salted his food even before he tasted it. And whenever eating meat, he demanded that it be well cooked. One of his favorite expressions was "That's burnt, man." Whether he was talking about a steak or a song, something that was "burnt" was good.

As a frequent diner at New York City's posh Le Cirque restaurant, **Frank Sinatra** would indicate his satisfaction with a meal by writing the word *yes* or *no* on a note and leaving it behind. When Sinatra and his dining pals were misbehaving one night, Le Cirque's owner used Sinatra's code to register his disapproval, placing a note marked *no* on the singer's table. Sinatra was furious and didn't return to Le Cirque for many years. Even when his wife dined there, Sinatra waited outside in his limousine. The restaurant's peace offering to the pouting crooner was—what else?—food, delivered by Le Cirque staff to Sinatra's limo.

Rockers particularly like to use food as a metaphor for sex, with the **Rolling Stones**' "Brown Sugar" being just one prominent example. And here's a news flash: **Little Richard**'s "Tutti Frutti" is not a tribute to a flavor of ice cream. In fact, the original lyrics—changed before the song hit the charts—include raunchy sexual references and use the phrase "Tutti Frutti, good booty" instead of the more familiar "Tutti Fruity, all rooty."

The song's risqué nature was in the tradition of other hip African American tunes, such as Julia Lee's "I Didn't Like It the First Time," subtitled "The Spinach Song," which may have referred to sex or marijuana. The double-entendre lyrics were so controversial in the late 1940s that jazz great **Benny Carter** used a pseudonym to claim credit for composing the music.

One of the Beatles' greatest hits started out as a food song. **Paul McCartney** came up with the melody, but the band struggled for months to decide on its lyrics and title.

"We called it 'Scrambled Egg' and it became a joke between us," **John Lennon** said. "We almost had it finished, we had made up our minds that only a one-word title would suit—and believe me, we just couldn't find the right one."

According to Beatles record producer George Martin, McCartney had thought of a one-word title for the song but worried that it sounded corny. Martin persuaded the Fab Four that McCartney's title, "Yesterday," was a fine name for the song. The public seemed to agree.

Elvis Presley loathed seafood, disgusted by the smell. He even asked his wife, Priscilla, not to eat fish when he was around. When Presley was urged to try escargot, he refused, saying, "Man, I don't want to eat something I could step on when I walk out the door."

One of the legendary stories about an out-of-control, apparently drug-addled Presley involved seafood. The so-called catfish incident occurred on July 20, 1975, when Presley gave a concert in Norfolk, Virginia. He was in a dangerous mood for someone armed with a microphone. First, he insulted the audience by complaining about having eleven thousand people breathing on him. Then he said he smelled green peppers and onions and suggested that his quartet of black backup singers, the Sweet Inspirations, had been eating catfish. It was not a compliment. Two of the "Sweets" walked off the stage in disgust. Some people took the comment as a racial insult, but it was more likely the culmination of a series of bizarre remarks that Elvis had made to his backup singers—both black and white—during the tour. The offended Sweets returned for the next night's concert in Greensboro, North Carolina, and Presley publicly apologized.

Many strange but true stories about rock stars and food have come from the contract riders for their concerts that sometimes include bizarre demands about food, drink, and other arrangements.

When the **Beatles** played New York's Shea Stadium in 1965, their backstage demands were modest: a black-and-white television set and a case of Coca-Cola. Rockers would soon get more tyrannical. The hard rock group **Metallica** declared that it was "very important that bacon be available at every meal and during day." Pop singer **Janet Jackson** demanded clean ice. "NO FISH ICE!" a clause read. "If it had never happened, I wouldn't have to write this."

The rider of the rock group **Van Halen** has often been cited as the most ridiculous. The Rock 'n' Rock Hall of Famers wanted a bowl of M&M's candies to be available backstage—with all the brown ones removed. But singer David Lee Roth explained that the demand wasn't as stupid as it seemed. The group inserted the clause as a tripwire: If the bowl had brown M&M's, the group could be suspicious of more important arrangements—whether the electrical requirements had been met, whether the stage would bear the weight of the equipment, and so on. After all, details matter.

Every month, songwriter **Cole Porter** had nine pounds of fudge shipped to him from a store called Arnold's Candies in his hometown of Peru, Indiana.

Elvis Presley hired his stepbrother, Billy Stanley, as a personal assistant, but fired him over food. As Stanley watched Elvis devour a pizza and start on a second one, he blurted: "Where you gonna put it?" Presley canned him on the spot.

Today, many dishes are named for **Gioacchino Rossini,** classical music's greatest gourmet. The best known is a preparation of steak with foie gras and truffles called tournedos Rossini. According to lore, the dish was devised at tableside in Paris's Café Anglais, with the customer Rossini orchestrating. The maitre d' disapproved of the meal's excess and therefore prepared it with his back to the other diners. The French phrase *tourner le dos* ("to turn one's back") led to the name tournedos.

Other dishes named for the maestro include poulet Rossini (chicken with ham and mushrooms), filets de sole Rossini (Dover sole with foie gras and truffles), and veal Rossini (medallions of veal with shallots, foie gras, and either truffles or truffle oil). There's also pizza Rossini, featuring the usual tomato and cheese, but with a special encore of egg and mayonnaise on top.

Other musicians have inspired their own specialty dishes.

Luisa Tetrazzini, an Italian soprano popular in the United States in the early 1900s, lent her name to two American inventions, chicken tetrazzini and turkey tetrazzini. The food-loving soprano once said, "I must not diet. If I diet my face sag."

Then there's an Australian soprano named Helen Porter Mitchell, who retitled herself **Nellie Melba,** choosing that moniker because she grew up in a suburb of Melbourne. She traveled to Europe to sing, establishing herself at London's Covent Garden as the nineteenth century turned into the twentieth. Her voice and personality made her an international star, but she is most remembered today for two food items named in her honor by French chef Auguste Escoffier: peaches melba and melba toast.

On August 16, 1977, **Elvis Presley** was killed by a mixture of prescription drugs at the age of forty-two. His diet didn't help. The King's final food was six chocolate chip cookies and four scoops of ice cream. Two of the scoops were peach-flavored, and the flavor of the other two scoops is unknown—a rare missing detail in an excruciatingly public life.

How many calories did Elvis consume in a day? By one well-publicized estimate, ninety-four thousand. By another, sixty-five thousand—described as the average daily intake of an Asian elephant.

But both of those figures are utterly implausible.

Presley reportedly weighed 250 pounds or so at his death. Let's do the math—or ask Dawn Jackson Blatner, an American Dietetic Association spokesperson, to do the math for us. She estimates that a person weighing 300 pounds would consume about four thousand calories to maintain his weight and would consume about twelve thousand calories if he was gaining 10 pounds or more a week. "Hard to imagine how someone could eat much more than that regularly," she says.

That means Presley's daily calorie intake was not elephantine. At most, it approached the average diet of eight Eritreans. Which is either wretched excess, or an American success story. Or as Elvis might have put it: That's burnt, man.

CHAPTER 10

Business Lunch

Entrepreneurs were eccentric eaters

*I*N 1966, BILLIONAIRE entrepreneur **Howard Hughes** moved to Las Vegas, where he turned the top floor of the Desert Inn into his private residence. Soon after moving into the hotel, Hughes learned that Baskin Robbins was discontinuing his favorite ice-cream flavor: banana-nut. Hughes had his personal staff place a special order for 350 gallons of Baskin Robbins banana-nut ice cream.

Hughes later took a fancy to a new ice cream flavor: French vanilla. This left the Desert Inn's restaurant with a lot of banana-nut ice cream on its hands. The restaurant staff worked hard to promote this ice-cream flavor, but it took the hotel roughly a year to exhaust the supply that it had stored specially for Hughes.

Warren Buffett's heart belongs to Cherry Coke.

In 2007, Buffett wrote a letter to shareholders explaining his wish to find a successor to guide his firm, Berkshire Hathaway. Buffett reassured the company's shareholders that his search was not motivated by concerns about his health. "It's amazing what Cherry Coke and hamburgers will do for a fellow," Buffett wrote to shareholders.

When he wants to drop some pounds, Buffett's diet of choice is to cut out all of the Cherry Coke he would normally drink.

Interestingly, it was Coke's rival that initially claimed Buffett's loyalty. During the 1950s and '60s, Buffett's offices stocked ample supplies of Pepsi-Cola. His financial interest in Coca-Cola may have been stirred in the late 1980s when Donald Keough, the soft drink giant's chief executive, persuaded Buffett to try Cherry Coke. Within months, Buffett's investment firm, Berkshire Hathaway, bought more than twenty-three million shares of Coca-Cola stock.

Reporters who follow Buffett have learned to follow the Cherry Coke. "Whenever I lost track of Buffett," wrote a *BusinessWeek* reporter, "Coke often appeared to guide me—a carbonated version of the proverbial trail of crumbs. . . . When I arrived at [London's] Berkeley Hotel, I did not have to wonder for long whether Buffett had preceded me. A bellhop approached with a shopping bag. 'Is this yours?' he asked. Inside were two six-packs of Cherry Coke."

Estée Lauder never would have built her successful cosmetics empire if she had heeded her father's advice to stop "fiddling with other people's faces."

Although she always wanted to look her best, one thing she didn't fiddle with was dieting. In 1981, she told a reporter why she didn't go on diets.

"It's a false way of eating," Lauder explained. "I believe in eating well. Everybody should have a pat of butter, for example. You need it for your bones so they don't dry up. I have my pat for breakfast."

Oysters Rockefeller has no direct connection with magnate **John D. Rockefeller,** or any other Rockefeller for that matter. In

1899, the chef of the venerable New Orleans restaurant Antoine's devised a new way to serve oysters with a lavish sauce. He chose the Rockefeller name simply because it was a synonym for "rich"—fitting for a recipe that features so much "green," including celery, parsley, and green onions.

As America slid into the Great Depression in the early 1930s, workers at Ford Motor Company appealed to the automaker's founder, **Henry Ford,** for financial assistance. His response? Eat more vegetables.

Ford ordered each employee to plant a vegetable garden or to sign up for a plot within the four-thousand-acre company tract known as Ford Farms. Because the workers were commanded by their boss to start these plots, they were known as "shotgun gardens."

Apple Computer founder **Steve Jobs** is a vegetarian who named the firm for his favorite fruit. After high school, he worked in an apple orchard. And when he dropped out after one semester of college, he experimented with an all-apple diet, believing it might eliminate the need for him to bathe. It didn't.

Jobs is a friend and follower of Dr. Dean Ornish, who recommends a low-fat vegetarian diet. Jobs is particularly fond of broccoli and other green veggies.

Investors were concerned in 2004 when they learned that Jobs was battling cancer. After all, he

personally had made so many of Apple's decisions—even choosing the chef for the company's cafeteria—that it was hard to imagine anyone replacing him.

In 2009, as disgraced investment guru **Bernard Madoff** endured house arrest, a New York City artist began selling bottles of hot sauce named for him: "Bernie in hell."

Before he cofounded Sony, **Akio Morita** was a World War II naval veteran in search of a postwar trade to support himself in his native Japan. Morita and his friends pondered what they could produce that Japanese consumers would truly need to buy. Rice was the staple of the country's diet, so Morita and his comrades decided that one of their first products would be an electric rice cooker.

The trickiest part was finding the metal—then in short supply—for making their rice cookers. Their solution? They gathered the discarded fuel tanks that American B-29 bombers had jettisoned during their wartime raids over Japan.

Bored with working as an IBM salesman, **H. Ross Perot** quit and started a company he called Electronic Data Systems, which he eventually sold to General Motors for $2.5 billion.

EDS staff who met Perot learned quickly that the wealthy Texas native expected them to anticipate needs and handle them without excuses. Once, during a 3 a.m. hotel conversation with EDS recruiter Rob Brooks, Perot confided that he craved a chocolate malt. Brooks persuaded the hotel's night manager to open the hotel's kitchen so he could prepare his boss a malt. "The word 'impossibil-ity' was not in his vocabulary," Brooks remembered.

John D. Rockefeller made a fortune from oil refineries, and his net worth approached one billion dollars by 1913. But unlike many billionaires, he did not hire a chef schooled in French cooking.

Rockefeller liked to eat an apple right before he retired for the night, and for many years he kept a sack of apples on a windowsill near his bed.

In his final years, Rockefeller battled digestive problems that reportedly led him to rely on milk for his sustenance. But it didn't come from the local grocery: It was provided by wet nurses whom he kept on his household staff.

By the time he died in 1917, railroad tycoon **"Diamond Jim" Brady** had built a reputation as the ultimate glutton. A New York City restaurateur once called Brady the "best twenty-five custom-ers I ever had."

According to stories of his ravenous appetite, he ate enor-mous breakfasts of eggs, muffins, grits, pancakes, steaks, fried potatoes, and breads—washed down with pitchers of orange juice. In between lunch and dinner, Brady would supposedly devour a few dozen oysters or clams. Then lunch would include copious amounts of crabs, oysters, lobsters, beef, pie, and more orange juice. He would eat a midafternoon snack, followed by a supper of game birds and more orange juice. This gorging, we are told, was Brady's daily ritual.

Many tales of Diamond Jim's feasting were exaggerated. But ac-counts provided by Brady's urologist, Dr. Hugh Hampton Young, are only slightly less sensational. "I have seen him eat six cantaloupes and quantities of eggs," Dr. Young wrote. "His principal libation was orange juice, of which I have seen him consume two quarts."

During his collegiate years, future General Electric chief executive **Jack Welch** was frustrated by his stutter. Welch would frequent a certain restaurant on Fridays and order a tuna sandwich on toast for lunch.

"Inevitably, the waitress would return with not one, but a pair of sandwiches, having heard my order as 'tu-tuna sandwiches,'" he recalled.

The most flamboyant signature on the Declaration of Independence belonged to **John Hancock,** and that seems only fitting. The wealth he acquired by inheriting and growing his uncle's mercantile firm enabled Hancock to live and eat with a lot of style.

To acquire one of the first salmon of the season, he paid a guinea—an amount equal to a full week's wage for most skilled English craftsmen. Hancock was known for the elaborate codfish dinners that he hosted. He so loved the cod found in Massachusetts Bay that even after advancing British troops forced him to flee Boston, Hancock paid to have codfish from the bay shipped to his temporary homes in Philadelphia and Baltimore.

When **Mary Kay Ash**—the queen of door-to-door cosmetics— went grocery shopping, she always made a list and stuck to it.

"I have always said that the smartest salesperson who ever lived was the fellow who invented the shopping cart," Ash said. "How many times have you stopped at the grocery for a single item and ended up filling that empty cart?"

By 1937, Phillips Petroleum was producing sixty-seven thousand barrels of oil daily and annual sales of nearly $120 million. Its future looked bright. And its wealthy founder, **Frank Phillips,** insisted on eating in rooms that were bright.

Dimly lit restaurants annoyed Phillips, and he would ask the maitre d', "What's the matter, can't you pay your light bill?"

Bill Angel, Phillips's traveling secretary, once led the oil executive to a swank restaurant with its lights turned down low. Phillips complained to the headwaiter and then walked out. With few appealing dining options, the two men ended up going to a cheap, but brightly lit, eatery.

"All we could get were hot dogs and orange juice and we had to stand," Angel said, "but the lights were shining like the noonday sun. He ate his hot dog and said, 'This is great.' Course, I knew he was disappointed but that he'd never admit it."

In the years before the U.S. Civil War, **Mayer Lehman** and his brother Emanuel built a cotton brokerage business in Alabama. The firm later moved to New York City, where it would become one of the most illustrious investment banks in Wall Street's history.

Relatively little is known about Lehman's personality, but his daughter, Settie, had a notorious temper. Chocolates—in the form of éclairs, chocolate-coated wafers, and other delicacies—were the typical form of apology she offered to friends, family, or others who had been on the receiving end of her verbal explosions. Her tantrums provided a steady stream of business for Dean's Pastry Shop, which delivered her chocolate apologies.

Settie also had a compassionate side. Once, after purchasing an apple from a fruit stand, she learned that the female vendor had neither the time nor money to eat lunch. Settie gave the woman a dollar and agreed to tend the apple stand while the vendor bought and ate her meal. Within a few hours, neighborhood gossip circulated the shocking news that the daughter of Mayer Lehman had lost all her money and was out on the street corner selling apples.

Hamburgers, french fries, and honey-roasted peanuts are **Warren Buffett**'s favorite foods. And the billionaire is horrified when a restaurant server delivers a plate on which a vegetable is touching his hamburger.

Long before the hedge fund business made him a billionaire, Hungarian-born **George Soros** was struggling to make ends meet in London soon after World War II. Both before and after he was admitted to the London School of Economics, Soros worked at restaurants.

First, he washed dishes at a diner called The Better 'Ole. Then he landed a job as a busboy at a stylish London restaurant called Quaglino's. The headwaiter at Quaglino's eventually learned that Soros had lied when he claimed he had experience working in a hotel dining room. But the headwaiter overlooked the fib because Soros was doing a good job. He even promoted Soros to demi-chef, the person who delivers food to diners, and he offered Soros the promise of more: If Soros kept working hard, he might one day become assistant headwaiter.

"I was being paid as a sub waiter," Soros recalled, "but I was beginning to get a share of the kitty. They pooled the tips and used a point system to divide the money, and years later I introduced something like that at Soros Fund Management."

When a judge ordered the arrest of the Erie Railroad's board of directors in the late 1860s for contempt of court, tycoons **Jim Fisk** and **Jay Gould** hastily prepared to leave New York City. The two Erie board members planned to cross the Hudson River to New Jersey, where they would be one step farther from the court's reach.

But first things first. They decided to enjoy an extravagant dinner at Delmonico's, a Manhattan restaurant known for its upscale French food. The two men were only halfway through their meal of steak and champagne when a messenger alerted them that police were closing in. Fisk and Gould fled Delmonico's, traveled by carriage to the foot of Canal Street, and hired a small boat that transported them to New Jersey.

When he died in 1996, **Arthur G. Gaston** was one of the wealthiest African Americans in the United States, amassing more than $130 million from a hotel, a savings and loan company, and other businesses. But the first business that Gaston created capitalized on his mother's tasty home cooking.

While working in an Alabama coal mine, Gaston noticed that many of his fellow miners were impressed by the boxed lunch he brought with him each morning, which typically included chicken, sweet potatoes, and flaky biscuits. Gaston found that other miners would eagerly buy such a lunch, and that allowed his mother to spend time doing something she loved: cooking.

There was nothing particularly Southern, however, about the breakfast beverage that became Gaston's routine—a mixture of orange juice and raw eggs.

Howard Hughes was a man of routine. On most evenings during the 1930s, Hughes ate the same dinner: a very lean, ten-ounce steak; a serving of canned—never fresh—peas; and one scoop of vanilla ice cream with caramel sauce.

Even if his glass, plate, and eating utensils were sparkling clean, Hughes insisted on carrying all of these dining accessories into the kitchen and hand-washing them before every meal.

Martha Stewart's cooking and craft-making skills helped her build a business that has made her one of the richest women in America. Yet she may owe her culinary smarts to genetics. Stewart's father had the ability to walk into a kitchen, smell what was cooking or baking, identify the ingredients, and later bake or cook the same dish.

Stewart often stayed up to the wee hours of the morning with her father, eating onion sandwiches as they played Scrabble or chatted.

Food was a source of anxiety for **Henry Ford.** The man who founded one of the world's largest automakers would not eat chicken because chickens ate bugs. He also worried about eating granulated sugar—wouldn't the sharp crystals of sugar tear into his stomach and cause internal bleeding? Even after a scientist showed him a microscopic image of sugar crystals easily dissolving in water, Ford could not shake his fear.

The elaborate Ponzi scheme that investment broker **Bernard Madoff** devised swindled clients out of nearly sixty-five billion dollars. After spending the day at his office in New York City's so-called Lipstick Building, Madoff frequently joined his wife at Primola, an Italian restaurant that was his favorite dining destination in the city.

The couple typically arrived at about 6:30 p.m.—much earlier than most New Yorkers dine—and asked for a quiet table in the rear of the restaurant. Visit after visit, the couple ordered the same meal: a small salad, followed by chicken scarpiello for him and seafood for her. Madoff drank a Diet Coke or red wine. Neither of them ordered dessert or coffee. They typically finished their dinner in under an hour and left a tip of 20 percent.

Months after the Madoff scandal broke, an employee of Primola told a reporter, "Now everybody is asking for 'the Madoff table,' but I always say, 'The F.B.I. already has it.'"

As a married woman in the 1930s, **Estée Lauder** balanced homemaking duties with her desire to prepare skin-care products that she could sell to neighbors and beauty parlors. In the family's kitchen, Lauder often heated multiple pots atop the stove. Her husband had to be cautious before dipping his finger into one of the pots for a taste. Some pots contained the family's meals while others held her latest concoction of face cream.

New York City has seen more than its share of banquets, but in 1903 wealthy businessman **C. K. G. Billings** arranged a one-of-a-kind dinner.

The dinner was organized by Billings—the 1910 census identified him as a "capitalist at large"—to celebrate the opening of his stable at 196th Street. According to *The Strand* magazine, each of the thirty-two people who attended Billings's banquet at Sherry's restaurant mounted a horse and "from little tables placed upon the pommels, they ate their splendid dinner."

Billings didn't forget about the horses' needs. Feeding troughs were filled with oats and brought to the horses so they could eat while their riders did.

What won't the French eat? That question must have popped into **Milton Hershey**'s head while the chocolate candy magnate was dining with his wife in southern France.

At a restaurant in Marseille, Hershey ordered a pork dish. After he heard the waiter call out "*jambon*," Hershey thought he heard "Jumbo"—the name of the famous elephant in P. T. Barnum's circus. Hershey shouted, "I don't want an elephant!"

Boston merchant **John Hancock,** attending the Continental Congress in March 1777, wrote a letter to his wife, Dolly, who was living in Baltimore. He complained about the papers that covered his table and interfered with mealtime. When someone brought him a plate of minced veal, Hancock grumbled, there was no tablecloth and "not room on the table to put a plate, [for] I am up to the eyes in papers."

Hancock signed off his letter with "my dear girl, yours most affectionately," but he added an unromantic postscript: "Buy and bring 1 or 2 bushels of parsnips. Bring all the wine, none to be got here."

The years that Body Shop founder **Anita Roddick** worked in her family's restaurant may have influenced some of the unconventional products she later launched through the Body Shop—from banana shampoo to blueberry body butter.

During the late 1990s, a typical day in the life of media mogul **Rupert Murdoch** began with a bowl of porridge for breakfast because he was a big believer in "roughage." He worked the rest of the morning at the Fox corporate headquarters in southern California and then ate lunch at the network's commissary. Although he carefully read the commissary's lunch menu, he always ordered the same meal: grilled chicken, vegetables, and a Diet Coke.

In 1884, New York City's *World* newspaper printed a front-page cartoon mocking the lavish dinner that financial bigwigs had arranged with Republican presidential nominee James Blaine. The cartoon depicted **Cornelius Vanderbilt**, **John Jacob Astor**, and other wealthy men eating "lobby pudding" and drinking "monopoly soup" while poor people begged for crumbs.

The influential publisher **Henry Luce** dined at many fancy restaurants, and he left a lot of stories behind. Once at a French restaurant, he ordered a classic dish, duck a l'orange, but asked for applesauce in place of the orange sauce. At another restaurant, Luce curtly asked a maître d', "Got anything good to eat here?" He also liked to puncture soufflés as he babbled on to fellow diners.

Immediately after dinners at **J. Paul Getty**'s Sutton Place estate in England concluded, doors to the dining room were closed and locked—as if, wrote a biographer, "the host expected some member of the invited party to make off with the silver."

Television executive **William Paley** was a perfectionist. When CBS built its headquarters on New York City's Sixth Avenue, he analyzed every detail of its construction. The same was true for the small park being built less than a block away, which was to be named after Paley.

Even the hot dogs that would be sold at the park's concession stand caught his attention. After sampling dozens of different frankfurters for the stand, Paley was dissatisfied. He ordered that a hot dog be created to reflect his taste—then instructed employees precisely how they were to cook it.

While her mother worked long hours outside the home, a very young **Mary Kay Ash** bore the hefty responsibility of cooking the family's dinner.

"At the tender age of seven, I could hardly be considered a master chef," she recalled. If her father wanted something to eat that she didn't know how to cook, Mary Kay picked up the telephone and called her mother at work.

Mrs. Ash gave her daughter careful cooking instructions over the phone and concluded her remarks with the pep-talk phrase: "Honey, *you can do it.*"

John D. Rockefeller was one of many prominent individuals who followed the advice of Horace Fletcher, a man with no scientific credentials who was dubbed "the great masticator" because he urged eaters to chew every spoonful of food roughly one hundred times per minute.

After Rockefeller received a container of oatmeal from **Andrew Carnegie**—ground and packaged by one of Carnegie's own manufacturers—Rockefeller sent Carnegie a thank-you note and an instruction on how Carnegie should enjoy his own product: "Be sure to eat it very slowly, and masticate well."

Soon after Google cofounders **Larry Page** and **Sergey Brin** launched the Internet search engine company, they embarked on a search of their own. The young executives sought a chef to manage the café at Google's headquarters.

Google's ad sought a chef who could produce meals for employees "with a craving for epicurial delights" and asserted that this was the only chef's position that came with stock options. Google gave tryouts to—and rejected—twenty-five chefs before hiring Charlie Ayers, who had cooked for the Grateful Dead during the rock band's tours.

In a 1988 speech to business leaders in Beijing, Chrysler chief executive **Lee Iacocca** praised the inventions and ideas that had originated in China. He mentioned the wheelbarrow and the blast furnace, then said that "the one I'm most grateful for is noodles, which I call pasta."

The father of McDonald's founder **Ray Kroc** belonged to a singing group that frequently met at the family's home. Ray and his brother were exiled upstairs while Mr. Kroc and the other singers crooned to piano melodies played by Mrs. Kroc. But the brothers took solace in knowing they eventually would receive a snack—delivered in a strange and furtive manner.

Once the music stopped below, Ray would retreat to the room directly above the kitchen and remove an air grate out of the floor.

"My mother would put a dish of whatever refreshments she was serving on a tray that my father had affixed to an old broom handle," Ray recalled, "then she would hoist it up to us. It was a delightful feeling of adventure because my mother pretended to be sneaking the food away without letting the other adults know."

An executive for a competing software company once quipped that Microsoft was like "the fox that takes you across the river and then eats you." But for most of **Bill Gates**'s life, eating has been an afterthought.

Right after his high school graduation in the early 1970s, Gates was employed as a programmer at a computer facility near Portland, Oregon, frequently working with colleagues through the night. During this period, his nourishment often came from an iconic food of the seventies: Tang. This powdered product was supposed to be stirred into a glass of water to produce a beverage remotely resembling orange juice. But Gates and his comrades would simply scoop the powder raw, directly from the jar to their mouths, "giving their fingertips a perpetual orangish glow," wrote one biographer.

In Microsoft's early days, Gates occasionally skipped meals. Miriam Lubow, the company's receptionist, would often intervene.

"I would buzz him and say, 'Bill, you know, it's way past one-thirty. I think your people would like to have lunch,'" recalled Lubow. "And he'd say 'oh, thank you,' and they would traipse out to lunch. But he was oblivious to that."

Identifying and eating the ideal diet was an obsession of **Henry Ford.** "If people would learn to eat the things they should," he stated, "there would be no need for hospitals."

Ford soon decided that soybeans were it—the common ingredient for a practical, wholesome human diet. At Ford's direction, a team of cooks prepared an all-soybean dinner and served it at the 1933–34 Chicago Century of Progress exposition. The menu included celery stuffed with soybean "cheese," soybean croquettes, and apple pie with a soybean crust.

Ford hoped to make these soybean-based foods the staple of executive lunches at his company. But the reception was less than enthusiastic, which infuriated Ford. One day, he picked up a piece of white bread from a table in the executive lunchroom, rolled it into a ball, and then threw it at a window, which broke from the impact.

"That's what you're putting into your stomachs!" Ford shouted.

On March 5, 2004, a jury found **Martha Stewart** guilty of charges that she obstructed a federal investigation over the insider trading of a stock. Seven months later, Stewart began serving her jail time at a federal prison for women in Alderson, West Virginia. The prison was nicknamed "Camp Cupcake," but the moniker predated Stewart's arrival and reflected the less than harsh conditions—not her baking skills.

Stewart requested a job in the prison kitchen, but she was assigned other duties. Not surprisingly, she was unimpressed by the prison food. Her mother had an explanation for Martha's disapproval: "Most of the food is government surplus; that's why it's so bad."

Martha lost twenty pounds by passing up dinners served in the prison cafeteria. Instead, she used a microwave to cook meals using ingredients such as pasta, kale, and other vegetables from the prison garden that inmates tended.

In 1947, during his only visit to the United States, **Eiji Toyoda** was intrigued by the regular availability of freshly delivered milk in grocery stores. This cow-to-consumer pipeline inspired him to create the horizontal structure he called *kanban*, which he implemented as president of the Toyota Motor Corporation.

Some psychiatrists believed that **Howard Hughes** was afflicted with obsessive-compulsive disorder, a diagnosis that is buttressed by ample evidence, including a note from a member of his personal staff.

"The next time he has dessert," wrote Hughes's staffer, "he wants the cake put on the plate he used before which has the nut crumbs on it and which was put in the refrigerator."

Hughes sometimes used a ruler to confirm that a cook or restaurant had sliced his piece of chocolate cake into a perfect square. If it wasn't a perfect square, Hughes would return the dessert to the kitchen.

In the late 1950s, Hughes forbade kitchen staff from preparing pancakes or French toast for his wife, Jean Peters, in a frying pan in which sausage or bacon had been cooked.

Biographers write that the ex-aviator had "full-blown food fetishes" that included an obsession with the precise thickness of roast beef, the shapes of vegetables, and the precise number of chocolate chips in a batch of cookies.

For a while, Hughes requested dinners that came with a side order of twelve green peas—no more, no less. He ate the peas by threading each one onto his fork. If Hughes had difficulty sliding a pea onto the tines of his fork, he asked a waiter to replace the pea with a new one from the kitchen.

Writing on his blog in 2006, **Donald Trump** complained about "how poorly some people treat waiters and waitresses." He urged readers to "think twice the next time you sit down at a table and get ready to order. And don't forget to leave a big tip."

Although Trump may be generous with his restaurant gratuities, the most widely circulated story about Trump's tipping habits turned out to be an Internet-generated hoax. In 2007, a web blog leaked a bogus tale—facilitated by Trump's own "leave a big tip" suggestion—that the real estate mogul had tipped $10,000 on a total bill of $82.87 at a Santa Monica, California, restaurant.

Although Google cofounder **Larry Page** eventually benefited from his father's 1978 decision to purchase a home computer, he recalled that the computer was so costly that "we couldn't afford to eat well after that." As a billionaire, Page can afford to eat whatever he wants these days.

Milton Hershey believed Americans ate too much meat, and he was determined to help steer them away from a meat-centered diet. The alternative: a chocolate bar that contained cornmeal, carrots, and raisins.

Hershey urged one of his assistants to think of an additional ingredient that would give this chocolate bar the unique appeal required to hook consumers. He became impatient when his assistant failed to offer a solution. "Jesus Christ, boy, you're a college man," he said.

In 1954, **Hugh Hefner** launched *Playboy* to salute what the magazine called "the Good Life." Within its pages, *Playboy* defined "the

Good Life" as young and beautiful women, good things to read, and "good food and drink."

Although the magazine reviewed swank restaurants and featured articles with titles such as "Pleasures of the Oyster," Hefner's tastes—in food, at least—were quite ordinary. Cheeseburgers and fried chicken were among the entrées that Hefner enjoyed during the 1950s. And each day *Playboy*'s founder drank more than twenty bottles of Pepsi-Cola.

In spite of the wealth his oil business provided, **Frank Phillips** didn't think his life was all that different from the lives of ordinary people. In 1935, he told a reporter in Omaha, "Why, I can't eat any more ham and eggs for breakfast than you, and it's a cinch I can't take any more money with me when I die."

In advance of a 1995 trip to China with other business leaders, **Warren Buffett** informed the trip's planners of his dietary needs. "I don't eat Chinese food," he declared.

Yet the Oracle of Omaha was willing to show appropriate respect to his hosts. "If necessary," he added, "serve me rice and I'll move it around on my plate, and I'll go to my room afterward and eat peanuts."

While his cohorts sipped champagne with Chinese officials in Beijing, Buffett drank Cherry Coke. He was served hamburgers and french fries, while the others ate the local fare.

Whether or not he had a large appetite on a given evening, **John D. Rockefeller** was rarely the first person at the dinner table to taste a bite of food. The oil magnate didn't like to eat hot food.

So he would encourage fellow diners to dig in while he talked—
and while his meal cooled to his desired temperature.

Howard Hughes enjoyed eating Swanson's frozen TV dinners, and
his favorite was the turkey entrée. But Hughes had two complaints.
First, it bothered him that white and dark meat were served together. Second, he wished the turkey dinner came with a dessert of
peach cobbler instead of apple cobbler.

Hughes instructed one of his staff to ask Swanson to switch
cobblers. After being turned down, Hughes tried but failed to buy
the frozen-food company.

Before she launched her cosmetics business, **Mary Kay Ash** and
her husband struggled to make ends meet by selling kitchen cookware. The couple would invite potential customers to a dinner
they had prepared using the cookware. The dinner menu never
changed: ham, green beans, sweet potatoes, and a cake.

"Each dinner was fabulous," Ash said, "but it was food we
couldn't afford to buy for ourselves. If there was any food left over
after the demonstration, it became our dinner. If our prospective
customers ate it all, we just didn't eat that night."

In 1992, a butler who was fired by **George Soros** and his wife told
his side of the story to Britain's *Daily Mail* newspaper. One of the
reasons he'd run afoul of the Soroses, the butler contended, was
that he got into a dispute with the family's cook over which spoon
should be used to serve a soufflé.

While visiting **Henry Ford** in Dearborn, Michigan, George Washington Carver mentioned that he regularly ate a lunch of weed sandwiches. The automobile magnate was intrigued. He enthusiastically joined Carver in picking weeds and using them to make sandwiches, which they heartily munched.

CHAPTER 11

Playing with Their Food

Sports stars feasted on more than peanuts and Cracker Jacks

*W*HEN A PROFESSIONAL baseball team traveled for an out-of-town game at the start of the twentieth century, two players typically shared a double bed in the team's hotel. For Hall of Fame pitcher **Rube Waddell,** that roommate was catcher Ossie Schreckengost. And Schreckengost wouldn't sign his own baseball contract with the Philadelphia Athletics unless there was a clause in Waddell's contract forbidding the pitcher from eating animal crackers in bed.

Referring to this bizarre contract provision, Athletics manager Connie Mack said, "I wrote it in there, and the Rube stuck to it."

While **Joe Louis** was in Chicago, his trainer had an unsettling technique for trying to enhance the heavyweight boxer's toughness. Chappie Blackburn would lead Louis to the city's stockyards, where the boxer drank blood fresh from the slaughterhouse.

When Blackburn died in 1942, Louis's blood cocktail died with him. The boxer's next trainer took a similar but less gruesome approach—regularly applying beef or fish brine to Louis's hands and face.

Eating out can be a very cheap affair if one is lucky enough to be at the same restaurant where **Kurt Warner** and his family are dining. Warner, the quarterback who won Most Valuable Player honors for Super Bowl XXXIV, always picks up the bill for one other table and asks the restaurant staff not to tell the party who paid for its meal. Five years before he won that Super Bowl ring, Warner was facilitating eating in a different way—stocking shelves at a grocery store because he had failed to make the squad of any National Football League team.

A beverage comprised of equal portions of lemonade and unsweetened iced tea is called an **"Arnold Palmer,"** named for the professional golfer who loved to drink this concoction as he racked up one tournament win after another.

The first tiff that Palmer had with his wife, Winnie, was over food. Soon after they were married, Palmer asked her to cook a sausage breakfast while he ran a quick errand away from home. He returned to find Winnie crying and the sausage lying cold in the skillet.

Winnie's secret was out. Other than making an icebox cake, she "couldn't cook a lick," Palmer later wrote.

During his Hall of Fame pro basketball career, **Charles Barkley** ate with the same intensity that he shot the basketball. Barkley's appetite was so prodigious that he earned the nickname "the Leaning Tower of Pizza."

Baltimore Colts head coach **Weeb Ewbank** liked to keep his team together on the morning of an away game. He took breakfast orders from all of his players the night before—"Anything you want," Ewbank would tell them—so the requested food would be ready in the morning.

This practice prevailed on the morning of December 28, 1958, as the Colts prepared to play the New York Giants for the National Football League championship.

Art Donovan, a defensive tackle and future Hall of Famer, was a notorious late-night binger who feasted on pizzas, hot dogs, and other high-fat foods. But with the big game only hours away, Donovan chose a surprisingly light breakfast: two bowls of consommé soup. His teammate **Gene "Big Daddy" Lipscomb** ordered a root beer float. The quirky breakfast was followed by Baltimore's 23–17 victory.

Sports Illustrated chose heavyweight boxer **Muhammad Ali** as its "Sportsman of the Century." Yet Ali also made his mark outside the boxing ring during the 1960s as a vocal critic of America's foreign policy and racial attitudes.

Ali sometimes used a sugar-laden example to illustrate what he saw as the subliminal language through which pop culture stigmatized blacks as notorious or dangerous. "Devil's food cake was the dark cake, and angel food cake was the white cake," he wrote.

Tiger Woods made golf history even before he turned pro. By capturing the 1996 U.S. Amateur, Woods became the first golfer to win the tournament in three consecutive years.

During the third of these victories, Woods made it a nightly habit to stop at a McDonald's restaurant in North Plains, Oregon. His growing star status and fondness for McDonald's drew the attention of the restaurant's staff, who posted a photo of Woods and a list of the Big Macs and other foods he had purchased.

Although he enjoyed fast-food meals, financial realities reinforced Woods's eating habits. Before the big bucks from his tournament wins and product endorsements started rolling in, Woods said, "I'm still broke. I guess I'll still be eating at McDonald's for a while longer."

Baseball star **Ted Williams** liked seafood. He believed that Atlantic salmon made for "wonderful eating," and he ate a lot of meals at the oldest surviving restaurant in Boston, the Union Oyster House.

Baseball wasn't the only game Williams liked to play. When he stayed at a certain hotel in Boston, Williams would order an enormous breakfast from room service and—using a stopwatch—track how long it took for his food to be delivered.

When he became the youngest tennis player to win Wimbledon—and did so without losing a set—twenty-year-old **Björn Borg** may have felt there was nothing he couldn't accomplish. Away from the tennis court, however, Borg could feel downright helpless.

He and his wife, Mariana, had a heated quarrel, prompting her to pack her bags and leave Borg to the mercies of his coach, Lennart Bergelin.

"Two hours later," Borg recalled, "Lennart and I realized Mariana wasn't there to cook dinner. We panicked. Lennart volunteered to cook some hamburgers, and in a few minutes the kitchen was filled with smoke."

Ten minutes later, Mariana returned "as if nothing had happened," wrote the Swedish tennis star. "We all laughed like crazy, and Mariana went into the kitchen and cooked us a great dinner."

A resounding victory in football's Super Bowl XXIV left the game's Most Valuable Player, **Joe Montana,** feeling jubilant, yet hungry.

Right after the game, wrote Montana, "everything got so crazy with the celebration and award ceremony and media interviews, my father and I hid in the coaches' dressing room eating cheeseburgers with [teammate] **Ronnie Lott**—while we were still wearing our game pants and undershirts."

Olympic athletes closely monitor their own diets, but champion swimmer **Michael Phelps** had extra help. As his mother explained, "Our family became a team, and [his sisters] paid attention to Michael's eating habits."

During the 2004 Olympic Games in Athens—where he won six gold medals—Michael Phelps built his diet around pizza and pasta.

After Phelps made history at the 2008 Olympics, a British newspaper reported that the "secret" to the swimmer's success was his twelve-thousand-calorie-a-day diet. But Phelps called that calorie count an exaggeration, saying that he consumed between eight thousand and ten thousand calories each day—a range that's still about four times the caloric intake recommended for a typical adult male.

Hall of Fame baseball pitcher **Jim Palmer** was sometimes called "Cakes" because he loved pancakes. But the nickname that hockey star **Brett Hull** earned early in his career may have misled fans. Hull, who scored more than fifty goals in five straight seasons, was dubbed "Pickle" because of his hefty build—not because he had a special affection for pickled cucumbers.

The winning driver of the Indianapolis 500 traditionally celebrates victory by drinking milk. But it was buttermilk—not regular milk—that was guzzled by **Louis Meyer,** the three-time winner who started this tradition in 1936.

In 1964, winning driver **A. J. Foyt** nearly broke with the milk-drinking custom. That year Foyt, who won the Indy 500 four times during his career, drove into Victory Lane at the racetrack and was handed a bottle of milk. He initially pushed it away. "I don't want that," said Foyt. "I want water." Moments later, he changed his mind, grabbed the milk bottle, and took a swig.

When tennis star **Martina Navratilova** defected from Czechoslovakia to the United States in 1975, she was tempted by American fast food and reportedly gained twenty-five pounds in the first month.

But she seemed to change diets almost as often as she changed rackets. At first, she was a meat eater, but then she shunned red meat. Later, she deleted chicken from her diet, too. Even later, she stopped eating dairy products.

Ken Griffey Jr. hit his six hundredth home run in 2008. But nineteen years before Griffey drove that ball over the outfield wall, a man named Mike Cramer created and marketed a milk chocolate bar named for the slugger. The candy bar initially sold well, but Griffey could do only so much to contribute to sales; he's allergic to chocolate.

Romanian gymnast **Nadia Comăneci,** who stunned the world in 1976 by earning the first score of 10.0 in modern Olympic gymnastics history, sometimes smelled like the kitchen in a trattoria.

In the weeks before a gymnastics competition, Romanian coach Béla Károlyi ordered his gymnasts to consume raw garlic each day, believing that it would prevent them from falling ill.

"We hated garlic because when we worked out and sweat, we smelled like hell," Comăneci said.

Coaches from other countries learned of the Romanians' garlic regimen and instructed their gymnasts to follow suit.

"Pretty soon, every gymnast in Europe was eating raw garlic," said Comăneci. "I remember saying to myself, '*It's not the garlic, people, it's the training!*' We simply worked harder."

When he was fourteen years old, tennis phenom-to-be **Roger Federer** boarded with the Christinet family, who lived near the Swiss tennis school that he attended. Federer ate no meat and unnerved his surrogate mother, Cornelia Christinet, by his vast consumption of breakfast cereal.

"I thought it wasn't very healthy," she said, "but I let him do it and his parents knew about it."

In the year before he won college football's Heisman Trophy, University of Georgia running back **Herschel Walker** was preparing to play in the 1982 Sugar Bowl game when a reporter asked him to name his favorite candy bar. Walker gave the first answer that came to mind: "Snickers."

When he returned to college for the next semester, Walker walked to his dormitory room one day and discovered a large box in front of his door.

"It was a box filled with a dozen cases of Snickers bars," he said. "Now I don't know if the people at M&M Mars who make them sent me the box or if some fan who read that interview stepped up and did it; all I know is that I had more Snickers bars than I'd ever eaten in my whole life."

In the months that followed, Walker built his diet around Snickers. "I don't recommend the Snickers bar diet to anyone, but it is possible to live off them and to compete at a high level while doing it."

When he and his Pittsburgh Pirates teammates made road trips to New York in the 1950s, **Roberto Clemente** often ate at a Puerto Rican restaurant—the rice, beans, fried bananas, and steaks served there reminded the ballplayer of his youth on the island.

One day during a 1969 road trip in San Diego, Clemente went looking for food and found trouble instead. As he left a restaurant with a box of take-out fried chicken, a car with four men in it suddenly pulled up beside the future Hall of Famer. One of them pointed a gun at Clemente and ordered him into the vehicle.

The men drove Clemente to an isolated part of San Diego and ordered him to strip down to his underwear. They took his wallet and All-Star game ring. Clemente pleaded with the men not to kill him, and he told them who he was.

The bandits had a change of heart and gave Clemente back his wallet, ring, and clothes, then let him out of the car and drove away. Only moments later, however, Clemente heard the car returning at a high speed. He feared the men might have decided to kill him after all. But they were only returning his box of chicken.

Before he achieved soccer stardom, a youthful **Pelé** tried to earn money by selling meat pies at a rail station in his native Brazil. But Pelé—born with the name Edison Arantes do Nascimento—had little success.

The unsold pies that he returned to Dona Filomena, the woman who made them, usually could not be reconciled with the money he'd collected. This typically created a confrontation as Filomena accused Pelé of eating pies for which he didn't pay. "It was a poor choice of jobs for a growing boy," he admitted.

Kevin Garnett has led the National Basketball Association in defensive rebounds five times. But when the star tried to rebound from an ankle injury during the 1999–2000 season, his mother suggested a remedy: tomato soup. Garnett was skeptical. "I'm like, 'Ma, how is that going to help?'" he said. "But then you know what I did, right?" He took her advice and ate the soup.

Golfer **Jack Nicklaus** won more than seventy tournaments on the pro tour. Along the way, he was prone to high-fat eating binges. During the 1962 Masters tournament, Nicklaus dined one evening with fellow golfer **"Chi-Chi" Rodriguez.** Rodriguez recalled what happened when he cut the fat off of his steak.

" 'What are you doing?' Jack asked. 'That's the best part.' I gave him the portion I'd cut off and he ate it," Rodriguez said.

In 1959, Nicklaus played as an amateur in his first Masters. He and fellow amateur Phil Rodgers may have missed a few fairways, but they didn't miss a meal.

Taking advantage of a policy that allowed players to simply "sign" for their meals, Nicklaus and Rodgers devoured steaks and shrimp cocktails nightly until tournament officials stepped in. "They changed the rules on us," said Rodgers. "I guess ordering chateaubriand for two did the trick."

When he broke major league baseball's color barrier in 1947, **Jackie Robinson** endured a torrent of racist abuse. Some ballpark Neanderthals even threw chunks of watermelon at him.

But Robinson's fans also showered him with meals, extending invitations to public banquets and private dinners to satisfy his hearty appetite. "His attack on a wedge of apple pie, topped with two scoops of vanilla ice cream, was an exercise in passion," one baseball writer noted.

"Jackie's admirers fed him until he was fat and futile," wrote columnist Carl Rowan.

Entering the 1948 season, Robinson's weight had ballooned so much that his new manager, Leo Durocher, complained that "he looks like a black tub of lard."

When ESPN listed the best North American athletes of the last century, track and golf star **Babe Didrikson Zaharias** was the only female in the top ten. Zaharias took a simple approach to her diet.

"I eat anything I want, except very greasy foods and gravy," she said. "I just pass the gravy. That's just hot grease anyway, with some flour or water in it."

True to her Scandinavian heritage, Zaharias liked Swedish meatballs—presumably without any gravy. But there were at least two things she loved consuming more than meatballs: onion sandwiches and strawberry soda.

Early in his career, future baseball Hall of Famer **Joe DiMaggio** received an endorsement deal with Huskies Cereal. Executives at Quaker Oats, which produced the cereal, must have bristled when DiMaggio was asked on a national radio show what he ate in the morning, and he answered: "A heaping bowlful of Wheaties!"

One morning in 1965, New York Jets quarterback **Joe Namath** left his home with a pair of sunglasses, an apple, and a saltshaker. He hailed a taxi and asked to be driven to an army induction center for a physical exam. (The military's subsequent announcement that Namath was unfit for service raised public suspicions of preferential treatment.)

Namath emerged from the taxi with the apple in his mouth. When someone asked the Jets rookie why he carried a saltshaker, Namath replied that he used it to salt his apple. "I always eat apples that way," he said.

St. Louis Cardinals pitcher **Dizzy Dean** turned heads and raised eyebrows—both for the thirty games he won in 1934 and for his eccentric behavior.

During sultry summer days, Dean sometimes amused fans by frying eggs atop the dugout roof. On one steamy afternoon, he shouted sarcastically for a ballpark vendor to bring him a hot chocolate.

Joining a baseball team in the cosmopolitan city of St. Louis did not easily break Dean of the eating habits that reflected his rural, sharecropper roots. Corn bread and beans anchored his diet during his early years in baseball. Dean ate four or five meals a day, and they were usually large.

In 1934, he was fined for failing to show up for an exhibition game in Detroit. Manager Frank Frisch later learned that Dean had been at a friend's cookout while his teammates were traveling north by train.

"While we were on our way to Detroit," Frisch wrote, "Dizzy and [his brother] were gnawing on fried chicken, enjoying it no end, and no doubt laughing heartily over the much better time they were having."

The husband of **Margaret Court,** the Australian tennis star who swept all four women's Grand Slam singles titles in 1970, had plenty of reasons to brag about her. Barry Court once told a reporter, "Margaret makes a great roast lamb, you know."

Baseball star **Pete Rose** was as aggressive at a restaurant as he was on the ballfield. Before a waiter could place a menu on the table, the all-time hits leader typically barked his order: "Gimme a steak, medium rare, baked potato, salad, iced tea." Regardless of who was dining with him—even a woman—Rose would order first.

After **Gabriele Schöpe** won the gold medal in a women's diving event at the 1960 Olympic Games, a German pastry chef who worked at the Olympic village made a rum cake for her. But Schöpe and her roommate had to eat the cake behind the closed door of their room to avoid a stern lecture. Their trainer frowned on both the alcohol and high-calorie desserts.

Two-time Olympic medal winner **John C. Thomas** believed he'd discovered a reliable way to prevent an upset stomach right before a track competition: The American high jumper ate baby-food fruit out of a jar.

When Hall of Fame basketball star **Michael Jordan** said that he and Chicago Bulls teammate Scottie Pippen engaged in "ham and egging," he wasn't describing what they ate for breakfast. To Jordan, the phrase meant that one of them had played well early in the game, and then the other had performed superbly later in the contest.

Bill Rodgers won the Boston and New York City marathons four times each, earning the nickname "King of the Roads." His eating habits could have produced another nickname: King of the Junk Food.

"What struck me most about Bill," said fellow runner Pablo Vigil, "was that he would stop at every corner bakery and buy the gooiest pastries he could find, the kind with green frosting on them."

The quality and variety of **Pelé**'s food improved greatly when the fifteen-year-old joined a soccer team in the Brazilian city of Santos.

"Foods we had rarely been able to afford in our house in Bauru became common," said Pelé. He was able to eat chicken and other meat as often as he wanted, as opposed to the starchy dishes on which most of Brazil's poor subsisted.

Yet his appetite for meat had its limits. While playing in Egypt, he and his fellow Brazilian players were served a regional specialty for dinner. "Well," wrote Pelé, "anyone who has ever smelled a camel for the first time can hardly get excited about eating anything that smells like that."

Two weeks before his fights, boxer **Joe Louis** vanquished fat from his diet, including the bacon he normally loved. It must have been tough for Louis to get pork bellies off his mind during his first professional fight—it occurred at Bacon's Arena in Chicago.

In 1904, the year before he began playing baseball for the Detroit Tigers, **Ty Cobb** was patrolling center field for a minor league team in Augusta, Georgia. During one game, a base runner scored because Cobb was munching on popcorn as a ball flew toward him.

Soon after the game, Augusta manager George Leidy told the young player that he had a bright career ahead of him if "you don't focus all your attention on popcorn."

Three years later, it was Cobb's Detroit teammate "Germany" Schaefer who raised eyebrows by eating popcorn on the field during a game. Unlike Cobb, Schaefer was nibbling on popcorn for deliberate spectacle—his way of showing that he didn't take the Tigers' opponents seriously.

Australian tennis star **John Newcombe** captured the U.S. Open title twice, but he lost the 1966 U.S. Open final. According to Billie Jean King, Aussie tennis fans "just didn't tolerate [runners-up], even when it came to John Newcombe." This became evident when Newcombe hosted a large party in Australia.

As guests helped themselves to chicken from a silver dish, they noticed that the dish had been inscribed. "What the hell is this, mate?" someone asked Newcombe. The tennis star said it was the silver dish he received as runner-up to the 1966 U.S. Open champ.

Apparently, that didn't sit well with a few guests who made derisive comments and then carried the silver dish outside, urinated on it, and left it in some bushes.

When nineteen-year-old **Babe Ruth** joined the Boston Red Sox, teammate Harry Hooper determined that there were two important differences between Ruth and other young ballplayers: "He could eat more than anyone else, and he could hit a ball farther."

When stacks of sandwiches or a platter of hot dogs were placed before Ruth, they quickly disappeared, usually washed down by several bottles of soda. Ruth loved large steaks, and he preferred them uncooked with ample amounts of hot sauce on the side. "He ate every day like a man released from prison," noted one Ruth biographer.

Ruth's snacking during ball games prompted Red Sox manager Bill Carrigan to ban food in the dugout.

After a ball game, Ruth's voracious appetite resumed its rampage. According to Ty Cobb, it wasn't unusual for Ruth to "send out for five or six club sandwiches—those huge triple-deckers with all the fixings—and then sit in bed and polish them off before going to sleep."

Sugar Ray Robinson won the middleweight boxing title five times from 1951 to 1960, and his reputation for arrogance extended beyond the boxing ring.

One day he asked his second wife, Edna Mae, to cook him

lunch. Although she had filed for legal separation, Edna Mae was willing to prepare the meal—until she realized the lunch was intended for Robinson and his girlfriend.

Fruit was the mainstay of **Lou Gehrig**'s diet. "It is my notion," said the Yankee slugger, "that the most important part of my diet is the fruit and fruit juices that I eat or drink morning or night." When it came to fruit, he added, "I am practically an addict."

South African–born golfer **Gary Player** won nine major tournaments on the Professional Golf Association tour. As tournament locations changed, so did the high-energy foods that Player kept close at hand.

During one stage of his career, raisins were his favorite energy snack. During another period, he would sip honey from a jar kept in his golf bag. And there was the banana phase.

When rain began to fall during one tournament, Player asked caddie Wally Armstrong to retrieve his rain slicker from a pocket in the golf bag. Armstrong reached in the pocket and discovered a few bananas he had stuffed in there days earlier. "It was like black tar," said Armstrong. The rotten bananas had congealed onto Player's slicker. After that round of golf, Player fired Armstrong.

Satchel Paige offered nuggets of advice to anyone who would listen. "Avoid fried meats, which angry up the blood," the legendary pitcher urged. He instructed others that "if your stomach disputes you, lie down and pacify it with cool thoughts."

If "you are what you eat," then baseball star **Wade Boggs** would have grown feathers. Boggs collected more than three thousand hits during his impressive baseball career, and he ate a lot of chicken along the way.

His poultry-centered diet reflected Boggs's superstition that eating chicken several hours before a game contributed to his on-the-field success. It was a routine that Boggs stuck to for nearly all of his eighteen years in the major leagues.

"I noticed that I always seemed to hit best after [eating] chicken," said Boggs. "So I started having [my wife] Debbie fix it every day."

Boggs liked his pregame chicken meal prepared in a variety of ways, but he insisted on having lemon chicken once a week after he ate the dish and then stroked seven hits in a doubleheader. The recipe for lemon chicken can be found in *Fowl Tips,* the chicken cookbook that Boggs and his wife wrote in the 1980s.

As a teenager in England, **David Beckham** spent a lot of time on the soccer field, preparing himself for stardom. But on Sunday mornings, the young Beckham was typically in the kitchen of his family's home, making breakfast for his parents—"cooking was something I'd always enjoyed," Beckham explained.

He also prepared his own dinner, and the menu never changed. "When Mum and Dad came up to the new house and I cooked for them in my own home for the first time, I don't think they were all that surprised at what I'd made: chicken stir-fry," said Beckham.

Hall of Fame baseball pitcher **Walter Johnson** reportedly consumed about a quart of ice cream per day.

The football career of Hall of Famer **Jim Parker** spanned eleven years with the Baltimore Colts, starting in 1957. Although hydration is now viewed as essential during games and practices, Baltimore head coach **Weeb Ewbank** had a different take back then. Ewbank considered it a sign of weakness for a player to take a drink of water during summer training camp—even when the heat and humidity were intense.

One day during a sweltering summer practice, Parker wanted a beverage so badly that he defied Ewbank's rule against hydration. The offensive lineman's son brought him a cup of lemonade, and Ewbank fined Parker for drinking it.

Years later, Parker proudly showed an author a photograph taken on that day. "That's me with a five-hundred-dollar lemonade," Parker said.

In the early 1930s, **Ben Hogan** was struggling to make his living as a golfer. His meager finances forced him to take an unusual step to satisfy his hunger: picking oranges off trees that lined the fairways of California golf courses.

Benny Parsons won both the Winston Cup and Daytona 500, but auto racing was only one of his loves. Parsons was so fond of eating and cooking that he earned the moniker "Buffet Benny" and coauthored a cookbook.

As a broadcaster for NASCAR, Parsons produced television segments about the food sold at various racetracks.

When he walked through the spectators' stands to reach the broadcast booth, racetrack fans would sometimes hand him cookies or cake. Fellow broadcaster Allen Bestwick remembered a phrase he frequently heard from Parsons. " 'Wanna stop and get a bite?' was not a question," said Bestwick.

Baseball star **Ty Cobb** ate two meals a day, skipping lunch. "It's easy to adjust to and surely makes you enjoy your dinner a lot more," said Cobb.

Gary Stevens's fame as a thoroughbred racing jockey required him to constantly monitor and restrict his diet. When Stevens ate a heavy meal, he sometimes forced himself to throw up. But Mister Frisky, the horse that Stevens rode to victory in the 1990 Santa Anita Derby, did not share his rider's anxiety about eating.

"This horse was a pig," Stevens wrote. "A garbage collector. He would eat anything that happened to be in front of him."

At one point, the California Racing Board reported that Mister Frisky had tested positive for barbiturates. It took a while for racing officials to determine that the "drug" was really a poppy seed bagel that the horse had eaten.

If Hall of Fame quarterback **John Elway** had to order the last meal of his life, it would be a concoction he calls "hamburger soup." It's a vegetable soup with ground beef, garlic, and green beans.

When he went out for dinner and drinks with his fellow New York Yankees, **Joe DiMaggio** insisted on picking up the check. If they tried to pay their share, DiMaggio would slap their hands away. "When you eat with the Dago," he would say, "the Dago pays."

Throughout his Hall of Fame coaching career, Boston Celtics head coach **Red Auerbach** regularly ate Chinese food after his team's basketball games. He would phone ahead, pick up the food on his way back to the team's hotel, and eat it in his room. Auerbach always ordered his Chinese food to be steamed, not fried.

Bobby Knight was another basketball coach who adored Chinese food. By his own admission, the former college basketball coach probably ate a thousand such meals from 1971—his first season as head coach at Indiana University—to 2002. The number of Chinese meals that he ate outnumbered the 902 victories in his coaching career.

As he concluded his first-ever Chinese meal, Knight opened and read the message in his fortune cookie. For the next thirty years, he never read another fortune.

That cookie's message read: "You will find success, but it will be slow in coming."

The next season, Knight's Indiana Hoosiers won the Big Ten conference title. Four seasons after that, Indiana won the NCAA championship.

Babe Ruth met his first wife, Helen Woodford, over breakfast. She waited tables at Landers' Coffee Shop, where Ruth frequently ate his morning meal in Boston.

In 1958, **Pelé** became the youngest soccer player ever to score a goal in a World Cup match. He was seventeen. When Pelé and the rest of the Brazilian team returned home from Sweden with the World Cup trophy, there was little time to rest or eat because of the rigorous schedule of parades and appearances.

Pelé described the Brazilian team as "worn out, half-starved, ready to trade our medals for a sandwich." Ushered from one city to the next, the players eventually drew the line. They refused to continue the appearances until their stomachs were placated. Sandwiches were quickly provided for Pelé and the other players.

In the book *The Soul of a Butterfly,* Hana Ali praised her father, **Muhammad Ali,** because he showered her "with affection and love" and—among other things—because he "helped me eat my vegetables, so I could have dessert."

In November 1999, a rare liver disease claimed the life of football great **Walter Payton.** After his illness was diagnosed, Payton made a strange request to his former Chicago Bears teammate, Matt Suhey: Purchase a Zagat's restaurant guide for Chicago.

"[Payton] said, 'You know, I haven't eaten in that many restaurants in Chicago,'" Suhey remembered. Payton's goal was for them to identify the city's top ten restaurants and eat a meal at each of them before Payton died.

"We picked out a few, but never got to finish the project," said Suhey. "All he wanted to do was go eat an appetizer, look at the atmosphere, check it out, look around."

Anyone who placed a fork and spoon on a dining table for **Shoe-less Joe Jackson** quickly learned that these utensils were rarely employed by the baseball star. Jackson primarily used his knife and his hands.

Jackson's small-town Southern background gave his teammates some good ideas for pranks. One time they tricked Jackson into drinking from the finger bowl after dinner.

Carl Lewis won four consecutive Olympic gold medals in the long jump, but one of his greatest leaps was dietary.

In 1990, halfway through his Olympic career, Lewis adopted a vegan diet. "I was competing in Europe," he recalled, "and ate a meal of Spanish sausage on a Saturday and on the following Monday started eating vegan."

Lewis wrote the introduction to *The Complete Vegan Kitchen*, a cookbook published in 2007.

In 1939, **Lou Gehrig** found his energy and performance on the baseball field deteriorating. The Yankees' star was perplexed and turned to physicians for answers.

One of them, Dr. Israel Wechsler, suspected a vitamin E deficiency might be the culprit. Wechsler advised the Yankees' star to start eating a diet centered on lettuce, kale, whole wheat bread, egg yolks, bananas, and other fresh, unprocessed foods. This treatment and other suggestions did nothing to counter the effects of amyotrophic lateral sclerosis—now known as Lou Gehrig's disease. He died on June 2, 1941.

Boston Celtics head coach **Red Auerbach** imposed a food rule that governed his basketball team: no pancakes could be eaten on the day of a game. The coach believed that pancakes lingered in the stomach and made a player lethargic on the court.

Auerbach once caught Sam Jones taking a bite of pancakes at International House of Pancakes and told the player he was fined.

"This isn't game day," Jones protested. "We just played." But Auerbach stood his ground. "It's one a.m.," he replied. "We're playing at eight o'clock *tonight*."

Both **Ty Cobb** and Coca-Cola were born in the state of Georgia in 1886, and the ballplayer was connected with the soft drink in other ways as well. Cobb appeared in several advertisements for Coke, and he amassed a fortune in Coca-Cola's common stock. The loyalty he felt for his home-state beverage was intense.

John McCallum, a journalist who took a road trip with Cobb after the star had retired, recalled one particular stop at a gas station. Cobb used a nickel to buy a bottle of Coke. "Just to be different," said McCallum, "I dropped my coin into the 7-Up machine. That was a mistake." Cobb threw a fit.

The experience taught McCallum a lesson: "Never drink a 7-Up in the company of a person who owns 20,000 shares of stock in Coca-Cola!"

Tacos tame Tiger's temper.

In 1992, after playing one of his worst rounds of golf on the amateur circuit, **Tiger Woods** stormed off the course. Asked later how long it took him to get over his anger, Woods replied, "Dinner." He had eaten ten tacos.

Jim Thorpe is the only Olympic athlete to win gold medals in both the decathlon and pentathlon. His athletic travels took him to fine restaurants in many major cities. Yet his favorite dishes remained the fried squirrel, baking powder biscuits, and other country fare that his mother prepared during his youth in rural Oklahoma.

English jockey **Lester Piggott,** the only nine-time winner of the Epsom Derby, grew up during World War II, when sweets were strictly rationed. The deprivations of his youth meant Piggott the adult was not severely tempted by dessert foods, with one exception: ice cream.

"Any ice cream stall near the exit gate of a racecourse acted on him like a magnet," wrote one biographer, "and on a hot day, tired after riding, he couldn't resist this appeal."

Piggott's description was terser. "Mad for it," said the jockey, who added, "American ice cream is best. They have forty-two varieties in those Howard Johnson restaurants."

A foot injury and her father's rapidly declining health drove tennis star **Monica Seles** to eating binges. She recalled waiting "anxiously by the toaster as my frosted Pop-Tarts turned a perfect golden brown" and watching television "armed with bags of chocolate-covered pretzels." She could limit calories during the day, but her self-control disappeared late at night. "I turned into a food vampire," she noted. Seles began to turn the corner only after hiring a "food warden" who supervised all of her meals and briefly moved into a guest room right next to Seles's kitchen.

When eight-time batting champion **Honus Wagner** wasn't at the ballpark, the Pittsburgh Pirates star was often fishing. While on the road, Wagner brought notes on good fishing sites that weren't too far from the team's hotel. If he caught a fish, he would often ask a hotel cook to prepare it for dinner.

As he boarded a Europe-bound ship with America's Olympic athletes in 1936, U.S. Olympic Committee president Avery Brundage was probably worried. Brundage remembered what had happened to U.S. athletes on a similar transatlantic journey to the 1912 Olympics in Stockholm.

"Exposure to the unlimited menus on shipboard was fatal to some," he noted, "and several hopes of Olympic victory foundered at the bounteous dinner table."

U.S. track competitor **Jesse Owens**'s bout of seasickness during the 1936 journey may have curbed any temptations to overeat. Owens was pleased with the food in the host city of Berlin. There were "steaks and plenty of it . . . bacon, eggs, ham" and other foods to satisfy Owens's hunger pangs.

Owens captured four gold medals that year, but he bristled at the later criticism of his endorsement deals. "I had four gold medals," he said, "but you can't eat four gold medals."

For the first five years of his career with the New York Yankees, **Babe Ruth** ate like a starving man, but his gluttony appeared to have no ill effect on his hitting. During these years, Ruth was virtually unstoppable. By 1925, however, he was on the verge of eating his way out of baseball.

That spring, Ruth tried but failed to lose weight during the Yankees' preseason training in Florida. In early April, before the regular season began, Ruth and his teammates boarded a train headed to New York. En route, Ruth fainted inside a train station.

Dr. Charles Jordan diagnosed Ruth with influenza and indigestion, and the doctor made it clear that the slugger's eating habits threatened his career.

"All I can say is that unless somebody is appointed to act as guardian over him at the dining table, he won't be a baseball player very long," said Jordan.

Ruth was defensive. "Every time anything happens to a fellow they say he's overeating," he complained.

To regain his health for the 1926 season, Ruth entered an intensive exercise and nutrition program run by former boxer Artie McGovern.

McGovern eliminated red meat, sweets, and snacks from Ruth's diet. His new breakfast consisted of poached eggs and a single slice of toast. Lunch was a salad. Ruth's meals came without beverages because McGovern wanted to make sure Ruth chewed his food throughly, instead of washing it down.

A New York tabloid published Ruth's nine goals for the upcoming season, and one of them was: "To watch his diet carefully." Six weeks after entering McGovern's program, Ruth had lost forty-four pounds. The Babe enjoyed a successful season in 1926, helping the Yankees reach the World Series, in which Ruth hit a record four home runs.

During baseball's spring training season, Seattle Mariners manager Lou Piniella once made a bet with star slugger **Ken Griffey Jr.**

"Hey, Junior, I bet you a steak dinner you can't hit one of the next three pitches out of the park," said Piniella. Griffey took the bet but lost.

Did he know that Piniella had a prior conversation with the pitcher, who agreed to throw three pitches to Griffey that were virtually unhittable? It's unclear whether Griffey knew, but that could explain why Griffey paid off his bet by having a live—and perturbed—steer brought into Piniella's office.

In the sport of thoroughbred racing, jockeys must control their weight—a challenge that can encourage strange behavior. Consider the transcontinental flight that all-time great **Laffit Pincay Jr.** took in 1982.

Pincay refused the dinner brought to him by a flight attendant. Instead, the Panamanian-born jockey accepted a bag of peanuts. He opened the bag and took out a single peanut. At first, he ate half the peanut. Several hours later, Pincay had dessert: the other half of the peanut.

CHAPTER 12

Delicious Discoveries

Explorers plunged into uncharted meals

By the time of **Christopher Columbus**'s fourth visit to the New World, he was wearing out his welcome. Anchored in Jamaica, he and his men relied on food from the natives that seemed to grow ever more meager, as if the hosts were sending them a message to go home.

Columbus knew from his almanac that a lunar eclipse was drawing near, and he devised a devious plan. He told the natives that his god would punish them for withholding food. The first action would be to blot out the moon. Some of them scoffed, until a shadow fell over the moon and the frightened natives desperately begged for forgiveness.

The Jamaicans got their moon, and Columbus got his dinner.

Polynesian explorer **Hawaii-Loa** sailed twenty-four hundred miles to discover the Hawaiian islands around the fifth century, living on taro root during the arduous voyage. Once they had settled in Hawaii, the Polynesians cultivated taro and used it to make the islands' signature dish, poi.

In 1928, **Amelia Earhart** became the first woman to fly across the Atlantic. She was listed as the pilot, but she readily admitted that her two male crew members were at the controls. The two weeks before the crossing, as they waited in Newfoundland for decent weather, proved agonizing—not the least because they were served rabbit and mutton repeatedly. When they finally took off, they carried coffee, mineral water, oranges, egg sandwiches, chocolate, oatmeal cookies, malted milk tablets, and pemmican, a dried meat product. During their more than twenty hours in flight, the men ate sandwiches while Amelia dined on three oranges and about a half-dozen malted milk tablets. She tasted the pemmican, but didn't like it.

Four years later, Earhart's repeat crossing was much more appetizing. For one thing, she flew alone, defying her critics. She drank chicken soup from a thermos and tomato juice from a tin can, which she opened with an ice pick.

Another high point came in 1935, when Earhart made the first solo flight by anyone—man or woman—from Hawaii to California. She packed tomato juice, chocolate, water, a thermos of hot chocolate, and more malted milk tablets. The wife of a naval radio expert contributed a picnic lunch. As Earhart flew through a starry night, she drank "the most interesting cup of hot chocolate I have ever had," as she later wrote. Before landing in California, she sipped tomato juice and ate a hard-boiled egg.

John Glenn was the first American to eat in space. On a five-hour orbit of the Earth in 1962, he sucked pureed applesauce from a toothpaste-like tube. Before Glenn ate, there was suspense over whether human beings could swallow properly amid weightlessness, but Glenn broke that barrier.

More than three decades later, a seventy-seven-year-old Glenn returned to space aboard the shuttle *Discovery*, and the fare was more filling. His menu included shrimp cocktail, macaroni and cheese, peanut butter and jelly, tortillas, beef with barbecue sauce, rice with butter, dried apricots, banana pudding, apple cider, scrambled eggs, oatmeal with raisins, and candy-coated peanuts. Like other senior citizens concerned about proper digestion, Glenn also chewed on Metamucil wafers.

Captain James Cook, Britain's greatest explorer of the Pacific, flirted with death near New Caledonia in 1774 when he and two other crew members ate blowfish, which contains a poison that can paralyze and kill the diner.

Cook and his colleagues were lucky. They took only a taste and survived the scare.

In his memoir, Cook wrote: "About 3 or 4 o'clock in the morning we were seized with extraordinary weakness in all our limbs attended with a numbness or sensation like to that caused by exposing one's hands or feet to a fire after having been pinched much by frost, I had almost lost the sense of feeling nor could I distinguish between light and heavy bodies, a quart pot full of water and a feather was the same in my hand. We each of us took a vomit and after that a sweat which gave great relief."

Afterward, Cook wrote, they discovered that "one of the pigs which had eaten the entrails was found dead."

Zheng He, a Muslim eunuch who became China's greatest explorer, led a series of fifteenth-century ocean voyages that dwarfed Western expeditions of the time. With more than three hundred ships and about twenty-seven thousand crew members, Zheng He had to maintain careful supplies. His tanker ships carried water, and his food supply ships were like farms, with vegetables growing in large tubs of dirt.

The Chinese explorer seemed less fascinated by exotic food than some Western mariners. While he brought back food items such as crabapples, spices, and crop seeds, his most celebrated prize was a live giraffe that some Chinese thought was the mythical qilin, or unicorn.

Six years before aviator **Charles Lindbergh** would achieve international fame with his flight across the Atlantic, the motorcyclist Lindbergh conducted a rehearsal that required just as much concentration and self-discipline. Lindbergh rode his motorcycle from Kentucky to Florida in eight days, drinking quarts of milk at intervals but not eating a real meal until the third day, when he stopped to munch on an egg sandwich.

As the Lewis and Clark expedition explored the western wilderness of North America, the Shoshone guide **Sacagawea** helped find edible plants. She was especially fond of wapato root, which tasted similar to potato when cooked. Others in the expedition also enjoyed the root, but they rejected her advice to camp for the 1805–6 winter where wapato was readily available. They ended up short of food and had to trade with natives for wapato.

Other native vegetation was not so well received. When Sacagawea prepared the edible bulbs of the camas plant, **William**

Clark complained: "This root is palatable but disagrees with us in every shape we have used it. The natives are extremely fond of this root and present [it] to their visitors as a great treat." He recalled that when the Nez Perce tribe shared camas root with the explorers, his hungry men "made so free a use of this root it made them all sick for several days after."

The space shuttle *Columbia* disintegrated upon reentry in 2001, killing all seven crew members. One of those aboard was **Ilan Ramon,** Israel's first man in space, who had arranged for NASA to include kosher food on the flight. Ramon described himself as a secular Jew, and he ate both kosher and nonkosher food. His first meal in space was kosher chicken and noodles, green beans with mushrooms, crackers, strawberries, trail mix, a brownie, and orange juice.

One of the most famous stories of seafaring, the mutiny on the *Bounty,* happened because of breadfruit—a fruit that, when cooked, has a texture and smell similar to freshly baked bread.

The British ship, captained by **William Bligh,** was dispatched to Tahiti in 1787 to fetch breadfruit trees to the West Indies to grow cheap food for slaves. Bligh's strict rules and the sensual pleasures of the South Pacific created a discipline problem among the crew. Even the breadfruit itself raised tensions: Sailors suspected that the plants were getting more fresh water than *they* got.

Dissidents led by **Lieutenant Fletcher Christian** mutinied, herding Bligh and his loyalists into a small boat and setting them adrift.

When Bligh reached civilization, he was given another ship, the *Providence,* and made good on his original mission, bringing breadfruit to Jamaica and St. Vincent in the West Indies. For the first half century, breadfruit got a poor reception. Rejected by slaves, it was fed to pigs. But it is now a versatile and popular food in the Caribbean, used in salads, puddings, flour, and wines.

On the *Gemini 3* mission in 1965, astronaut **John Young** smuggled a corned beef sandwich in his spacesuit. Once in orbit, he offered the sandwich to fellow astronaut **Gus Grissom,** who happily accepted. Others were not so pleased. Technicians worried that floating bits of sandwich debris would foul equipment, endangering the mission and the crew. Later, a National Aeronautics and Space Administration official appeared at a congressional hearing and promised to "prevent the recurrence of corned beef sandwiches on future flights."

The incident highlighted NASA's philosophical clash—happy-go-lucky flyboys versus serious-minded scientists. But the no-nonsense crowd soon gained the upper hand as it became apparent that the margin for error was frighteningly thin. Less than two years after the corned beef sandwich incident, Grissom died with two others in a training accident aboard the *Apollo I* command module.

When **Christopher Columbus** landed in the New World in 1492, he sent two members of his party into Cuba's interior to seek treasure. The pair failed to find gold—in a literal sense at least. They returned with "a sort of grain . . . which was well tasted, bak'd, dry'd, and made into flour," according to an early history. The natives called the grain maize, but the Europeans later labeled it "Indian corn."

Columbus brought maize back to Spain, and it was planted in the country's south. Historians once believed that corn spread through Europe from that planting. But recent genetic studies indicate that it's more likely that the mother strain was brought to Europe a few decades later by Italian explorer **Giovanni da Verrazzano,** who traveled along the East Coast of North America.

Not only were **Christopher Columbus** and his fellow explorers the first Europeans to eat maize, but they also got early samples of other foods, such as chile peppers, pineapples, and plantains.

Diego Cheka, a physician traveling with Columbus, described "a tree whose leaf has the finest smell of cloves that I have ever met with." It was allspice.

They also ran into what Cheka called "a sort of turnip"—sweet potato.

Columbus described how the Indians "sow little shoots, from which small roots grow that look like carrots. They serve this as bread, by grating and kneading it, then baking it in the fire." The crop was cassava. Columbus was guest of honor at a dinner hosted by the king of Hispaniola featuring two or three types of cassava, plus cassava bread, shrimp, and game.

British explorer **James Cook** ordered the flogging of crewmen who refused to eat what they were served. When they rebelled at helpings of walrus, he rebuked them for failing to embrace "novelty" in dining. Cook considered the walrus to be "marine beef," with fat as "sweet as marrow." But one crew member wrote that the walrus meat was "too rank both in smell and taste as to make use of except with plenty of pepper and salt, and these two articles were very scarce."

When flogging proved ineffective, Cook ended up restoring his crew's ration of "salt meat," which was beef or pork boiled and cured with salt.

Sixteenth-century Italian explorer **Amerigo Vespucci** was described as a "pickle-dealer" by American writer Ralph Waldo Emerson, who was offended that his homeland was named for Vespucci instead of Christopher Columbus. But the naming of the Americas wasn't Vespucci's idea, and he was an aristocratic merchant of naval supplies—no mere pickle dealer.

After his travels, Vespucci wrote vivid chronicles about the dining habits of American natives: "Their mode of life is most barbarous; they do not eat at regular intervals; but it is a matter of indifference to them whether appetite comes at midnight or at mid-day, and they eat upon the ground at all hours, without napkin or tablecloth."

But Vespucci approved of the acorns served to him by one tribe, finding them "savory to the taste and healthy to the body." He also enjoyed a wine made of acorns.

He was repelled by another tribe's roasting of "a certain animal that looked like a serpent . . . and was so disgusting in appearance that we were astonished at its deformity." Vespucci and his aides thought it was poisonous and wouldn't touch it, much less eat it. Scholars have identified the "serpent" as an iguana.

When **Sacagawea** joined the Lewis and Clark expedition, she was eating for two. The Shoshone woman, pregnant with her first child, went into a difficult labor. **Meriwether Lewis** resorted to an Indian folk remedy, giving her the crushed rattle of a rattlesnake mixed with water. She drank it up and gave birth within minutes.

Food killed **Vitus Bering**—or lack of the right food. The Danish-born explorer who served in the Russian navy gave his name to the Arctic's Bering Strait and Bering Island—where he died in 1741 of scurvy, caused by a deficiency of vitamin C.

Bering, who completed a groundbreaking journey through Siberia and mapped parts of the Arctic, died battling the elements on his way home. Some of his men survived through methods of hunting that were described in cringe-worthy detail by a member of Bering's expedition, Georg Steller.

They clubbed seals, which did not die easily. "When the cranium is broken into little bits, and almost all the brains have gushed out and all the teeth have been broken, the beast still attacks the men with his flippers and keeps on fighting."

After a manatee was harpooned and left in the sun for days, Steller recalled that its fat was "as pleasantly yellow as the best Dutch butter."

One of **James Cook**'s greatest achievements was his aggressive attention to scurvy, a problem that had plagued mariners for centuries. Following the research of naval surgeon James Lind, Cook packed his ships with such provisions as malt, sauerkraut, salted cabbage, soups, lemon and orange concentrate, and carrot marmalade. Even more important, he ordered his crew to find fresh fruit and vegetables whenever in port. In seven years of exploration, Cook did not lose a single crewman to scurvy.

Astronaut **Peggy Whitson** was aboard the International Space Station in October 2002 when the grocery delivery guy came by. Jeff Ashby, commander of the space shuttle *Atlantis,* radioed that he and his crew were arriving—with salsa.

"OK, we'll let you in then," said Whitson.

Salsa was an obsession on the space station during Whitson's six-month stint. "We choose our meals based on what goes well with salsa," she said, adding, "We could probably eat paper if we had it with salsa."

Atlantis also brought fresh oranges, grapefruits, and garlic, as well as a surprise gift from Whitson's husband: a pecan pie.

New Zealand explorer **Sir Edmund Hillary** and Sherpa guide **Tenzing Norgay** dined on chicken noodle soup and canned apricots in a chilly tent as they prepared to make history. A few hours later—at 11:30 a.m. May 29, 1953—they became the first human beings to reach the summit of Mount Everest.

Hillary later wrote: "I noticed Tenzing digging a little hole in the snow and watched him place in it some pieces of chocolate and other food, small gifts to the gods which he believed spent some time on the summit of Everest."

Descending to their tent afterward, they enjoyed a hot lemon-and-sugar drink. Farther down, they reached Hillary's friend George Lowe.

"Well, George," said Hillary, "we knocked the bastard off!"

"Thought you must have," said Lowe, who poured them hot tomato soup.

The Aztecs who lived in Mexico during the sixteenth century ate almost anything that moved—and at least one thing that didn't. They used fine nets to gather a substance, probably algae, from the surface of lakes. According to Spanish conquistador **Hernán Cortés,** who conquered the Aztecs, this soggy substance was "spread out on floors, like salt, and there it hardens. It is made into cakes resembling bricks . . . [and] eaten as we eat cheese." Cortés sampled an algae cake that had been seasoned with a chili sauce and declared it "delicious."

Australian police officer **Robert O'Hara Burke** led a government-financed mission in 1860 to cross the continent from south to north for the first time. He and three others reached the northern coast in about six months, but their return to civilization became a race against starvation. A key mistake was Burke's choice of route, which aimed for the aptly named Mount Hopeless. As their desperation deepened, Burke and his comrades ate their camels and their horse. Aborigines provided some fish and nardoo, the seeds of a fern that could be pounded into flour. But that only slowed the end for Burke, who died before help arrived. His last meal was nardoo and a crow.

Amelia Earhart made an agreement with her husband-manager, George Putnam: She would sign twenty-five autographs before going to sleep at night. When she awoke, she would sign ten more autographs before having her orange juice at breakfast. Then, before moving on to the bacon and eggs, she had to sign fifteen more.

Portuguese explorer **Ferdinand Magellan** named an ocean, calling it the Pacific, which means peaceful. But as his ships crossed the ocean in the sixteenth century, any tranquil thoughts were banished by a desperate hunger.

Not realizing how wide the Pacific was, Magellan packed inadequate provisions. Eventually, the only food left was biscuits that a crewman described as "powder of biscuits swarming with worms." As if that was not disgusting enough, he added, "It stank strongly of the urine of rats."

Soon even the crumbs of biscuits were gone. Desperate crewmen tore leather off the ship, but it was too tough to chew. So they attached the leather to cords, and threw it overboard to soften in the saltwater. After a few days, they brought up the leather, cooked it, and ate it.

When that, too, was gone, they ate sawdust and hunted for the ship's resident rats.

Finally, they reached an island where the natives fed them bananas and coconuts. But when the natives stole a small boat, Magellan retaliated by burning part of a village. As Magellan's ships left, the natives followed them in boats and held up fish, presumably to mock them for their hunger.

Magellan later was killed in fighting with natives on another island. But members of his crew pushed on, completing the first circumnavigation of the world. They arrived in Spain in 1522 with enough cloves to make the journey a commercial success, though costly in human terms.

The seventeenth-century sea voyage of Dutchmen **Jacob Le Maire** and **Willem Schouten** was remarkable for its discovery of a new passage below South America—and for its smart food choices.

The expedition stopped at Sierra Leone in western Africa and traded a few beads and knives for twenty-five thousand lemons, which helped the crew avoid scurvy. Near Patagonia at the southern end of South America, the expedition found a remarkable island. According to a contemporary account, "Our men landed on the island, which was almost entirely covered with eggs. A man standing still, with his feet together, could touch with his hands fifty-four nests, each containing three or four eggs.... They belonged to the black-backed gull, and we brought them on board by thousands and ate them."

Remarkably for a voyage of that time, only three of eighty-seven men died during the fifteen-month adventure.

After members of the Lewis and Clark expedition killed an elk in 1805, **Sacagawea** ate the marrow out of the shank bones and then cut up the bones and boiled them to make grease for oiling boots and guns.

Charles Lindbergh didn't care about in-flight meals.

The pilot took note that French war ace René Fonck, who attempted a nonstop Atlantic flight in 1926 with a crew of three, had packed a bag of croissants and a hot celebratory dinner in anticipation of arriving in Paris. But Fonck's plane crashed on takeoff, killing two of his crewmen.

Lindbergh would have no such culinary indulgences. The manufacturer of a vegetable extract called Vegex sent Lindbergh some samples that could be "taken into the plane in a thermos bottle like coffee or . . . eaten with crackers or bread." But Vegex did not make the flight.

Instead, Lindbergh brought only a few cans of army rations and five sandwiches. He didn't eat a single sandwich over the Atlantic and finally chewed on one just before landing.

When asked before his flight whether he'd packed enough sandwiches, he had said: "If I get to Paris, I won't need any more, and if I don't get to Paris, I won't need any more, either."

Marco Polo's thirteenth-century travels to the Far East were like trips to an exotic supermarket.

The Italian explorer stopped at the Persian island of Hormuz and reported that its residents thrived on dates, salt tuna, and onions. In India, Sumatra, and the Nicobar islands, he ran across coconuts, which he called pharoah's nuts.

For centuries, historians credited Polo with bringing pasta from China and introducing it to Italy. But modern scholars now believe that Italy already had pasta, and that the mistaken credit to Polo came from liberties taken by a sixteenth-century editor of Polo's memoirs.

While in China, Polo claimed to have encountered giant white pears "which weigh ten pounds apiece." But his tales seemed so fantastic that many disbelieved him. Children were said to have trailed behind him in his old age, taunting him with shouts of "Messer Marco, tell us another lie!"

When **Père Jacques Marquette** was exploring the southwestern shore of Lake Michigan in 1674, he survived on wild onions, including *Allium tricoccum*, a member of the onion family known as a ramp or wild leek. The pungent plant grew so abundantly in one area visited by Marquette that Indian tribes gave the location the same name they used for both the plant and the striped skunk. The place was called Chicago.

The problem of feeding long-term space explorers has challenged the imagination of modern scientists.

Peggy Whitson, the first female commander of the International Space Station, grew soybeans in space. Dubbed "cosmic beans" by the news media, they were brought to earth for further analysis. NASA envisions that a farm unit—nicknamed "the salad machine"—will be built into future space vehicles.

In the 1960s, Grumman Aircraft researcher Sydney Schwarz offered another possible food source: the spacecraft itself. Schwarz mixed common grocery items—flour, corn starch, powdered milk, powdered bananas, and hominy grits—and baked them into hard objects. Schwarz thought the edible substance could be used for spacecraft fixtures, such as partitions and control knobs, and later could be broken off, soaked in water, and eaten by hungry astronauts.

"With sugar and cream, it's delicious," Schwarz said. "But then, anything is."

Spanish conquistador **Francisco Vásquez de Coronado,** leading a 1540 expedition in what is now the southwestern United States, searched for a rumored civilization of seven great cities. What he found instead was the "country of the cows"—the buffalo.

Coronado and his men criticized the Indians' consumption of the buffalo, noting that they ate the meat raw and drank the partially digested food that they found in the buffalo stomachs. But the explorers also survived on buffalo meat and used a hunting tool unknown to the Indians: the horse. In a month's time, Spaniards riding horses and throwing spears killed five hundred buffalo—and transformed the way Indians would hunt their primary prey.

To Coronado, the buffalo wasn't just for nutrition—it was for navigation, too. As his forces moved through unfamiliar country, they piled buffalo dung into mounds to mark the way home. Presumably, Coronado delegated that important task to his subordinates.

In the fourteenth century, a Moroccan named **Abu Abdullah Muhammad Ibn Battuta** spent nearly three decades traveling the known Islamic world and beyond.

Ibn Battuta visited Azak—now the Russian town of Azov—and was greeted with a meal of boiled horse and sheep, millet gruel, and a fermented mare's milk called koumiss that he found "disagreeable."

In Maqdashaw—now the Somalian city of Mogadishu—Ibn Battuta was welcomed with betel leaves and areca nuts, followed by a stew of meat, fish, and vegetables poured over rice cooked in clarified butter. Other dinner items included green bananas in milk, green ginger, mangoes, and pickled lemons and chilies. Ibn Battuta was amazed at the locals' appetite: "A single person . . . eats as much as a whole company of us would eat, as a matter of habit, and they are corpulent and fat in the extreme."

Japanese adventurer **Naomi Uemura** was not much of a team player. He was the first to travel solo by dogsled to the North Pole. He floated the length of the Amazon River by himself. And he was the first to climb Alaska's Mount McKinley alone.

His lonely travels put a serious crimp in his dining. When he attempted a solo crossing of Greenland by dogsled, he was blocked by a deep crevasse in the ice and resorted to eating dog food before being airlifted.

During his Mount McKinley achievement in 1970, he lived for eight days on bread, salmon, and salmon eggs—less energy-producing food than many climbers might have chosen. In 1984, he attempted a further feat on McKinley, climbing it solo in the winter. This time he carried caribou meat, and he succeeded in reaching the summit, but on the way down he disappeared and has never been found.

While exploring the West Indies, **Christopher Columbus** met a tribe called the Galibi, meaning "brave people." Some Europeans pronounced the name as Carib or Caniba, leading to two new words—*Caribbean* and *cannibal*. The latter word was associated with the Galibi because Columbus suspected them of being maneaters. But many historians now consider that a rash conclusion arising from the fact that the Galibi sometimes left skulls and bones unburied.

South Korea's first astronaut, **Yi So-yeon,** brought her engineering expertise to the International Space Station in 2008. But most of the media attention went to something else she brought: kimchi.

South Korean researchers spent several years and millions of dollars perfecting a space version of the pickled cabbage dish, trying to ensure it would not be too stinky for Yi's foreign comrades and that conditions in space would not cause the food to react unpredictably. Lee Ju-woon of the Korean Atomic Energy Research Institute explained the risk: "Imagine if a bag of kimchi starts fermenting and bubbling out of control and bursts all over the sensitive equipment of the spaceship."

As it turned out, no cabbage catastrophe occurred.

For centuries, explorers searched for the Northwest Passage, a hoped-for sea route above North America that would lead from the Atlantic Ocean to the Pacific. But ultimately, such hopes were put on ice.

A leading searcher was Britain's **Sir John Franklin,** who traveled along five thousand miles of frigid coastline in the early 1800s. On an early voyage, Franklin and his crew were so racked with hunger that they survived by scraping lichen off rocks and eating spare shoes. Afterward, Franklin was nicknamed "the Man Who Ate His Boots."

On a later, better organized effort, he brought along an expert fisherman to provide food. On his final expedition, beginning in 1845, Franklin and 133 crew members packed impressive provisions, including thirty-two thousand pounds of pork, nine thousand pounds of chocolate, and one thousand pounds of raisins.

But much of the food was stored in cans that had been contaminated by lead. Combined with scurvy and frigid conditions that immobilized ships, the lead poisoning doomed Franklin and his crew. There were no survivors.

David Livingstone, a Scottish medical missionary in Africa, lost contact with the outside world for several years, and the *New York Herald* sent reporter **Henry Morton Stanley** to find him. In 1871, Stanley encountered the missionary in what is now Tanzania and uttered the famous line, "Dr. Livingstone, I presume."

They celebrated by eating what Stanley called "hot hashed-meat cakes," along with curried chicken, stewed goat meat, and rice. Stanley recalled that although Livingstone complained of a poor appetite, he "ate like a vigorous, hungry man; and, as he vied with me in demolishing the pancakes, he kept repeating, 'You have brought me new life!' "

Stanley happened to have a bottle of Sillery champagne and silver goblets, and he issued a toast: "Dr. Livingstone, to your very good health, sir."

"And to yours," Livingstone said.

The weightlessness of outer space causes fluids to collect differently in the human body, and many astronauts experience a dramatic change in their tastes for food.

"One of my favorite foods on the ground is shrimp, and up here I can't stand it," said International Space Station astronaut **Peggy Whitson**. "The guys like it because they get all my shrimp that I selected on the ground before flight. I'm really hoping my tastes will go back [to what they were on Earth] and I will enjoy shrimp as much as I did before."

Captain James Cook met a violent end in a clash with Hawaiian villagers in 1779. Cook's crew members fled to their ship, leaving his body behind.

A day later, two Hawaiian priests visited the ship, returned a piece of flesh from Cook's hindquarters, and left. Cook's outraged crew reacted with a spasm of violence, killing dozens of Hawaiians. Later, the Hawaiians surrendered more pieces of Cook, including his scorched limbs and his skull.

Because some body parts were still missing, and because the Hawaiians were viewed as savages, some Europeans believed that Cook was cannibalized. Did Cook—a significant figure in the history of food—become a menu item?

Not likely. Experts believe the Hawaiians accorded Cook their version of high respect, treating him as they would a dead chief. Because the Hawaiians wanted to save a chief's bones as prized relics, they would roast the body long enough for the bones to be easily separated from the flesh. Presumably, they did the same with Cook.

Which means the intrepid captain was most certainly cooked, but in all likelihood, he was not eaten.

Woe be unto dogs when humans are desperate and hungry.

Álvar Núñez Cabeza de Vaca, a sixteenth-century Spanish visitor to North America, arrived in a party of six hundred and was among only a handful of Europeans to survive the struggles with hostile natives and nature. Traveling vast uncharted areas of what is now the southwestern United States, Cabeza de Vaca at first ate prickly pears for subsistence but later bought two dogs from the natives in a desperate bid for survival.

"After we ate the dogs . . . we had the strength to be able to go on ahead," he wrote.

On a later North American adventure in 1804, **Meriwether Lewis** wrote: "Having been so long accustomed to live on the flesh of dogs, the greater part of us have acquired a fondness for it, and our original aversion for it overcome by reflecting that while we subsisted on that food we were fatter, stronger, and in general enjoyed better health than at any period since leaving buffalo country."

American adventurer **Robert Peary** laid siege to the North Pole several times, finally claiming success in 1909. During his expeditions, he ordered that his weakest sled dogs be killed and eaten by his crew. It appears that Peary did not himself eat dog, but his aide, African American explorer **Matthew Henson,** certainly did, complaining that "raw dog is flavorless and very tough."

At the South Pole a couple years later, Norwegian explorer **Roald Amundsen** and his crew made their own mark. When Amundsen reached the pole, he celebrated by giving his crew double rations. Then his party headed back to civilization, eating all of its sled dogs on the return trip.

Britain's **Robert Scott,** who lost the race to the South Pole, was a meticulous explorer who inspected canneries before accepting their food for his missions. But he was softhearted toward dogs, never willing to use them as aggressively as Amundsen for either motility or meals. To reach the South Pole without reliance on dogs, Scott wrote, "would make the conquest more nobly and splendidly won."

Scott tried to use ponies as his main beasts of burden instead of dogs, but that failed, forcing his men to haul the sleds themselves. Scott managed to reach the South Pole five weeks after Amundsen, but he never made it back, dying of exposure and starvation—but without ever eating a dog.

ACKNOWLEDGMENTS

This book is not an academic tome, but rather it relies on work by millennia of scholars and enthusiasts. Some of our favorite experts are Paul Freedman, Waverley Root, and James Trager. We also thank the libraries that fed our project—the Skokie Public Library in Illinois and the Martin Luther King Jr. Library in Washington, D.C. In the case of the former, library staffers Laurence Johnson, Gary Gustin, and Frances Roehm offered strong support.

We are indebted to our agent, Gary Heidt of the Signature Literary Agency. He believed in our book and found the right publisher. This book could not have happened without him.

Editing was vital. The credit goes to Stephanie Chan and the rest of the Three Rivers Press team, including Lucinda Bartley and Jude Grant. They challenged our illogical notions and untangled our tortured sentences.

Others played special roles. Charlie Manzo of the PaceWildenstein Gallery in New York helped us find out whether Maya Lin really ate those mashed potatoes. The words that French writer Denis Diderot spoke before he ate an apricot—and died moments later—were translated by Richard Lutz. Archives assistant Lesley Zlabinger of the Louis Armstrong House Museum in Corona, New York, shared details of Satchmo's unique approach to food and "physics." Nutrition expert Dawn Jackson Blatner provided a reality check on how many calories Elvis Presley could have consumed.

We are grateful for friends and colleagues who offered fresh ideas, spicy feedback, and solid support: Christina Bartolomeo, Cate and Richard Cahan, Jim Conzelman, Larry Doyle, Paul Gordon, Bill Hearst, Tom and Lucy Keating, Lauren Luchi, Kyle Mantyla, Dan Murphy, Rob Reinalda, Nathan Richter, Vincent Russell, Gael Sammartino, John Schlitt, Esther and Richard Triffler, Ted Weinstein, and Michael Williams.

Mark thanks his *Chicago Tribune* colleagues, especially Gerry Kern, Jane Hirt, Peter Kendall, Phil Jurik, Robin Daughtridge, John Kass, Kerry Luft, Stephan Benzkofer, Monica Eng, and Colin McMahon.

Finally, love and gratitude to the great, supportive family with whom we've shared many a meal and tale: our spouses, Lisa and Jeff; our parents, John and Jane; our siblings and their families: Tim, Kathleen, Paul, and Anne; and Mark's daughters (otherwise known as Matt's nieces), Maureen and Katherine.

SELECTED BIBLIOGRAPHY

CHAPTER 1: CHICKEN À LA KING

Afkhami, Gholam Reza. *The Life and Times of the Shah.* Berkeley: University of California Press, 2009.

Barnes, John. *Evita, First Lady: A Biography of Eva Perón.* New York: Grove Press, 1978.

Bhutto, Benazir. *Daughter of Destiny: An Autobiography.* New York: HarperCollins, 2008.

Bullock, Alan. *Hitler: A Study in Tyranny.* New York: HarperCollins, 1971.

Burkett, Elinor. *Golda.* New York: HarperCollins, 2008.

Chandler, David P. *Brother Number One: A Political Biography of Pol Pot.* Boulder, CO: Westview Press, 1999.

Chang, Jung, and Jon Halliday. *Mao: The Unknown Story.* New York: Anchor Books, 2005.

Flandrin, Jean-Louis, Massimo Montanari, and Albert Sonnenfeld. *Food: A Culinary History from Antiquity to the Present.* New York: Columbia University Press, 1999.

Fleming, David Hay. *Mary Queen of Scots, from Her Birth to Her Flight into England: A Brief Biography.* London: Hodder & Stoughton, 1897.

Fletcher, Nichola. *Charlemagne's Tablecloth: A Piquant History of Feasting.* New York: St. Martin's Press, 2004.

Ford, Franklin L. *Political Murder: From Tyrannicide to Terrorism.* Cambridge, MA: Harvard University Press, 1985.

Frank, Katherine. *Indira: The Life of Indira Nehru Gandhi.* New York: Houghton Mifflin, 2002.

Fraser, Antonia. *Cromwell.* New York: Grove Press, 2001.

Frieda, Leonie. *Catherine de Medici: Renaissance Queen of France*. New York: HarperCollins, 2003.

Hanfstaengl, Ernst. *Hitler: The Missing Years*. New York: Arcade, 1994.

Hibbert, Christopher. *George III*. New York: Basic Books, 1998.

———. *Queen Victoria: A Personal History*. Cambridge, MA: Da Capo Press, 2001.

Hochschild, Adam. *King Leopold's Ghost: A Story of Greed, Terror, and Heroism in Colonial Africa*. New York: Houghton Mifflin, 1998.

Hume, Martin Andrew Sharp. *The Love Affairs of Mary Queen of Scots: A Political History*. McClure, Phillips & Company, 1903.

Khrushchev, Sergei. *Memoirs of Nikita Khrushchev*. Vol. 3, *Statesman (1953–1964)*. University Park: Pennsylvania State University Press, 2007.

Keyes, Ralph. *The Quote Verifier: Who Said What, Where, and When*. New York: Macmillan, 2006.

Kiernan, Ben. *The Pol Pot Regime: Race, Power, and Genocide in Cambodia Under the Khmer Rouge, 1975–79*. New Haven, CT: Yale University Press, 2008.

Langworth, Richard, ed. *Churchill by Himself: The Definitive Collection of Quotations*. New York: PublicAffairs, 2008.

Levi, Anthony. *Louis XIV*. New York: Carroll & Graf, 2004.

Li Zhisui, *The Private Life of Chairman Mao*. New York: Random House, 1994.

Lloyd, Hannibal Evans. *George IV: Memoirs of His Life and Reign*. London: Treuttel & Wurtz, 1830.

Mango, Andrew. *Atatürk*. New York: Overlook Press, 2000.

Martin, Bradley K. *Under the Loving Care of the Fatherly Leader: North Korea and the Kim Dynasty*. New York: Thomas Dunne Books, 2004.

Moorehead, Alan. *The White Nile*. New York: Dell, 1960.

Mussolini, Rachele. *Mussolini: An Intimate Biography by his Widow*. New York: William Morrow, 1974.

Pacepa, Ion Mihai. *Red Horizons: The True Story of Nicolae and Elena Ceauşescu's Crimes, Lifestyle, and Corruption*. Washington: Regnery Gateway, 1990.

Rawski, Evelyn S. *The Last Emperors: A Social History of Qing Imperial Institutions*. Berkeley: University of California Press, 1998.

Reader, John. *Potato: A History of the Propitious Esculent*. New Haven, CT: Yale University Press, 2008.

Rempel, William C. *Delusions of a Dictator: The Mind of Marcos as Revealed in His Secret Diaries*. Boston: Little, Brown, 1993.

Rounding, Virginia. *Catherine the Great: Love, Sex and Power*. New York: Macmillan, 2007.

Sampson, Anthony. *Mandela: The Authorized Biography*. New York: Vintage Books, 1999.

Service, Robert. *Stalin: A Biography.* Cambridge, MA: Harvard University Press, 2005.

Smith, Denis Mack. *Mussolini: A Biography* (abridged ed.). New York: Alfred A. Knopf, 1982.

Somerset, Anne. *Elizabeth I.* New York: St. Martin's Press, 1991.

Takekoshi, Yosaburō. *The Economic Aspects of the History of the Civilization of Japan.* London: Routledge, 2004.

Wałęsa, Lech. *The Struggle and the Triumph: An Autobiography.* New York: Arcade, 1992.

Weir, Alison. *Henry VIII: The King and His Court.* New York: Ballantine Books, 2001.

———. *Queen Isabella: Treachery, Adultery, and Murder in Medieval England.* New York: Ballantine Books, 2007.

CHAPTER 2: EATING THEIR WORDS

Angelou, Maya. *A Song Flung up to Heaven.* New York: Bantam Books, 2002.

Barry, Joseph. *Infamous Woman: The Life of George Sand.* Garden City, NY: Doubleday, 1977.

Bell-Villada, Gene H., ed. *Conversations with Gabriel García Márquez.* Jackson: University Press of Mississippi, 2006.

Berry, Faith. *Langston Hughes: Before and Beyond Harlem.* New York: Citadel Press, 1992.

Boswell, James. *Boswell's Life of Johnson: Tour to the Hebrides (1773) and Journey into North Wales (1774).* Edited by George Birkbeck Hill. London: Oxford/Clarendon Press, 1887.

Boyd, Brian. *Vladimir Nabokov: The American Years.* Princeton, NJ: Princeton University Press, 1993.

Boyd, Herb. *Baldwin's Harlem: A Biography of James Baldwin.* New York: Atria Books, 2008.

Bryer, Jackson R., and Cathy W. Barks. *Dear Scott, Dearest Zelda: The Love Letters of F. Scott and Zelda Fitzgerald.* New York: Macmillan, 2003.

Chatfield-Taylor, H. C. *Molière: A Biography.* New York: Duffield & Co., 1906.

Clarke, Gerald. *Capote: A Biography.* New York: Ballantine Books, 1988.

Clymer, William Branford Shubrick. *James Fenimore Cooper.* Boston: Small, Maynard & Company, 1900.

Conn, Peter. *Pearl S. Buck: A Cultural Biography.* New York: Cambridge University Press, 1998.

Donaldson, Scott. *By Force of Will: The Life and Art of Ernest Hemingway.* New York: Viking Press, 1977.

Dostoevsky, Ann. *Dostoevsky: Reminiscences.* New York: Liveright, 1975.

Feinstein, Adam. *Pablo Neruda: A Passion for Life.* New York: Bloomsbury USA, 2004.

Forster, John. *The Life of Charles Dickens.* Philadelphia: J. B. Lippincott & Co., 1874.

Frank, Joseph, and David I. Goldstein, eds. *Selected Letters of Fyodor Dostoyevsky.* New Brunswick, NJ: Rutgers University Press, 1987.

Gottfried, Martin. *Arthur Miller: His Life and Work.* Cambridge, MA: Da Capo Press, 2003.

Gussow, Mel. *Edward Albee: A Singular Journey.* New York: Simon & Schuster, 1999.

Ingham, Patricia. *The Brontës.* Oxford, England: Oxford University Press, 2006.

Jones, Leslie Ellen. *J. R. R. Tolkien: A Biography.* Westport, CT: Greenwood Press, 2003.

Jordan, Ruth. *George Sand.* New York: Taplinger, 1976.

Kjetsaa, Geir. *Fyodor Dostoyevsky: A Writer's Life.* New York: Elisabeth Sifton Books/Viking Press, 1987.

Knowlson, James. *Damned to Fame: The Life of Samuel Beckett.* New York: Grove Press, 2004.

Lee, Hermione. *Edith Wharton.* New York: Alfred A. Knopf, 2007.

Lingeman, Richard R. *Sinclair Lewis: Rebel from Main Street.* St. Paul: Minnesota Historical Society, 2005.

Loving, Jerome. *Walt Whitman: The Song of Himself.* Berkeley: University of California Press, 2000.

Ludwig, Emil. *Goethe: The History of a Man, 1749–1832.* New York: G. P. Putnam's Sons, 1928.

Maher, Paul. *Kerouac: The Definitive Biography.* New York: Rowman & Littlefield, 2004.

Marzials, Frank Thomas. *The Life of Charles Dickens.* New York: The University Society, 1908.

McKenna, Neil. *The Secret Life of Oscar Wilde: An Intimate Biography.* New York: Basic Books, 2005.

Minter, David. *William Faulkner: His Life and Work.* Baltimore, MD: Johns Hopkins University Press, 1997.

Morehouse, Ward. *Inside the Plaza: An Intimate Portrait of the Ultimate Hotel.* New York: Hal Leonard/Applause Books, 2001.

Motion, Andrew. *Keats.* New York: Farrar, Straus & Giroux, 1997.

Murray, Nicholas. *Aldous Huxley: A Biography.* New York: Macmillan, 2003.

Nel, Philip. *Dr. Seuss: American Icon.* New York: Continuum, 2004.

Paine, Albert Bigelow. *Mark Twain, a Biography.* New York: Harper & Bros., 1912.

Parini, Jay. *John Steinbeck: A Biography.* New York: Henry Holt, 1995.

————. *Robert Frost: A Life.* New York: Macmillan, 2000.

Pawel, Ernst. *The Nightmare of Reason: A Life of Franz Kafka.* Toronto: Collins Publishers, 1984.

Peters, Sally. *Bernard Shaw: The Ascent of the Superman.* New Haven, CT: Yale University Press, 1998.

Rampersad, Arnold. *The Life of Langston Hughes: 1914–1967: I Dream a World* (2nd ed.). New York: Oxford University Press, 2002.

Richardson, Joanna. *Victor Hugo.* New York: St. Martin's Press, 1976.

Robb, Graham. *Balzac: A Biography.* New York: W. W. Norton, 1996.

Salamo, Lin, Victor Fischer, and Michael B. Frank, Bancroft Library Mark Twain Projects, eds. *Mark Twain's Helpful Hints for Good Living: A Handbook for the Damned Human Race.* Berkeley: University of California Press, 2004.

Sandars, Mary F. *Honore de Balzac, His Life and Writings.* Teddington, England: Echo Library, 2006.

Sawyer-Lauçanno, Christopher. *E. E. Cummings: A Biography.* Naperville, IL: Sourcebooks, 2004.

Simon, Linda. *The Biography of Alice B. Toklas.* Lincoln: University of Nebraska Press, 1991.

Simpson, Melissa. *Flannery O'Connor: A Biography.* Westport, CT: Greenwood Press, 2005.

Stape, John. *The Several Lives of Joseph Conrad.* New York: Pantheon Books, 2007.

Tadie, Jean-Yves. *Marcel Proust: A Life.* New York: Viking Press, 2000.

Tagore, Rabindranath, with Krishna Dutta and Andrew Robinson. *Rabindranath Tagore: An Anthology.* New York: St. Martin's Press, 1997.

Turnbull, Andrew. *Scott Fitzgerald.* New York: Grove Press, 2001.

Wilson, A. N. *Tolstoy: A Biography.* New York: W. W. Norton, 2001.

Worthen, John. *D. H. Lawrence: The Early Years, 1885–1912.* Cambridge, MA: Cambridge University Press, 1992.

CHAPTER 3: SOUL FOOD

Augustine. *The Confessions of Saint Augustine.* Translated by Carolinne White. London: Frances Lincoln, 2001.

Alighieri, Dante. *Purgatorio.* Translated by John Ciardi. New York: New American Library, 2001.

Bair, Deirdre. *Simone de Beauvoir: A Biography.* New York: Summit Books, 1990.

Brown, Judith M. *Gandhi: Prisoner of Hope.* New Haven, CT: Yale University Press, 1989.

Brunson, Matthew. *The Pope Encyclopedia.* New York: Crown Trade, 1995.

Burgan, Michael. *Confucius: Chinese Philosopher and Teacher.* Minneapolis, MN: Compass Point Books, 2009.

Burroughs, John. *Locusts and Wild Honey: The Writings of John Burroughs.* Boston: Houghton Mifflin, 1907.

Bushman, Richard L. *Joseph Smith and the Beginnings of Mormonism.* Urbana: University of Illinois Press, 1988.

Chalmers, Irena. *The Great Food Almanac.* San Francisco: Collins Publishers San Francisco, 1994.

Chamberlin, Eric Russell. *The Bad Popes.* New York: Barnes & Noble, 1993.

Chin, Ann-ping. *The Authentic Confucius.* New York: Scribner, 2007.

Clarke, Desmond. *Descartes: A Biography.* New York: Cambridge University Press, 2006.

Craig, Mary. *Kundun: A Biography of the Family of the Dalai Lama.* Washington, DC: Counterpoint, 1998.

Damrosch, Leo. *Jean-Jacques Rousseau.* Boston: Houghton Mifflin, 2005.

Davidson, Ian. *Voltaire in Exile: The Last Years, 1753–78.* New York: Grove Press, 2004.

Forsberg, Clyde R. *Equal Rites: The Book of Mormon, Masonry, Gender, and American Culture.* New York: Columbia University Press, 2004.

Greene, Meg. *Mother Teresa: A Biography.* Westport, CT: Greenwood Press, 2004.

Jacquette, Dale. *The Philosophy of Schopenhauer.* Montreal, Quebec, Canada: McGill-Queen's University Press, 2005.

Jacob, H. E. *Six Thousand Years of Bread: Its Holy and Unholy History.* Translated by Richard and Clara Winston. New York: Lyons & Burford, 1944.

Kelhoffer, James A. *The Diet of John the Baptist.* Tubingen, Germany: Mohr Siebeck, 2005.

Laird, Thomas. *The Story of Tibet.* New York: Grove Press, 2006.

Marvin, Frederic Rowland. *The Last Words (Real and Traditional) of Distinguished Men and Women.* New York: Revell, 1901.

McBrien, Richard P. *Lives of the Saints.* San Francisco: HarperSanFranciso, 2001.

McElrath, Jessica. *The Everything Martin Luther King Jr. Book.* Avon, MA: Adams Media, 2008.

Morley, John. *Diderot and the Encyclopedists.* New York: Macmillan, 1897.

New American Standard Bible. Anaheim, CA: Foundation Publications, 1995.

Rawlinson, George. *Moses, His Life and Times.* London: James Nisbet & Co., 1887.

Rogerson, Barnaby. *The Prophet Muhammad.* Mahwah, NJ: HiddenSpring, 2003.

Rowley, Hazel. *Tête-à-tête: Simone de Beauvoir and Jean-Paul Sartre.* New York: HarperCollins, 2005.

Rumble, Victoria R. *Soup Through the Ages: A Culinary History with Period Recipes.* Jefferson, NC: McFarland, 2009.

Shaw, Brent D. *Spartacus and the Slave Wars: A Brief History with Documents.* Boston: Bedford/St. Martin's, 2001.

Spink, Kathryn. *Mother Teresa: A Complete Authorized Biography.* San Francisco: HarperSanFrancisco, 1997.

Stewart, Whitney. *The 14th Dalai Lama.* Minneapolis, MN: Lerner, 2000.

Strong, John S. *The Buddha: A Short Biography.* Oxford, England: Oneworld, 2001.

CHAPTER 4: WHAT EDVARD MUNCHED

Bailey, Anthony. *Standing in the Sun: A Life of J. M. W. Turner.* New York: Michael di Capua Books, HarperCollins Publishers, 1997.

Baldwin, Neil. *Man Ray: American Artist.* Cambridge, MA: Da Capo Press, 2001.

Bockris, Victor. *The Life and Death of Andy Warhol.* New York: Bantam Books, 1989.

Bull, George. *Michelangelo: A Biography.* New York: St. Martin's, 1995.

Burroughs, Polly. *Thomas Hart Benton: A Portrait.* Garden City, NY: Doubleday, 1981.

Chagall, Marc. *My Life.* Cambridge, MA: Da Capo Press, 1994.

Coughlan, Robert. *The World of Michelangelo, 1475–1564.* New York: Time, 1966.

Freedman, Paul, ed. *Food: The History of Taste.* Berkeley: University of California Press, 2007.

Friedman, B. H. *Jackson Pollock: Energy Made Visible.* New York: Da Capo Press, 1995.

Hanson, Lawrence. *Renoir: The Man, the Painter, and His World.* New York: Dodd, Mead, 1968.

Kimball, Roger. *Lives of the Mind.* Chicago: Ivan R. Dee, 2002.

Lane, Richard. *Hokusai: Life and Work.* New York: E. P. Dutton, 1989.

Lisle, Laurie. *Portrait of an Artist: A Biography of Georgia O'Keeffe.* New York: Seaview Books, 1980.

Madsen, Axel. *Chanel: A Woman of Her Own.* New York: Henry Holt, 1990.

Marnham, Patrick. *Dreaming with His Eyes Open: A Life of Diego Rivera.* New York: Alfred A. Knopf, 1998.

Olivier, Fernande. *Picasso and His Friends.* New York: Appleton-Century, 1965.

Penrose, Roland. *Picasso: His Life and Work.* New York: Harper & Brothers, 1958.

Prideaux, Sue. *Edvard Munch: Behind the Scream.* New Haven, CT: Yale University Press, 2005.

Secrest, Meryle. *Frank Lloyd Wright: A Biography.* New York: HarperPerennial, 1992.

———. *Salvador Dalí.* New York: Dutton, 1986.

Spurling, Hilary. *The Unknown Matisse.* New York: Alfred A. Knopf, 1998.

Sweetman, David. *Van Gogh: His Life and His Art*. New York: Crown, 1990.

Warhol, Andy. *The Philosophy of Andy Warhol: From A to B and Back Again*. New York: Harcourt Brace Jovanovich, 1975.

CHAPTER 5: HAIL TO THE BEEF

Angelo, Bonnie. *First Families: The Impact of the White House on Their Lives*. New York: HarperCollins, 2005.

Boller, Paul F., Jr. *Presidential Anecdotes* (rev. ed.). New York: Oxford University Press, 1996.

Bradford, Sarah. *America's Queen: The Life of Jacqueline Kennedy Onassis*. New York: Viking/Penguin Putnam, 2000.

Burstein, Andrew. *Jefferson's Secrets: Death and Desire at Monticello*. New York: Basic Books, 2005.

Cannon, Poppy, and Patricia Brooks. *The Presidents' Cookbook*. New York: Funk & Wagnalls, 1968.

Coletta, Paolo E. *The Presidency of William Howard Taft*. Lawrence: University Press of Kansas, 1973.

Dallek, Robert. *Lone Star Rising: Lyndon Johnson and His Times, 1908–1960*. New York: Oxford University Press, 1991.

Donald, Aida D. *Lion in the White House: A Life of Theodore Roosevelt*. New York: Perseus, 2007.

Dos Passos, John. *The Head and Heart of Thomas Jefferson*. Garden City, NY: Doubleday, 1954.

Ellis, Joseph J. *American Sphinx: The Character of Thomas Jefferson*. New York: Alfred A. Knopf, 1997.

Ewald, William Bragg, Jr. *Eisenhower the President: Crucial Days, 1951–1960*. Englewood Cliffs, NJ: Prentice-Hall, 1981.

Gartner, John. *In Search of Bill Clinton: A Psychological Biography*. New York: St. Martin's Press, 2008.

Graff, Henry F. *Grover Cleveland*. New York: Henry Holt, 2002.

Grant, James. *John Adams: Party of One*. New York: Farrar, Straus & Giroux, 2005.

Landau, Barry H. *The President's Table: Two Hundred Years of Dining and Diplomacy*. New York: HarperCollins, 2007.

MacMillan, Margaret. *Nixon and Mao: The Week That Changed the World*. New York: Random House, 2008.

Mesnier, Roland. *All the Presidents' Pastries: Twenty-Five Years in the White House*. New York: Rizzoli, 2007.

Morris, Edmund. *Theodore Rex*. New York: Random House, 2001.

O'Brien, Michael. *John F. Kennedy: A Biography*. New York: St. Martin's Press, 2005.

Packard, Jerrold M. *The Lincolns in the White House: Four Years That Shattered a Family.* New York: St. Martin's Press, 2005

Reeves, Richard. *President Nixon: Alone in the White House.* New York: Simon & Schuster, 2001.

Singleton, Esther. *The Story of the White House.* New York: McClure, 1907.

Smith, Marie. *Entertaining in the White House.* Washington, DC: Acropolis Books, 1967.

Smith, Sally Bedell. *Grace and Power: The Private World of the Kennedy White House.* New York: Random House, 2004.

Weik, Jesse W. *The Real Lincoln: A Portrait.* Cambridge, MA: Riverside Press, 1922.

Whitcomb, John, and Claire Whitcomb. *Real Life at the White House: Two Hundred Years of Daily Life at America's Most Famous Residence.* New York: Routledge, 2000.

CHAPTER 6: DINNER THEATER

Adir, Karin. *The Great Clowns of American Television.* Jefferson, NC: McFarland, 2001.

Andersen, Christopher. *Barbra: The Way She Is.* New York: HarperCollins, 2006.

Borgnine, Ernest. *Ernest: The Autobiography.* New York: Citadel Press, 2008.

Capra, Frank. *The Name Above the Title: An Autobiography.* Cambridge, MA: Da Capo Press, 1997.

Chandler, Charlotte. *Ingrid: Ingrid Bergman, A Personal Biography.* New York: Simon & Schuster, 2007.

———. *It's Only a Movie: Alfred Hitchcock, A Personal Biography,* New York: Simon & Schuster, 2005.

———. *Nobody's Perfect: Billy Wilder, A Personal Biography.* New York: Simon & Schuster, 2002.

Clarke, Gerald. *Get Happy: The Life of Judy Garland.* New York: Dell Publishing, 2000.

Coleman, Terry. *Olivier.* New York: Macmillan, 2006.

Conner, Floyd. *Hollywood's Most Wanted: The Top 10 Book of Lucky Breaks, Prima Donnas, Box Office Bombs, and Other Oddities.* Dulles, VA: Brassey's, 2002.

Curtis, Tony, with Peter Golenbock. *American Prince: A Memoir.* New York: Random House, 2008.

DiSilvestre, Rob. *Collectible Meals: Real Menus from History and Hollywood.* Bloomington, IN: Unlimited Publishing, 2002.

Douglas, Kirk. *Climbing the Mountain: My Search for Meaning.* New York: Simon & Schuster, 2001.

Eliot, Marc. *Cary Grant: A Biography.* New York: Three Rivers Press, 2005.

Fishgall, Gary. *Gregory Peck: A Biography.* New York: Scribner, 2002.

Flynn, Errol. *Wicked Wicked Ways: The Autobiography of Errol Flynn*. Lanham, MD: Rowman & Littlefield, 2002.

Goudsouzian, Aram. *Sidney Poitier: Man, Actor, Icon*. Chapel Hill: University of North Carolina Press, 2004.

Grobel, Lawrence. *Al Pacino: In Conversation with Lawrence Grobel*. New York: Simon & Schuster, 2006.

Jolie, Angelina. *Notes from My Travels: Visits with Refugees in Africa, Cambodia, Pakistan, and Ecuador*. New York: Simon & Schuster, 2003.

Kanfer, Stefan. *Ball of Fire: The Tumultuous Life and Comic Art of Lucille Ball*. New York: Alfred A. Knopf, 2003.

Kellow, Brian. *Ethel Merman: A Life*. New York: Viking Press, 2007.

Meade, Marion. *Buster Keaton: Cut to the Chase*. Cambridge, MA: Da Capo Press, 1997.

Milton, Joyce. *Tramp: The Life of Charlie Chaplin*. New York: HarperCollins, 1996.

Munn, Michael. *Jimmy Stewart: The Truth Behind the Legend*. Fort Lee, NJ: Barricade Books, 2006.

Nelson, Nancy. *Evenings with Cary Grant: Recollections in His Own Words and by Those Who Knew Him Best*. New York: Citadel Press, 2002.

Porter, Darwin. *Katharine the Great: Secrets of a Lifetime Revealed*. New York: Blood Moon Productions, 2004.

Quick, Lawrence J., and William Schoell. *Joan Crawford: The Essential Biography*. Lexington: University Press of Kentucky, 2002.

Sheward, David. *Rage and Glory: The Volatile Life and Career of George C. Scott*. Milwaukee, WI: Applause Books/Hal Leonard, 2008.

Spicer, Chrystopher J. *Clark Gable: Biography, Filmography, Bibliography*. Jefferson, NC: McFarland, 2002.

Spoto, Donald. *The Dark Side of Genius: The Life of Alfred Hitchcock* (centennial ed.). New York: Da Capo Press, 1999.

Taylor, Elizabeth. *Elizabeth Takes Off: On Weight Gain, Weight Loss, Self-Image, and Self-Esteem*. New York: G. P. Putnam's Sons, 1988.

Thomas, Bruce. *Bruce Lee: Fighting Spirit* (2nd ed.). Berkeley, CA: Frog, 1994.

CHAPTER 7: GENERAL FOODS

Abbott, John Stevens Cabot. *History of Frederick the Second*. New York: Harper & Bros., 1871.

Alexander, Bevin. *How Great Generals Win*. New York: W. W. Norton, 2002.

Armstrong, Karen. *Holy War: The Crusades and Their Impact on Today's World*. New York: Doubleday, 1991

Beyer, Rick. *The Greatest War Stories Never Told*. New York: HarperResource, 2003.

Brown, Dee. *Bury My Heart at Wounded Knee*. New York: Henry Holt, 1970.

Davis, William C. *A Taste for War*. Mechanicsburg, PA: Stackpole Books, 2003.

D'Este, Carlo. *Warlord: A Life of Winston Churchill at War, 1874–1945*. New York: HarperCollins, 2008.

Edgerton, Robert B. *The Fall of the Ashante Empire*. New York: Free Press, 1995.

Eisenhower, John S. D. *General Ike: A Personal Reminiscence*. New York: Free Press, 2007.

Fleming, Thomas. *Washington's Secret War: The Hidden History of Valley Forge*. New York: Smithsonian Books/Collins, 2005.

Glatthaar, Joseph T. *General Lee's Army*. New York: Free Press, 2008.

Hastings, Max, ed. *The Oxford Book of Military Anecdotes*. Oxford: Oxford University Press, 1985.

Hirshson, Stanley P. *General Patton: A Soldier's Life*. New York: HarperCollins, 2002.

Howe, Russell Warren. *Mata Hari: The True Story*. New York: Dodd, Mead, 1986.

Knight, Ian, and Angus McBride. *The Zulus*. London: Osprey, 1989.

Longacre, Edward G. *General Ulysses S. Grant: The Soldier and the Man*. Cambridge, MA: Da Capo Press, 2006.

McLynn, Frank. *Napoleon: A Biography*. London: Jonathan Cape, 1997.

Newby, P. H. *Saladin: In His Time*. London: Faber & Faber, 1983.

Perry, James M. *Arrogant Armies*. New York: John Wiley & Sons, 1996.

Prange, Gordon William, Donald M. Goldstein, and Katherine V. Dillon. *God's Samurai*. Washington, DC: Brassey's, 2004.

Richard, Carl J. *Twelve Greeks and Romans Who Changed the World*. Lanham, MD.: Rowman & Littlefield, 2003.

Robertson, David. *Denmark Vesey: The Buried History of America's Largest Slave Rebellion and the Man Who Led It*. New York: Alfred A. Knopf, 1999.

Robertson, James I., Jr. *Stonewall Jackson: The Man, the Soldier, the Legend*. New York: Macmillan, 1997.

Root, Waverley. *Food: An Authoritative and Visual History and Dictionary of the Foods of the World*. New York: Simon & Schuster, 1980.

Shenkman, Richard. *Legends, Lies & Cherished Myths of World History*. New York: HarperCollins, 1993.

Wilberforce, Reginald Garton. *An Unrecorded Chapter of the Indian Mutiny*. London: John Murray, 1894.

Stevens, Patricia Bunning. *Rare Bits: Unusual Origins of Popular Recipes*. Athens: Ohio University Press, 1998.

CHAPTER 8: EXPERIMENTS IN DINING

Albala, Ken. *Beans: A History.* New York: Oxford University Press, 2007.

Biagioli, Mario. *Galileo, Courtier.* Chicago: University of Chicago Press, 1993.

Browne, Janet, *Charles Darwin: Voyaging.* New York: Alfred A. Knopf, 1995.

Bruce, Robert V. *Bell: Alexander Graham Bell and the Conquest of Solitude.* Ithaca, NY: Cornell University Press, 1990.

Bryson, Bill. *A Short History of Nearly Everything.* New York: Broadway Books, 2003.

Cheney, Margaret, Robert Uth, and Jim Glenn. *Tesla, Master of Lightning.* New York: Barnes & Noble Books, 1999.

Clary, David A. *Rocket Man: Robert H. Goddard and the Birth of the Space Age.* New York: Hyperion, 2004.

Cropper, William H. *Great Physicists.* Oxford, England: Oxford University Press, 2001.

Crouch, Tom. *The Bishop's Boys: A Life of Wilbur and Orville Wright.* New York: W. W. Norton, 1989.

Crumpacker, Bunny. *The Sex Life of Food.* New York: Thomas Dunne Books/St. Martin's Griffin, 2007.

Dommermuth-Costa, Carol. *Nikola Tesla: A Spark of Genius.* Minneapolis, MN: Lerner Publications, 1994.

Dyer, Frank Lewis, and Thomas Commerford. *Edison: His Life and Inventions.* New York: Harper Brothers, 1929.

Freud, Martin. *Sigmund Freud: Man and Father.* New York: Vanguard Press, 1958.

Goertzel, Ted, and Ben Goertzel. *Linus Pauling: A Life in Science and Politics.* New York: Basic Books, 1995.

Goldsmith, Barbara. *Obsessive Genius: The Inner World of Marie Curie.* New York: W. W. Norton, 2005.

Gratzer, Walter. *Eurekas and Euphorias.* Oxford, England: Oxford University Press, 2002.

Gribben, John. *The Scientists.* New York: Random House, 2002.

Henig, Robin Marantz. *The Monk in the Garden.* Boston: Houghton Mifflin, 2000.

Horvitz, Leslie Alan. *Eureka! Scientific Breakthroughs That Changed the World.* New York: John Wiley & Sons, 2002.

Howard, Jane. *Margaret Mead: A Life.* New York: Simon & Schuster, 1984.

Isaacson, Walter. *Benjamin Franklin: An American Life.* New York: Simon & Schuster, 2004.

Jones, Francis Arthur. *Thomas Alva Edison.* New York: T. Y. Crowell, 1908.

Jungnickel, Christa, and Russell McCormmach. *Cavendish.* Philadelphia: American Philosophical Society, 1996.

McMurry, Linda O. *George Washington Carver: Scientist and Symbol.* New York: Oxford University Press, 1981.

Ogilvie, Marilyn Bailey. *Marie Curie: A Biography.* Westport, CT: Greenwood Press, 2004.

O'Neill, John J. *Prodigal Genius: The Life of Nikola Tesla.* New York: Cosimo, 2006.

Pickover, Clifford A. *Strange Brains and Genius.* New York: HarperCollins, 1999.

Roberts, Royston M. *Serendipity: Accidental Discoveries in Science.* New York: John Wiley & Sons, 1989.

Simoons, Frederick J. *Plants of Life, Plants of Death.* Madison: University of Wisconsin Press, 1998.

Teller, Edward, with Judith Shoolery. *Memoirs.* Cambridge, MA: Perseus, 2001.

Watson, James D. *The Double Helix.* New York: Simon & Schuster, 1968.

CHAPTER 9: SINGING FOR THEIR SUPPER

Adler, David. *The Life and Cuisine of Elvis Presley.* New York: Crown Trade Paperbacks, 1993.

Cotten, Lee. *All Shook Up: Elvis Day by Day, 1954–1977.* Ann Arbor, MI: Pierian Press, 1985.

Edwards, Anne. *Maria Callas: An Intimate Biography.* New York: St. Martin's Griffin, 2003.

Everett, Walter. *The Beatles as Musicians: The Quarry Men Through Rubber Soul.* New York: Oxford University Press, 2001.

Furia, Philip. *Ira Gershwin: The Art of the Lyricist.* New York: Oxford University Press, 1996.

Gage, Nicholas. *Greek Fire: The Story of Maria Callas and Aristotle Onassis.* New York: Alfred A. Knopf, 2000.

Jones, Max, and John Chilton. *Louis, the Louis Armstrong Story, 1900–1971.* New York: Da Capo Press, 1988.

Kohler, Joachim. *Richard Wagner, the Last of the Titans.* Translated by Stewart Spencer. New Haven, CT: Yale University Press, 2004.

Morris, Edmund. *Beethoven: The Universal Composer.* New York: Atlas Books/HarperCollins, 2005.

Servadio, Gaia. *Rossini.* New York: Carroll & Graf, 2003.

Stravinsky, Igor. *Igor Stravinsky: An Autobiography.* New York: Steuer, 1958.

Watson, Derek. *Richard Wagner: A Biography.* New York: Schirmer Books, 1981.

Young, Bob, and Al Stankus. *Jazz Cooks: Portraits and Recipes of the Greats.* New York: Stewart, Tabori & Chang, 1992.

CHAPTER 10: BUSINESS LUNCH

Ackerman, Kenneth D. *The Gold Ring: Jim Fisk, Jay Gould, and Black Friday, 1869.* New York: Carroll & Graf, 2005.

Ash, Mary Kay. *Miracles Happen: The Life and Timeless Principles of the Founder of Mary Kay, Inc.* New York: HarperCollins, 2003.

Barlett, Donald L., and James Steele. *Howard Hughes: His Life and Madness.* New York: W. W. Norton, 2004.

Brown, Peter Harry, and Pat H. Broeske. *Howard Hughes: The Untold Story.* Cambridge, MA: Da Capo Press, 2004.

Burrows, Edwin G., and Mike Wallace. *Gotham: A History of New York City to 1898.* New York: Oxford University Press, 2000.

D'Antonio, Michael. *Hershey: Milton S. Hershey's Extraordinary Life of Wealth, Empire, and Utopian Dreams.* New York: Simon & Schuster, 2007.

Higham, Charles. *Howard Hughes: The Secret Life.* New York: Macmillan, 2004.

Israel, Lee. *Estée Lauder: Beyond the Magic.* New York: Macmillan, 1985.

Jeffers, Harry Paul: *Diamond Jim Brady: Prince of the Gilded Age.* Hoboken, NJ: John Wiley & Sons, 2001.

Jenkins, Carol, and Elizabeth Gardner Hines. *Black Titan: A. G. Gaston and the Making of a Black American Millionaire.* New York: One World/Ballantine Books, 2004.

Josephson, Matthew. *The Robber Barons: The Classic Account of the Influential Capitalists Who Transformed America's Future.* Boston: Houghton Mifflin Harcourt, 1962.

Kahney, Leander. *Inside Steve's Brain.* New York: Portfolio-Penguin Group, 2008.

Kaufman, Michael T. *Soros: The Life and Times of a Messianic Billionaire.* New York: Alfred A. Knopf, 2002.

Koehn, Nancy. "Estée Lauder: Self-Definition and the Cosmetics Market." In *Beauty and Business: Commerce, Gender, and Culture in Modern America,* edited by Philip Scranton, 217–53. New York: Routledge, 2001.

Kroc, Ray. *Grinding It Out: The Making of McDonald's.* New York: Macmillan, 1987.

Lenzner, Robert. *The Great Getty: The Life and Loves of J. Paul Getty—Richest Man in the World.* New York: Crown, 1985.

Lowe, Janet. *Bill Gates Speaks: Insight from the World's Greatest Entrepreneur.* Hoboken, NJ: John Wiley & Sons, 2001.

Manes, Stephen, and Paul Andrews. *Gates: How Microsoft's Mogul Reinvented an Industry—and Made Himself the Richest Man in America.* New York: Doubleday, 1993.

Morgenthau, Henry, III. *Mostly Morgenthaus: A Family History.* New York: Ticknor & Fields, 1991.

Morris, Charles R. *The Tycoons: How Andrew Carnegie, John D. Rockefeller, Jay Gould, and J. P. Morgan Invented the American Supereconomy.* New York: Macmillan, 2005.

Nasaw, David. *Andrew Carnegie.* New York: Penguin, 2007.

Price, Joann F. *Martha Stewart: A Biography.* Westport, CT: Greenwood Press, 2007.

Renehan, Edward. *Commodore: The Life of Cornelius Vanderbilt.* New York: Basic Books, 2007.

Schroeder, Alice. *The Snowball: Warren Buffett and the Business of Life.* New York: Bantam Dell, 2008.

Sears, Lorenzo. *John Hancock: The Picturesque Patriot.* Boston: Little, Brown, 1913.

Steele, Jay. *Warren Buffett: Master of the Market.* New York: HarperCollins, 1999.

Warren, Kenneth. *Triumphant Capitalism: Henry Clay Frick and the Industrial Transformation of America.* Pittsburgh, PA: University of Pittsburgh Press, 2000.

Watts, Steven. *Mr. Playboy: Hugh Hefner and the American Dream.* Hoboken, NJ: John Wiley & Sons, 2008.

Welch, Jack. *Jack: Straight from the Gut.* New York: Business Plus, 2001.

CHAPTER 11: PLAYING WITH THEIR FOOD

Ali, Muhammad, with Hana Ali. *The Soul of a Butterfly: Reflections on Life's Journey.* New York: Simon & Schuster, 2004.

Auerbach, Red, with John Feinstein. *Let Me Tell You a Story: A Lifetime in the Game.* New York: Little, Brown, 2004.

Baker, William J. *Jesse Owens: An American Life.* New York: The Free Press, 1986.

Barrow, Joe Louis, Jr., and Barbara Munder. *Joe Louis: 50 Years an American Hero.* New York: McGraw-Hill, 1988.

Borg, Björn. *My Life and Game.* New York: Simon & Schuster, 1980.

Comăneci, Nadia. *Letters to a Young Gymnast.* New York: Basic Books, 2004.

Cramer, Richard Ben. *Joe DiMaggio: The Hero's Life.* New York: Simon & Schuster, 2000.

Dodson, James. *Ben Hogan: An American Life.* New York: Broadway Books, 2004.

Eig, Jonathan. *Luckiest Man: The Life and Death of Lou Gehrig.* New York: Simon & Schuster, 2005.

Francis, Dick. *A Jockey's Life: The Biography of Lester Piggott.* New York: G. P. Putnam's Sons, 1986.

Freeman, Mike. *Jim Brown: The Fierce Life of an American Hero.* New York: Harper Entertainment, 2006.

Frommer, Harvey. *Shoeless Joe and Ragtime Baseball.* Lincoln: University of Nebraska Press, 2008.

Heidenry, John. *The Gashouse Gang.* New York: PublicAffairs, 2007.

Hittner, Arthur D. *Honus Wagner: The Life of Baseball's Flying Dutchman.* Jefferson, NC: McFarland, 2003.

Kahn, Roger. *The Era: 1947–1957, when the Yankees, the Giants, and the Dodgers Ruled the World.* Lincoln, NE: Bison Books, 2002.

Knight, Bob, with Bob Hammel. *Knight: My Story.* New York: St. Martin's Press, 2002.

Kriegel, Mark. *Namath: A Biography.* New York: Penguin Books, 2004.

Londino, Lawrence J. *Tiger Woods: A Biography.* Westport, CT: Greenwood Press, 2006.

Markusen, Bruce. *Roberto Clemente: The Great One.* Champaign, IL: Sports Publishing LLC, 2000.

McCallum, John D. *Ty Cobb.* New York: Praeger, 1975.

McMullen, Paul. *Amazing Pace: The Story of Olympic Champion Michael Phelps from Sydney to Athens to Beijing.* New York: Rodale, 2006.

Meola, Marc, and Lawrence Baldassaro. *Ted Williams: Reflections on a Splendid Life.* Lebanon, NH: University Press of New England, 2003.

Morelli, Jack, and Mark Chiarello. *Heroes of the Negro Leagues.* New York: Abrams Books, 2007.

Palmer, Arnold, with James Dodson. *A Golfer's Life.* New York: Ballantine Books, 1999.

Payton, Walter, with Don Yaeger. *Never Die Easy: The Autobiography of Walter Payton.* New York: Random House/Villard, 2000.

Pelé, with Robert L. Fish and Shep Messing. *My Life and the Beautiful Game: The Autobiography of Pelé.* New York: Skyhorse, 2007.

Seles, Monica. *Getting a Grip: On My Body, My Mind, My Self.* New York: Penguin, 2009.

Sokolove, Michael. *Hustle: The Myth, Life, and Lies of Pete Rose.* New York: Simon & Schuster, 2005.

Stauffer, Rene. *The Roger Federer Story: Quest for Perfection.* New York: New Chapter Press, 2007.

CHAPTER 12: DELICIOUS DISCOVERIES

Berg, A. Scott. *Lindbergh.* New York: G. P. Putnam's Sons, 1998.

Bown, Stephen R. *Scurvy: How a Surgeon, a Mariner, and a Gentleman Solved the Greatest Medical Mystery of the Age of Sail.* New York: Thomas Dunne Books, St. Martin's Press, 2004.

Cabeza de Vaca, Alvar Núñez. *The Narrative of Cabeza de Vaca.* Edited, translated, and with an introduction by Rolena Adorno and Patrick Charles Pautz. Lincoln: University of Nebraska Press, 2003.

Chien, Philip. *Columbia, Final Voyage.* New York: Copernicus Books, 2006.

Clark, Ella E., and Margot Edmonds. *Sacagawea of the Lewis and Clark Expedition.* Berkeley: University of California Press, 1983.

Colon, Ferdinand. *The History of the Life and Actions of Adm. Christopher Columbus, and of His Discovery of the West-Indies, Call'd the New World, Now in Possession of His Catholick Majesty.* London, 1732.

Cummins, Joseph. *History's Great Untold Stories.* London: Murdoch Books, 2006.

De Groot, Gerard J. *Dark Side of the Moon.* New York: New York University Press, 2006.

Derr, Mark. *A Dog's History of America.* New York: North Point Press, 2005.

Dickie, John. *Delizia! The Epic History of the Italians and Their Food.* New York: Free Press, 2008.

Dunn, Ross E. *The Adventures of Ibn Battuta, a Muslim Traveler of the Fourteenth Century.* Berkeley: University of California Press, 2005.

Eardley-Wilmot, Arthur Parry. *Manning the Navy.* London: W. J. Cleaver, 1849.

Van Spielbergen, Joris, and Jacob le Maire. *The East and West Indian Mirror, Being an Account of Joris van Spielbergen's Voyage Round the World (1614–1617) and the Australian Navigations of Jacob le Maire.* Translated, with notes and an introduction by J.A.J. Villiers of the British Museum. London: Printed for the Hakluyt Society, 1906.

Fernandez-Armesto, Felipe. *Pathfinders.* New York, London: W. W. Norton & Company, 2006.

Foley, William E. *Wilderness Journey: The Life of William Clark.* Columbia: University of Missouri Press, 2006.

Frost, Orcutt. *Bering: The Russian Discovery of America.* New Haven, CT: Yale University Press, 2003.

Glenn, John, with Nick Taylor. *John Glenn: A Memoir.* New York: Bantam Books, 1999.

Goldstein, Donald M., and Katherine V. Dillon. *Amelia: A Life of the Aviation Legend.* Washington, DC: Brassey's, 1999.

Gratzer, Walter. *Terrors of the Table.* Oxford, England: Oxford University Press, 2005.

Grossman, James R., Ann Durkin Keating, and Janice L. Reiff, eds. *Encyclopedia of Chicago.* Chicago: University of Chicago Press, 2004.

Henson, Matthew A. *A Negro Explorer at the North Pole.* Mountain View, CA: Widget Magic, 2000.

Hillary, Edmund. *View from the Summit.* New York: Pocket Books, 1999.

298 Selected Bibliography

Howard, Harold P. *Sacajawea*. Norman: University of Oklahoma Press, 1971.

Howitt, William. *The History of Discovery in Australia, Tasmania, and New Zealand*. London: Longman, Green, Longman, Roberts, & Green, 1865.

Irving, Washington. *The Life and Voyages of Christopher Columbus*. Leipzig, Germany: Baumgärtners Buchhandlung, 1832.

Jackson, Andrew. *Robert O'Hara Burke and the Australian Exploring Expedition of 1860*. London: Smith, Elder & Co., 1862.

Levy, Buddy. *Conquistador: Hernán Cortés, King Montezuma, and the Last Stand of the Aztecs*. New York: Bantam Books, 2008.

Lindbergh, Charles A. *The Spirit of St. Louis*. New York: Scribner, 1998.

Morton, Mark. *Cupboard Love: A Dictionary of Culinary Curiosities*. Winnipeg, Manitoba, Canada: Bain & Cox, 1996.

Pennington, Piers. *The Great Explorers*. New York: Facts on File, 1979.

Rich, Doris L. *Amelia Earhart: A Biography*. Washington: Smithsonian Institution, 1989.

Ross, Walter Sanford. *The Last Hero: Charles A. Lindbergh*. New York: HarperCollins, 2005.

Sanborn, Geoffrey. *The Sign of the Cannibal*. Durham, NC: Duke University Press, 1998.

Stanley, Henry Morton. *How I Found Livingstone*. New York: Scribner, Armstrong & Co., 1872.

Thomas, Nicholas. *Cook: The Extraordinary Voyages of Captain James Cook*. New York: Walker, 2003.

Toussaint-Samat, Maguelonne. *A History of Food*. Translated by Anthea Bell. Cambridge, MA: Blackwell Reference, 1993.

Towle, George Makepeace. *Magellan; Or, the First Voyage Round the World*. Boston: Lee & Shepard, 1902; New York: C. T. Dillingham, 1879.

Trager, James. *The Food Chronology: A Food Lover's Compendium of Events and Anecdotes, from Prehistory to the Present*. New York: Henry Holt, 1995.

Van Pelt, Lori. *Amelia Earhart: The Sky's the Limit*. New York: Tom Doherty Associates, 2005.

SELECTED PERIODICALS AND NEWS SERVICES

American Heritage, Anchorage Daily News, Baseball Digest, British Broadcasting System, Canadian Press, Chicago Sun-Times, Chicago Tribune, Condé Nast Traveler, Cornell Chronicle, Food and Wine, Forbes, Fortune, Guardian, GQ, GW Magazine, Hartford Courant, Independent, Indiana Daily Student, Jerusalem Post, Jet, Journal of the Abraham Lincoln Association, London Telegraph, Los Angeles Times, New Statesman, New York Daily News, New York Times, New Yorker,

Newsweek, People, Phoenix New Times, Popular Science, Press Association (Britain), Religion & Liberty, Reuters, The Strand, Sun Star (Cebu City, Philippines), Time, Times of India, Toronto Star, Vanity Fair, Wall Street Journal, Washington Post, and Weekly Standard.

SELECTED WEBSITES

(Status as of August 16, 2009)

The American Presidency Project at the University of California–Santa Barbara. www.presidency.ucsb.edu

Text of "Religion and Art" (1880) by Richard Wagner. Translated by William Ashton Ellis. http://users.belgacom.net/wagnerlibrary/prose/wlpr0126.htm

The story of Joe Ombuor, Idi Amin's cook. http://www.africamasterweb.com/AdSense/AminTalesOfChiefCook.html

Scott Myers's interview with Neil Simon. http://www.gointothestory.com/search?q=Neil+Simon

Mohandas Gandhi's address to the London Vegetarian Society in 1931. http://www.ivu.org/congress/wvc57/souvenir/gandhi2.html

Roman Catholic saints. http://www.catholic.org and http://www.newadvent.org

Patricia G. Solley's encyclopedia of soup. http://www.soupsong.com

General debunking of tempting myths. http://snopes.com

Space travel. http://spaceflight.nasa.gov

Historical context from Public Broadcasting System. www.pbs.org

A complete bibliography is available at whatthegreatate.org.

INDEX